The Keystone House, Inc.

Keystone, S. Dak. 57751

"*The Friendly Place*"

BOOT HILL

Historic Graves of the Old West

BOOT HILL

Historic Graves of the Old West

By

Lambert Florin

HERALD M. ENGLAND—CRESTED BUTTE, COLO.

OLD HEADBOARD apparently was once fastened to wooden enclosure, inscription almost gone, only part still decipherable being name with unusual spelling — "Herald". Old mining camp of Crested Butte, Colorado, shown in background, was laid out in 1879 when enormous deposits of coal were found nearby. Beds included good grade anthracite, first found west of Pennsylvania. Heavy fatalities in mines and from frequent snow avalanches soon filled large cemetery. Photo was made from edge of burial ground.

BONANZA BOOKS · NEW YORK

DEDICATION

This book is dedicated to Dr. David C. Mason who has done the endsheet drawing and in many other ways assisted in the preparation of this work.

FOREWORD

Whatever changes man has made in his physical form and manner of living from time immemorial, life has always come to an end. I should say "thus far" because I haven't read the latest scientific reports on possible breakthroughs in this field. But with death seeming to be universal and quite final, the principal problems facing the living are conceptions of life after death and what to do with the body.

There is a temptation here to lead up to the subject of western pioneer graveyards with a brief rundown on funeral customs and last rite ceremonies down through the ages but it would be audacious of me to try to cover this in a few paragraphs when there are many books available on all phases of burials from cremations in ancient Greece to mass interments of plague victims ad infinitum.

So here we are with western settlers, miners, gunmen, preachers and seamen—all seeing so much of death and wanting so much to keep on living themselves. They really had little time and often little sentiment to waste on a corpse. Would they put it in a boat, set it on fire and shove it out on the tide? Should they remove the heart and bury it separate from the body? Would they leave the body to be ravaged by wild animals or boil it first, then burn the flesh and enshrine the more durable bones? Should they burn the body on a pyre, preserve the ashes or cast them to the winds or on the water? Shall this body be laid in a box with others until the flesh has sloughed off the bones, then added to others in a pit? Or shall the corpse be placed in an elaborately carved canoe and the craft be mounted on a raised platform? If you were a western pioneer or an Indian you had all these choices and a lot more.

There is a possibility whoever was faced with burial could recall Sir Thomas Gray's immortal lines:

"The boast of heraldry, the pomp of power,

And all that beauty, all that wealth e'er gave,

Awaits alike the inevitable hour.

The paths of glory lead but to the grave."

And having dwelt on such profundity, what else could the mourners do, say out there on the rim of civilization with the snow a foot deep with no cortege of Cadillacs to take the body to church or chapel, no steaming cup to thaw out the feet of the pallbearers. Life was real, life was earnest. He was a good man, boys, but he's gone now, so let's bury him the best way we can and get on with the horseshoeing.

The Boot Hill Graveyard in Tombstone, Arizona, is about as representative of western burial as any one you could find. "The Town Too Tough To Die" is famous enough to warrant some details of personal experience. When rounding up material for *Western Ghost Towns* and having a deep distrust of blaring tourist traps, I deliberately shied away from Tombstone. Readers of the book missed it and called me on it. So for a later one on the old mining camps I made a trip to Tombstone and other old camps. Modern Tombstone surprised me, being full of relics of its wild days, almost every building being genuine and loaded with historic interest. Even so I avoided its Boot Hill as being too famous, having seen too many spurious epitaphs in fabricated or "restored" cemeteries and thinking the funny inscriptions you heard about in Tombstone's Boot Hill must be invented too.

Well I have been wrong a lot of times but never more than when I was finally forced to explore the avoided Boot Hill, in light of the book you have in your hands. I found the town full of old friends including the affable William Hunley of the Bird Cage Theater. I asked him, "Billy—is the Boot Hill Graveyard a phony?" It was almost an affront. He blazed back, "Certainly not!" and filled me in with detail.

After being well populated with the victims of violence of one sort and another, Boot Hill itself fell victim to neglect and decay. For many years it was deserted except by those getting rid of trash and garbage. Then a group of prideful Tombstone citizens cleared away the refuse, consulted old burial records, located most graves, placed stones and duplicate markers on them. Sufficient time has now passed to give a patina of old age to the comparatively new heardboards.

It is true you must pass by a novelty shop at the gate but no one is asked to buy and some of the merchandise, such as books on the history of the area, is worthwhile. And you can understand the shop people contribute to the upkeep of the graveyard and acting somewhat as guardians, almost eliminate the hazards of vandalism. Then once inside the cemetery you are at liberty to browse, take notes and make photographs.

One of the markers you will see bears the name of Emmet Nunelley who died in 1946. He was the main force in the effort to restore the graveyard, spending the last year of his life in this work. You will then note another headboard.

HERE LIES LESTER MOORE

FOUR SLUGS FROM A .44

NO LES, NO MORE

Moore was the Wells Fargo agent at Naco, tiny town on the Mexican border. He made the mistake of being too conscientious about duty on a package.

Three-fingered Jack, buried here, was shot by Jeff Milton in an attempted train robbery at Fairbank (see *Ghost Town Treasures*) and was left by his pals to die. Brought to Tombstone he lived long enough to inform on them. Other graves hold bodies of Rodrigues Petron, Margarita and George Johnson. Petron's body, well dressed but fatally stabbed, was found at the bottom of a mine shaft. "There was no identification of any kind," said the press and perhaps you can tell how the finders got his name. Two dance hall girls loved the same man and the problem was solved by one of them, Gold Dollar, stabbing Margarita. George Johnson innocently bought a stolen horse, was discovered riding it and was hanged. His headboard carries the apology — "Hanged By Mistake."

In Boot Hill are also bodies of Marshal White who attempted to disarm Curly Bill on the lot where the Bird Cage Theater now stands; Bronco Charlie, shot by Ormsby; Hancock, shot by John Ringo; Mike Noonan, killed by Indians; two Chinamen who died of leprosy; Campbell, a suicide; J. D. Dermit, who fell to his death; Dutch Annie, Queen of the Red Lights who in death was mourned by city officials and underworld alike, her funeral procession of 1,000 buggies exceeded in number only by the one for Ed Schieffelin who started things in Tombstone.

I mentioned vandalism up there and readers of my books know this is a *bete noire* of mine that almost drives me up the wall. Now strapped to my chair, I expound further. I have visited countless old burial grounds from the Arctic Circle to well below the Mexican border and have found few in the United States that have not suffered from the depredations of apparent psychopaths, none in Canada or Mexico that have. There are the common cases of pushed-over headboards and marble slabs, the upsetting of some of the larger ones seeming to require collective effort. In one pioneer cemetery it was recently noticed a wide, circular swath of destruction was made by a car that had smashed through the gates, driven among the stones, bumper knocking some over and breaking up others. And damage is done not only in cemeteries on main roads and streets. The little family plot of the Keils holds the graves of several children of William Keil, founder of the colony and town of Aurora, Oregon. The children died within a few days of each other from an epidemic, each one marked by a beautiful carved marble headstone. Only last summer — 1965 — all of these were not only pushed over but smashed into fragments by something like a sledge hammer. This old private burial plot is hidden behind brush and trees a quarter of a mile from the end of a private road.

Yet on the whole anyone wandering among the tombstones of old western cemeteries to study history, photograph the stones or simply to enjoy a period of peace and tranquillity will find little that is depressing or morbid. The grief associated with the departure of each person buried here has long been assuaged by the passing of time and melancholy is replaced by interest in the character and histories of the personalities and in the markers.

The techniques employed in photographing these are not much different from those suggested in my earlier books where most of the subjects are old buildings or ghost town relics. Perhaps I should stress the importance of a glancing side lighting, especially in the case of wooden headboards whose painted inscriptions have faded away with age. It will be noted that while the paint lasted it protected the wood under it while that of surrounding areas was eroded away. Although the painted marks may have vanished completely, leaving no visible inscription in a flat, head-on lighting, a strong light from the side will throw faint shadows revealing what would otherwise not be seen. The same lighting helps greatly to make more clear the chiseled inscriptions in marble, these often being obscured by growth of lichens and moss. In all cases, filters (I used a red A) help strengthen grain of wood, contour of marble and other details. Long exposures necessitated by filters require a tripod which should be used for steadiness in any case. Select one that will telescope to short length as the detail to be recorded will often be low on the stone.

If all this be reason, make the most of it.

Lambert Florin.

TABLE OF CONTENTS

Acknowledgments and Suggested Further Reading

Stone Age on the Columbia River by Emory Strong

Chief Seattle by Eva Greenslit Anderson

The Story of Seattle by Roberta Frye Watt

By Juan de Fuca Strait by James McCurdy

Sacajawea, Guide of the Lewis and Clark Expedition
    by Grace Raymond Hebard

Off the Beaten Trail by Ed Syers

University of Texas, Bureau of Economic Geology

Shallow Diggin's by Jean Davis

The Bonanza Trail by Muriel Sibell Wolle

Stampede to Timberline by Muriel Sibell Wolle

Shipwrecks of the Pacific Coast by James E. Gibbs

Pacific Northwest Indian Wars by Ray Howard Glassley

California's Golden Treasures by Charles Peters

East of the Cascades by Phil Brogan

Men of Champoeg by Caroline Dobbs

History of the Pacific Northwest by George W. Fuller

Life and Death of Julia Bulette by Zeke Daniels

Story of Two Others, Frontier Times, by D. E. Warren

Lost Mines and Buried Treasures by Ruby El Hult

Bethel and Aurora by Robert Hendricks

History of Columbia County, Columbia County Historical
    Society

Barkerville by Bruce Ramsey

History of Oregon by Charles Carey

Story of Early Mono County by Ella Cain

Story of Bodie by Ella Cain

American Guide Series, Oregon, Washington, Colorado, Utah,
    Arizona, Idaho, New Mexico, California, South Dakota,
    Texas

Pioneer Days in Idaho County by Sister Elfreda Elsensohn

Information on Billy the kid by Ed Bartholomew, Toyahvale,
    Texas

Here Rolled the Covered Wagons, by Jane and Albert
    Salisbury

Pacific Graveyard by James E. Gibbs

Mountain Men and the Fur Trade of the Far West by
    LeRoy R. Hafen

In addition I wish to express my gratitude to the personnel
of the many State Historical Societies and Libraries consulted, the families of many of those whose grave-markers
are pictured here, and the many individuals who have contributed information. In particular, I wish to thank Mr.
Jack Pollard and Mrs. Gertrude Pollard whose careful
proof reading has contributed so much to the accuracy of
this book.

SEATTLE,
Chief of the
Suquampsh, and
Allied tribes.
DIED JUNE 7, 1866.
The firm friend of the
whites, and for him the
CITY OF SEATTLE
was named by its
FOUNDERS.

SEALTH

SEATTLE THE NAME THAT HAUNTS

OPPOSITE PAGE
WHEN PIONEERS of infant town on Elliott Bay informed Indian chief the place would be named for him, he displayed great agitation, saying "It is very bad, do you not know that when the name of one who is dead is spoken, he will turn over in his grave? Every time name of Sealth is said, I will be disturbed in my tomb, I will never rest."

Inscribed on cross at top of seven-foot monument are letters I.H.S., sign for Jesus, a contraction of His name in Greek. Local Indians believe the letters mean "I Have Suffered." They gather at grave each final Saturday in August, maintain this is birthday of great chief. On other specified annual dates such varied organizations as Boy Scouts of America and Daughters of American Revolution also hold meetings at site.

CHIEF SEALTH ACCEPTED THE NEW DAY

". . . And when the last Red Man shall have perished," Chief Sealth told his people of the Suquamish and Duwamish tribes on Puget Sound gathered around him in 1854 when Governor Stevens came to arrange a treaty with them, "and the memory of my tribe shall have become a myth among the White Men, these shores will swarm with the invisible dead of my tribe, and when your children's children think themselves alone in the field, the store, the shop, upon the highway, or in the silence of the pathless woods, they will not be alone. In all the earth there is no place dedicated to solitude. At night when the streets of your cities and villages are silent and you think them deserted, they will throng with the returning hosts that once filled them and still love this beautiful land. The White Man will never be alone."

*   *   *   *   *

The kindness Capt. George Vancouver showed the Indians when he explored Puget Sound could well have been the reason for Chief Sealth's friendship toward the whites all through his life. In Vancouver's diary he entered in May, 1792, the line, "Today I met a rude, humble people . . ." Sealth was then a child, son of Schweable, Suquamish chief, and he grew to be a patriarch of the Puget Sound tribes, "patron saint" of the city of Seattle which Americanized his name.

CLOSE-UP OF INSCRIPTION of front of monument on grave of Indian who likely saved infant Seattle by holding back his Indians from participation in attacks on city. On rear of stone is briefer inscription reading "Baptismal Name Noah Sealth Age Probably 80 Years." Previous to his conversion, Sealth listened attentively to Bible stories expounded by Father Demers, was particularly intrigued by story of Noah and Ark, requested Demers to bestow this name upon him in baptismal ceremonies. However, few know of this and no one ever called him Noah.

Dr. Henry A. Smith translated Sealth's classic reply to Gov. Stevens, saying it was given in a "trumpet-toned voice". The aged chief was a continuing factor in peace between Indians and whites until his death, presumed to be at about 80, on June 7, 1866.

THE FOUNDERS OF A CITY

STRANGERS ON A TIMBERED SHORE

The Dennys

In Cherry Grove, Illinois, Arthur Denny stood by the fireplace and read a letter to his wife. It came to him from the far Northwest where some hardy adventurous souls were pioneering, most of them in the Oregon Country, and sending back alluring reports. "Flowers can be seen here in bloom all winter," Denny read, "and snow is a rarity."

Roberta Frye Watt, who would one day be born to Louisa Catherine, daughter of the Dennys, wrote years later of how Arthur, her grandfather-to-be, read the letter to his wife, Mary. He stood by the fire in reflective silence for a moment and then asked, "Will you go, Mary?" And Mary answered simply, "Yes, Arthur." Both question and answer came after the Dennys had given deep consideration to such a move — and by going started a chain of events that would result in the founding of the city of Seattle.

The Dennys who headed for Oregon were Arthur and Mary, their infant daughter Loretta, Arthur's parents, John and Sarah Denny, and Arthur's four single brothers — David, James, Samuel and Wiley. With them went the related Carson Borens with their daughters, small Gertrude and teenager Louisa.

The wagon train crossed the prairies and mountains with no more than the usual difficulties, although sometimes being short on supplies and water, and once being forced to race an Indian war party to a narrow pass through a ravine and going through just ahead of the savages. They heard later a family of Clarks going through a few weeks later was not as lucky, being caught and massacred at the same spot. Louisa Boren's beauty attracted young braves along the way, one going so far as to enter the emigrants' camp with a band of cayuses, offering to trade them for the girl. The rejected suitor followed the train for some distance and gave the travelers anxious moments.

The Dennys and John Lows, whose parties were joined along the Snake River, reached the village of Portland, Oregon Territory, via the Columbia River route through the gorge in August, having made a very good average of eighteen miles a day from Illinois. Though Arthur Denny heard good things about the Puget Sound area and was anxious to go there, he and Mary were taken by the "ague" and forced to stay where they were.

On September 10, 1851, young David Denny and John Low started north to see what the country around the Sound had to offer. In Olympia the two met Lee Terry who joined with them and the trio found a Capt. Robert C. Fay about to begin a voyage in his boat to buy salmon from the Indians around the Sound, and was willing to take the youths along. One of the first stops was at Skwudux on the west shore of the peninsula now called West Seattle and here occurred a historic meeting and welcome by Chief Sealth, who gave the city of Seattle its name. Cruising up the Duwamish River the next day the youths met Luther Collins whose claims, with others on the river, predated Seattle and were later to be engulfed by it.

The young men were entranced with a beautiful point of gravelly beach gently extending into the waters of Puget Sound, a spot to be known later as Alki and John Low at once hired David Denny and Lee Terry to build him a cabin. Waiting only long enough for David to write a letter to his brother, Low started back to Portland, riding as far as Olympia in Capt. Fay's boat, then tramping the rest of the way through the wilderness.

David's note to Arthur was short and simple, carrying the magic phrase, "There is plenty of room for a thousand settlers, come at once." The other Dennys immediately made plans to join him, taking with them new friends William Bell and Charles Terry, brother of Lee. In addition there would be a new baby boy born to Mary Denny shortly after the arrival in Portland. David's unmarried brothers remained behind with the grandparents.

At Alki David and Lee worked at the hard task of building a cabin with only the most primitive tools, while sleeping under a crude shelter. When they got the walls up they found they could not split shakes without a froe, so Lee went to Olympia to get one. Swinging an axe David let it slip and cut his foot badly, being forced to crawl under the cedar-bough shelter, hungry and cold, while the rain came down steadily. This brought on fever and ague which sent waves of discouragement through the nineteen year old.

On the morning of November 13, 1851, the *Exact*, under command of Capt. Isaiah Folger, came in view of the point and anchored off the beach just below the half-completed cabin. Aboard was the Portland contingent feeling fortunate at locating this place like a thousand others in the vast maze of wooded islands, points and tree-lined inlets. The party came ashore, the crew unloaded supplies, the ship departed and David limped around on the beach with little welcoming spirit, having only a cabin with no roof and only blind faith in the future.

The band of settlers numbered twenty-four — a few adults, the others teenagers, children or babies. Rain fell incessantly and everyone was soaked before another shelter of boughs could be put up. The women sat on logs and wept. They had exchanged snow and home comforts for rain and uncertainties in this raw, savage land. Arthur Denny's own heart sank but perhaps he found some consolation in David and Louisa Boren. They were not discouraged. On the long journey across country they came to realize they were in love, would soon marry now and start a new life of their own.

With the cabin roofed, a second one was built and some semblance of comfort established. The settlers would have been comparatively happy but for the constant annoyance of inquisitive Indians who were forever underfoot, in and out of the cabins. The situation was difficult, the whites not willing to antagonize them by direct rebuff.

Legend must be relied upon for the naming of the settlement on the point. There are several versions, one concerning a ship passing close enough for the captain to call out, "What place is this?" Quick with repartee, Terry called back, "New York!" The captain laughed and retorted, "New York Alki, maybe," Alki being "sometime" or "bye and bye" in Chinook jargon. The name stuck but being too cumbersome, the New York was soon dropped. Today a monument stands on Alki Point, inscribed with the names of the settlers who landed there.

A ship stopped one day to ask if there were

DRAPED URN surmounts tall column topping eminence in center of Seattle's old Lake View Cemetery. Monument conspicuously marks plot of Denny family, several members foremost among founders of city. Some, including Arthur and Mary were originally laid to rest in family plot on Denny Hill, later transferred here along with other pioneers when old site was leveled for occupation by business structures.

any pilings available for wharf building, to be transported to San Francisco. The settlers saw an idea here to make some money and began cutting timber for the purpose, wishing the water were deeper near shore so more and larger ships could tie up. To further the plan, the men took a canoe one day in January, 1852, sounding along the eastern shore of Elliott Bay, using Mary Denny's clothesline and Terry's unused horseshoes. As they left Mary called out a caution not to lose the precious line, Terry maintaining the horseshoes were even more important.

Somewhere near the inlet now called Smith's Cove the water proved deep, as it did near where Yesler Way would be. The soundings continued northward and the men stopped to eat lunch on the beach, concluding the place would be just right for a settlement. It was to prove very good for around this spot would grow the largest city in the Pacific Northwest.

The party returned to New York well satisfied, returning in a few days to stake out donation land claims which allowed 320 acres to each married couple, half that to single men. A stake was driven at the foot of Denny Way, another at First Avenue and King Street, and claims measured off from there, Arthur Denny getting the middle section. The claims were calculated on the north-south dimension only, no consideration given to how far they ran back into the dense forest, or up the steep hills.

Carson Boren was the first to get a cabin up, one built of split cedar puncheons, Indian style. Arthur Denny, still sick with ague at New York, was unable to accompany the others to the new site, still less build a cabin there. The others built him one on the bluff near the foot of Battery Street but when he moved his family in they found the location a poor one, access to the bay being difficult and well water insufficient. He built another cabin in a clearing at the northwest corner of First and Marion Streets.

The scattered collection of cabins was casually referred to as Duwamps. General opinion seemed to say the place should be called after the chief who had welcomed young David Denny and party to the area, the suggestion possibly Dr. David S. Maynard's, since his friendship with Chief Sealth was the longest. The Indian pronunciation of the word, as well as most others, was decidedly gutteral and the settlers modified it to Seattle.

As the town grew there were increasing grumblings that the whole area was still part of Oregon, though usually designated as Northern Oregon. Arthur Denny later related, "We were like two sisters; Oregon was the big sister and of course must be served first. I will be the first to admit that she was always willing to let her little sister have what was left after she was served." On the Fourth of July, 1852, he went with a delegation to the well-settled and larger Olympia to talk over the possibility of separating from Oregon but the matter was not resolved. It seemed necessary first of all to establish a newspaper. With it, the COLUMBIAN, arguments for separation using the Columbia River as a natural boundary could now reach the general public, scanty as it was, and Arthur Denny wrote a steady stream of articles agitating for the move.

As a result, in October of 1852, representatives of the more aspiring towns held a convention in Monticello (now Longview) to draw up a petition to Congress asking that the northern area be established as a separate territory. Bell, Maynard and Denny were among the delegates, the trip requiring a canoe paddle to Olympia, then walking or riding a horse on the old Hudson's Bay Trail to Monticello, a matter of two weeks time each way. A proper petition was drawn and the delegates returned home, except for Dr. Maynard who went on to Oregon City.

The settlers were too busy to do much exploring away from the waterfront but to check out rumors of prairie grass growing in the northeast interior which could be valuable for raising stock in the future, Arthur Denny led a party that way. After almost a full day breaking through virgin timber they came to a lake at first thought to be fresh water. Denny later wrote it was inadvisable for anyone to make the trip. "Anyone can get lost," he said, "between the bay and the lake."

There were some hard times. One winter brought a foot of snow and enough ice formed in the bay to hamper movements of canoes. Food grew scarce. In the fall Arthur Denny bought two barrels of pork for $90, "imported" as it were, getting one up to his house and leaving the other on the beach overnight where a high tide carried it away. Fortunately there was plenty of syrup, sugar, tea, coffee, venison and ducks. But potatoes and flour gave out, the people being without bread for six weeks. Arthur Denny, John Low and several Indians went up the Duwamish River and found a supply of "little red potatoes" which provided the yearned-for starch until a ship arrived.

David Denny's cabin at the foot of Denny Way was finished just about the date of his marriage to Louisa Boren. The wedding took place in his older brother's cabin on January 23, 1853, Louisa dressing for it in the loft. She told of it later. "I couldn't stand erect and could hardly pull on my white mull dress." She made it before leaving Illinois when there was no bridegroom in sight. The service was performed by Dr. Maynard in his capacity of Justice of the Peace, after which he presented the couple with an old hen and a rooster, valuable gifts under the circumstances. The young Dennys loaded their homely gifts in a canoe and paddled from Marion Street to Denny Way. Louisa's first supper for her husband was of salted meat and the "little red potatoes". In the windowless cabin the only furniture was the table and chairs David bought from a sailing vessel, bed made of cedar poles and slats and the stove a regulation ship's galley range with rail around the edges.

The old hen made a nest under the front step and soon had a clutch of eggs. When they were hatched the rooster took over the care of the chicks, leaving his mate free to start another family, an example of pioneer industry not confined to Seattle. Around the same front step Louisa planted sweet-brier seeds brought from Illinois and produced the first flower garden in the settlement, the bushes persisting until uprooted by a bulldozer almost eighty years later.

Arthur Denny continued to be the foremost citizen of Seattle. Among his great efforts was attempting to induce the Northern Pacific Railway, then well under transcontinental construction, to establish its terminal in Seattle. Every citizen fully expected this development and many invested entire fortunes in land and buildings on the presumption they would become valuable to the railroad on its arrival.

It was Denny's darkest moment when he read the telegram from Rice and Ainsworth, railway commissioners, reading, "We have located the terminus at Commencement Bay". This site would be the city of Tacoma. Seattle's efforts to improve the area for the expected road had defeated them. It had no interest in buying land already valuable. It would develop its own terminal facilities, expand its own real estate business with previously unwanted land. The disappointing decision caused a serious slump in the city's economy for some time.

FUNERAL FOR PRINCESS Angeline was odd combination of white tradition and ancient Indian custom. Coffin was built in shape of war canoe, complete with paddle resting on stern. Daughter of Chief Sealth was dressed as people saw her every day, in checkered shawl and old bandana. School children passed by grave to drop daisies in coffin and strew flowers on ground. Just before canoe coffin was closed, Mrs. Maynard placed on it a sprig of cedar which Angeline loved. Later children contributed enough dimes and nickels to erect granite monument, faced with bronze plaque. Henry Yesler monument is seen at left.

STRANGER IN HER OWN LAND
Princess Angeline

Rollie Denny and Van Wykoff were two of the small boys who taunted the aging Princess Angeline, daughter of Chief Sealth, in Seattle's early days. They often told of the old woman's losing her temper and cursing them in rich vernacular, a mixture of the old Suquamish and Indian-type pidgin English. Denny claimed to his death that his head still showed scars of wounds left by well-aimed rocks she threw at him and Van Wykoff said she had once become so irate over what she considered insults, she emptied a basket of clams and hurled them with practiced accuracy.

This was Angeline, daughter of a chief with noble bearing, of great dignity and courtesy, who in her old age came to be regarded as a virago, a shrewish, bad-tempered beggar, displaying only occasionally some qualities inherited from her illustrious father.

She was not always called Angeline. When Mrs. David S. Maynard, wife of Seattle's first doctor, met her as a young woman, widow of Kick-is om-lo Cud, she asked the girl, "And what is your own name?" The answer was, "They just call me Cud." Mrs. Maynard laughed. "You are far too handsome a woman for a name like that. We will call you Angeline."

She lived all her years in the reflected glory of her father. While young and pretty she had many friends among Seattle's early people but they grew fewer as she aged. Some were staunch, like Henry Yesler, *kloshe white tillicum*. In the former days Angeline worked hard at scrubbing white women's floors and doing their laundry but she became infirm and lazy.

In these latter times she lived in a shanty on the waterfront between Pike and Pine Streets. Being a confirmed packrat, accumulating all manner of junk until the small hovel was filled, she would have a "potlatch" for her equally miserable neighbors and get a fresh start. Without her half-breed grandson, Joe Foster, who lived in the shack when out of jail, she might have lived in comparative comfort but he was a drunkard and kept her destitute paying his fines or bail. On the verge of starvation, her plight would become known to Henry Yesler and the Princess would have money and food.

When she heard Yesler was dying she rushed to his home but was not allowed to see him. She remained on the porch until her weeping and wailing penetrated the failing consciousness of her benefactor. He had her admitted and tried to comfort her before he died. The incident appeared in the newspapers, reporters interviewing her and finding her not the vituperative person of public mind. She said, "Tell the people I feel bad over *kloshe Yesler memaloose*. He was good *tillicum* to me. Good *tillicums hyas papa.*" Mrs. Maynard went to see her soon after the funeral and the aged Angeline told her in her usual broken English, "When I die I want to be buried close to Henry Yesler."

The Princess lived eighty years, spending most of her last days sitting on the curbs of downtown Seattle trying to see some of her old friends in the passing throngs. She continued to live with grandson Joe who had compassion enough to care for her with some tenderness as she grew feeble. She died May 31, 1896 and her request was granted. She was buried on the Yesler lot near the four year old grave of the good *tillicum*.

THE BROTHERS WERE VALIANT
The Mercers

Some pioneer western towns needed money, some trade and most needed the army to keep the Indians quiet. They all needed more women and Seattle was one that did something about it. Asa Mercer went back East and brought back cargoes of brides, the first trip netting eleven—the historically famous Mercer Girls.

His older brother Thomas arrived on Puget Sound with Henry Yesler, full of tales he heard about the new country while living in Illinois. With wife and four daughters he crossed the plains in a

GRAVE MARKERS erected at turn of century and earlier often were pages of written history. No exception is square tomb marking plot of Thomas Mercer and his family, all four sides carrying heroic details of Seattle's founding.

covered wagon, arriving in Salem, Oregon, in the fall of 1852. His wife dying, he left the little girls in the temporary care of a pioneer woman and went north, staking a donation claim adjacent to David Denny's, extending south from Lake "Tenas Chuck". He retrieved his daughters, bringing with them a handsome team of horses, Tib and Charley, one white, one black.

Mercer immediately built a house facing the lake, neighbors helping cut a road through to it, and on the Fourth of July held a house-warming picnic. He proposed to the citizenry that Lake Duwamish be called Lake Washington and "his" Lake Tenas Chuck be Lake Union. "The smaller lake," he said, "may some day connect Lake Washington to Puget Sound."

In many ways Thomas Mercer became one of Seattle's first citizens, but far outshining him in colorful history was his younger brother, Asa. First teacher at the University of Washington, he had for students any and all available, whatever their ages, the University being derisively called "Seattle High School". First enrollment consisted of thirty, the school opening on November 4, 1861. After Asa's first term of five months the school was closed because of financial difficulties complicated by false accusations of financial mismanagement. When troubles were straightened out and school reopened, Mercer was offered the presidency but he had moved into other fields.

The main one was a one-man campaign to collect funds for him to go East to bring back a batch of marriageable and willing young females to balance the population of the fledgling Seattle. As can be surmised every bachelor he approached was eager to contribute and in a short time Mercer was in Boston giving lectures on Puget Sound's scenic beauties, business opportunities and marriage-eager men. Asa was personable, persuasive and there were many girls on the Eastern Seaboard orphaned

MERCER MONUMENT is in three sections. Upper part is cast in zinc. Metal section rests on carved stone, this in turn placed on foundation of concrete. Foundation shows signs of deterioration not displayed in more enduring materials.

during the Civil War. He brought eleven young women home with him in spite of the long ocean voyage to San Francisco, another north to Port Gamble on the lumber schooner *Torrent* and the final trip down Puget Sound to Seattle on the sloop *Kidder*.

The Mercer Girls were welcomed with open arms, even the women glad to see new faces, new clothes. A gala reception at the University, hosted by gallant Dr. Maynard, welcomed the venture-some eleven and Asa Mercer was cheered as the man of the hour. All the girls found jobs, many as teachers, and all but one fulfilled her destiny by marrying.

Full of fine purpose, young Mercer again went East to gather another parcel of girls, this time planning to see Abraham Lincoln and enlist his aid. He wrote later, "Having sat upon Lincoln's lap as a five year old lad listening to his funny stories and knowing the goodness of his heart, not a shadow of doubt existed in my mind as to the outcome." But on arrival Mercer was dismayed to hear the dreadful news of the President's assassination. "I was at sea without a compass," he said.

General Grant was sympathetic however, promising to see what he could do. While the wheels were turning, a very trouble-making article appeared in the NEW YORK HERALD which pointedly insinuated Mercer was taking the girls into prostitution. The feature was widely reprinted, delaying and almost canceling out Mercer's project. He had already written home that he was practically on the way with 300 young ladies and many of them who had agreed to come, withdrew after reading the story, others changing their minds simply because of the delay. But the ship did sail with forty-six single women, some widows, all suffering the rigors of sailing-vessel life, all subject to male influence. At one port several handsome Spanish officers came aboard and paid such devoted attention to the girls, several of them almost defected for a life in South America. Others were magnetized by a California gold field adventurer and had to be dissuaded from joining him. None were lost however in the group movement from San Francisco to Puget Sound on small schooners, some of the winsome cargo arriving at Port Gamble, Port Madison and other sawmill docks. If the waiting single men turned out in droves to greet them in Seattle, they never had a chance with Annie E. Stephens. With her Asa Mercer had the inside track — all the way from the East — and now married her.

THEY CALLED HER MOTHER DAMNABLE
Mary Ann Conklin

Seattle grew so fast in its early years there was almost no place for newcomers to eat or sleep under cover. Temporary relief came with a restaurant operated by a German, David Maurer, and in the homes of some residents. Notably for hospitality were the Andrew Butlers who never turned a stranger away. The first genuine hotel was the Felker House at Jackson Street and Western Avenue. Built by Capt. Leonard M. Felker of the brig *Franklin Adams,* it was an elegant structure of two stories with plastered walls.

The Felker House name soon became only a technicality, the hostelry becoming known far and wide as the Conklin House, dominated as it was by the cook and manager, Mrs. Mary Ann Conklin. Famous for her cooking, she was even better known to seamen for gusts of vile temper and a vocabulary of depth and richness. Her husband was only

THIS SPOT in Lake View Cemetery, is believed to be grave of Mrs. Conklin, better known in her day as Mother Damnable. No positive proof exists, original burial record being unavailable. Lake View records show entry about time bodies were transferred from Denny Hill Cemetery—name Conklin followed by small, hesitant "d". Site is surrounded by others positively known to have been brought from Denny Hill.

a dim figure in the background, it being generally accepted that any efforts to assert himself would be lost in a gale of invective. It was easy to see why the redoubtable woman became known up and down the Coast as Mother Damnable. One old map shows location of the hotel marked Mme. Damnable.

Hard and rough, she brooked no delay in payment of board and room but in at least one case she apparently made an exception. One of the interesting items in Vol. 1 of King County Deeds, is the record of sale and delivery to Mary Ann Conklin of one scow, fourteen feet in width, forty-five feet in length, in payment of board bill amounting to $110.00.

When Mary Ann died she was buried in the tiny cemetery on top of Denny Hill with other pioneer Seattleites. When the hill was cut down to provide more space for the expanding city, the graves were first moved to Lake View Cemetery. Mother Damnable's was undisturbed until almost all the others were exhumed and moved, and when workmen came to hers, it is related, they were unable to lift the coffin. When the lid was removed to clear up the mystery of all that weight, it was found that her body had turned to solid stone.

Such petrification, while somewhat unbelievable, is not unique. Numerous instances of the kind have been reported, notably that of Wild Bill Hickok. Some reputable archaeologists think the phenomenon possible, the "stone" being more likely only a partial mineralization of tissues.

RISING SUN symbol is unusual. When Martha Roberts was born in Wallulu (sic), Washington was still a territory.

MAN WITH A WILL AND A MILL
Henry Yesler

On a fine October day all the men of the infant town of Seattle were chopping spar timber in the "sag", about where Pioneer Place is now. They heard a canoe scrape on the beach and saw a stranger getting out. He proved to be Henry Yesler, forty-five, a ruddy and chunky German immigrant who would be a strong factor in the settlement's future.

David Denny invited him to the small cabin he occupied with his bride, Louisa, and Yesler told him he wanted to build a sawmill somewhere nearby. It was more than welcome information but Yesler's enthusiasm was somewhat dampened when he learned all the desirable land along the immediate waterfront was taken. So a day or so later Yesler took a claim on the opposite side of the bay for his sawmill site.

The Seattleites went into a huddle. It would never do to lose the mill, so some way must be devised to bring Yesler back. The matter was settled by Boren and Dr. Maynard paring off adjoining strips of their claims, narrow but widening at the beach like a wedge, and Yesler accepted, the piece of land following the Yesler Way of today. The German planned his mill building, the machinery to be powered by steam. the first of this kind in the area.

The cookhouse was built first, larger than needed but used later as a community center. With things going ahead, Yesler went to San Francisco to buy machinery and that same month an item appeared in the young newspaper *The Columbian* of Olympia, headlined: "Huzza For Seattle!" and predicting the mill would be a gold mine for Mr. Yesler, a boon to Seattle. This was the first news printed about Seattle.

As soon as the saw and machinery were unloaded from the vessel, Henry Yesler set it up and on March 28, 1853, the circular saw began cutting logs into timber for the mill to be built around the exposed machinery. The canny Dr. Maynard contracted to supply logs cut from the adjacent forest land he wanted to clear for his projected "Maynard town."

As fast as lumber was produced Yesler sold it at a good price to replace the split-cedar punchions and built a dock near the mill, as well as a small house, all at the flaring bay end of his land. It was a prosperous business for the genial "Dutchman" with a heavy accent but his generosity cut into his accumulated wealth. This was to come from the sale of his land which increased rapidly in value.

In 1865 Yesler collaborated with Charles Terry in initiating the town's first water system — springs tapped on the hills east of town and brought down in a V-shaped flume. When the system proved inadequate, Yesler bored logs to act as pipes to increase the volume of water, this line being used until 1886.

The city grew up rapidly around the tiny house at First and James where Yesler lived until 1883. Then he cut down the fine orchard he had planted and built an imposing mansion, on what is now the site of the County-City Building, where he lived out his life. The impressive monument on his grave is seen in the background of the photo of Princess Angeline's grave stone.

Soon after this event, Yesler and other city leaders initiated a movement to build a railroad over the mountains to Walla Walla. It was begun but never completed. After some years it did get as far as the rich coal beds at Newcastle and Wilkison.

During his lifetime Arthur Denny remained the dominant figure in Seattle's history. He lived to the end in his Victorian house on his claim in the heart of town. When friends suggested he move or build a more modern home he would say, "Maybe I would but what would I do with my cow?"

David became a rich man through his efforts to improve the city. He helped install water, electric and street railway systems but was completely ruined in the panic of 1893. He left the city and retired to a cabin in the woods, the only dwelling that remained of his once extensive holdings. And there he died.

DOCTOR OF ALL TRADES
Dr. David S. Maynard

Dr. David Maynard made a great success of his store in Olympia on Puget Sound — but no money. If a customer needed merchandise, it was his whether he could pay or not. Hail fellow, well met, the doctor was especially generous when in a convivial mood. As his friends increased, his business boomed while that of his competitors declined, all the while his books showing more red ink. "Something has got to be done," the doctor reflected ruefully. "I could make more money packing salmon and shipping it to San Francisco." Then a rival store owner made it clear it would be well if the physician-turned-merchant took his benevolent type of business elsewhere.

Dr. Maynard was in the habit of discussing his problems with the Suquamish Indian Chief Sealth, called Seattle, his close friend. The chief suggested that Maynard move north to the tiny new settlement of New York on the point later called Alki. There he could catch and pack salmon to his heart's content. Maynard did go there but not liking the location joined with settlers on the point in a move to the east shore of sheltered Elliott Bay. They even offered to shift their claim stakes a bit north to make room for him. On advice of Chief Seattle, Maynard considered a place somewhat south of the others, long used by the chief and his followers as a campsite, but after mature reflection he decided to accept the offer made by settlers Arthur Denny and William Bell.

For the fish shipping enterprise Maynard had Indians catch enough salmon to fill nearly a thousand barrels. The fish were properly salted (he thought) and shipped to the Bay City but something went wrong. As the barrels were unloaded on the docks the stench from them nearly overpowered the crew. The entire shipment was a total loss and so was Maynard's new business.

The doctor then opened a new store, determined to be less of an easy mark than at Olympia. He put up a large sign on the front reading, "Seattle Exchange", the village by this time having been named Seattle for the friendly chief. Olympia boasted a newspaper, the *Columbian,* and one of the earliest issues carried an advertising notice for the business: "We are now receiving direct from London and New York, via San Francisco, a general assortment of dry goods, groceries, hardware, crockery, etc. suitable for the wants of im-

DR. MAYNARD'S BURIAL was the first in the new Masonic Cemetery, later Lake View, where many other Seattle pioneers are buried. Huge sequoia tree near grave follows age pattern of many others in Northwest, dating back from about period of California gold rush, seeds probably brought north by returning miners. Marble slabs marking graves of Maynard, wife, and others were originally upright, but having fallen, have been replaced in horizontal position.

migrants just arriving. First come, first served."

In July of 1862 Maynard was appointed Justice of the Peace for the "Duwamps" precinct at the mouth of the Duwamish River. His first case concerned the mate of the brig *Franklin Adams*, accused of misappropriating ship's goods. Although the man was obviously guilty, the easy going doctor-justice let him off with a mild scolding and warning.

Before coming West, Maynard separated from his wife and now went to Oregon City to get a legislative divorce at the Territorial Legislature. Back in Seattle he married "the widow Broshears" whom he met and loved on the journey across the plains.

By 1853 the local government of Seattle was established, the town platted before the new clerk of probation, Henry Yesler, and Dr. Maynard's portion was fifty-eight blocks of what would be downtown in later years. He subdivided the property to become the town's first realtor, although he called his land Maynardsville. True to form, he

sold many lots for very little, just to keep them moving. He set up a young blacksmith with lot, shop and all equipment for ten dollars, the property now the southeast corner of First and Washington Streets.

After the Indian War in the 1850s, Seattle suffered a severe period of depression, the loss of business affecting even Dr. Maynard's characteristic optimism. He found that Charles Terry, still at Alki, had 320 acres there and would be willing to trade even for Maynard's still unplatted 260 acres in Seattle. So the doctor moved to Alki where he had almost settled earlier, Terry moving to Seattle.

Maynard found the going hard. Uncounted Indians camped around the house taking advantage of his well-known hospitality. As a farmer he decided he was a good doctor so he decided to go into practice in Seattle, finally realizing $450 for his remaining 315 acres of land at Alki. Now he gave his whole attention to medicine, opening in 1863 Seattle's first hospital in his home, Mrs. Maynard serving as nurse. Most of their first patients were injured loggers and sawmill workers.

During Maynard's final years he was assailed by much litigation. His donation land claim was acquired while he was still married to Lydia, his first wife. However he had separated from her and was not yet married to Catherine. Courts held he was not entitled to the "married man's claim" but only to half of it or 160 acres allowed to single men. This tied in knots the Alki property which had been traded even. Lydia came west to prove she had been his legal, if separated wife, but he lost the case and was left nearly impoverished. Catherine had joined him in welcoming Lydia at the steamer landing, the three walking to the Maynard home, the doctor with a wife on each arm. They all lived together at the house for several months.

Seattle's first physician, first realtor, first justice of the peace and founder of her first hospital died March 13, 1873. His funeral was held in Yesler's Pavilion and a brass band led the procession to the cemetery.

WHEN INDIANS ATTACKED settlers at Seattle, all settlers ran for shelter of fort built for just such emergencies. Volunteer soldiers remained just outside behind fort walls, firing on Indians. The sloop of war **Decatur** was fortunately in harbor, shells lobbed from its cannons likely turning tide of battle. Adventurous William Holgate, only fifteen years old, sheltered in the fort, decided to join soldiers outside. As he emerged from front door he became target for Indians, dying instantly. Only other fatality among whites was youth named Robert Wilson, who was killed in same manner while slipping from Mother Damnable's establishment.

ELISHA P. FERRY first served as a territorial governor of Washington and then when statehood arrived he was elected Washington state's first governor.

MISSIONARY FARMER
WHO STARTED A COLLEGE

Rev. Cushing Eells and wife

Rev. Cushing Eells went to the Oregon Country with the newly married Dr. Gray, Drs. Elkanah Walker and A. B. Smith, their wives and teacher Cornelius Rogers. In 1838 the Mission Board expanded its field, Eells and Walker being assigned to the Spokanes at Tshimakain, now Walker's Prairie, near Colville, 225 miles north of Waiilatpu —a strategic selection, it being the home of a chief and crossroads of Indian travel.

In 1840 the little log cabin of the Eells family was gutted by fire. The Indians were helpful, dragging out some of the Eells' belongings but most of their valuables were lost—books, the only clock, saddle and all bedding. Snow was deep, the temperature 10 degrees below zero but four men came from Colville to help make the cabin comfortable again.

Even more discouraging was the apathy of the Indians. Eells complained they were not at all concerned about their souls, persisting in their usual dances, incantations and gambling. One advised the minister he would get a far larger audience keeping the men supplied with plenty of tobacco rather than preaching. Mrs. Eells wrote to her mother in March, 1847, "We have been here almost nine years, and we have yet to be permitted to hear the cries of one penitent, or the songs of one redeemed soul."

After the Whitman massacre the Eells family moved to the Willamette Valley where they lived in a tiny log cabin with a puncheon floor. Mrs. Eells made the family's bread in a wash basin and baked it in a gallon can buried in hot coals.

By 1862 the family was at Waiilatpu, operating a farm near the massacre site. The whole valley was beset by horse thieves and a vigilante committee was organized to combat them. Myron, Dr. Eells' oldest son, was a member and the first shooting of a horse thief by the committee took place at the edge of the Eells farm. Soon after this they hanged six or eight men, causing about seventy-five of the worst offenders to leave the valley. All through the trouble the Eells boys slept with loaded guns within easy reach. Myron and his mother were alone one night when a man came to the house, asking to stay the night, saying he had been at Waiilatpu at the time of the massacre. He was allowed to stay, Myron keeping a close watch on him. After leaving the next morning he was caught with several articles belonging to the Eells and the vigilantes marched him out of town. The man stretched his luck too far by returning a short time later and he was strung up to a tree—the last lynching at Walla Walla.

Later Rev. Eells founded Whitman College and from 1874 to 1888 rode the preacher circuit, traveling hundreds of miles on his sorrel horse to reach different Indian villages and churches.

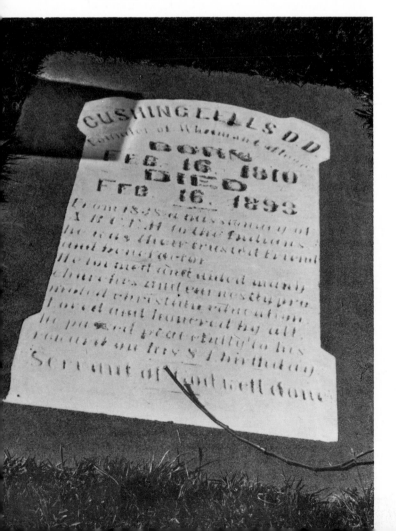

CUSHING EELLS, founder of Whitman College was fiery Methodist preacher, loudly accused Catholics of tolerating, even instigating tragic Whitman massacre. In rebuttal, Catholics blamed Methodists for allowing build-up of long smouldering resentments, suspicions, harbored by Indians. Originally in erect position, Eells marker has fallen to ground, is now placed horizontally.

THE CHIEF WAS BETRAYED

Chief Leschi

"The whites are plotting to send us all to a land called Polakly Illene. There the sun never shines everything is always in darkness. The rivers are so slimy fish cannot live. the mosquitos are so large one bite will kill a man." In such words Leschi spoke to his followers some of whom had been half convinced they should submit to the whites.

While Chief Seattle talked to his Suquamish Indians of peace, Nisqually Chief Leschi argued his tribesmen should join with fierce "Horse Indians, the Yakimas, in a concerted effort to wipe all white settlements from the Northwest. Natural enough was Leschi's friendliness with the Yakimas, his mother having come from that tribe on the eastern slope of the Cascades.

Earlier Leschi had been almost as friendly toward the whites as Seattle. He freely offered the use of his horses when J. E. Allen and his volunteers built the military road to Fort Steilacoom. When a party of immigrants bogged down on Naches Pass, they were saved by provisions carried in by Nisquallies under Leschi.

He was even willing to sign the Medicine Creek Treaty of 1854, third in the line of Indian chiefs signing the document proferred by Governor Stevens. Taking the paper in his hands he asked several questions about matters not clear and learned the deep, rich land his tribesmen held would be exchanged for bleak desert sand. In a rage he strode from the council, refusing to sign. His signature does appear in the place meant for it and could quite possibly be a forgery.

As rumors of an impending attack by hostiles

on Seattle built up the sloop *Decatur* anchored in Elliott Bay. On January 25, 1855, Capt. Guert Gansevoor sent out scouts to reconnoiter the woods around Lake Washington and they brought in reports of massed Yakimas and Klickitats preparing to join with the Nisquallies under Chief Leschi, their purpose only too clear.

Next day the attack came, Indian tribes spreading out on a line about where Third Avenue is now, and two whites — Robert Wilson and Milton Holgate — were killed. In all probability Seattle would have been ravaged and all inhabitants slain except for the *Decatur* and refusal of local Indians under Chief Seattle to join in the attack. Late in the evening the warriors retreated toward the Duwamish River, Leschi shouting that he would return and finish the extermination. As he passed small settlements on his way south he pillaged the houses and set them afire. Completely destroyed was Duwamish village which had been settled before Seattle.

Then came the inevitable reprisals. Gov. Stevens put a price in Leschi's head which drove the chief into hiding for three years. Then he offered to surrender to a man who had been his friend, Col. Casey at Fort Steilamoom. The colonel advised Leschi to remain in the woods for a time because of violent public feeling. Leschi stayed but was betrayed by his own nephew, Sluggia, who was offered 50 blankets to reveal the hiding place.

At the trial Leschi was defended by some white settlers and Army officers but the prosecution won its case largely by declaring, "Since Leschi had signed the Medicine Creek Treaty he had flagrantly violated its terms" and should be hanged.

CHIEF LESCHI mounted scaffold on Feb. 19, 1855. Said Charles Grainger, one of the executioners, "I felt . . . I was executing an innocent man." Tribesmen carried Leschi's body into woods for quiet burial. Thirty-five years later whites and Indians joined in movement to exhume body, rebury it on grounds of Tacoma Indian Sanatorium. Controversy is still revived occasionally—was Leschi a rescally renegade or was he sincerely attempting to do what he thought best for his people?

WALLA WALLA BING BANG

WHO DRANK THE WHISKEY?

Chief Peu-peu-mox-mox

It is said that an Indian, when imitating the sound of a gun firing, instead of using the white man's "bang-bang", said "peu mox", which could possibly shed some light on the strange name for the chief of the Walla Walla Indians.

During the summer and fall of 1855 marauding Yakimas and Walla Wallas had been making life miserable for settlers east of the Cascade Mountains while Gov. Stevens was attempting to complete treaties with the various tribes. Chief Peu-peu-mox-mox vowed that when Stevens showed up in his territory he would personally slay and scalp the governor. Col. James K. Kelly with six companies of Oregon Volunteers was sent to the area near Waiilatpu to prevent such an assassination.

Kelly and his troops found Walla Walla already pillaged and deserted and he took his men up the Touchet River in pursuit of the savages. On Dec. 5, 1855, the troops made camp for the night.

Next morning, Chief Peu-peu-mox-mox came to the camp bearing a white flag of truce. That he could be sincere seemed unbelievable to Kelly and he decided to break truce conventions and "detain" the suspiciously surly chief. No sooner had the party started for Waiilatpu than it was forced to stop by gunfire from Indians concealed in shrubs along the Touchet. Riding by were arrogant braves flaunting poles crowned by fresh and bloody scalps of white settlers.

The Indians were converging on the little village of Frenchtown and Kelly's troops pursued them. When the savages discovered they were being attacked from the rear they barricaded themselves in one of the settlers' houses and shot several of Kelly's men as they approached. Early next morning Kelley made a near hit with his howitzer and as Indians tumbled out doors and windows, Peu-peu-mox-mox, who had been growing wildly excited tried to grab a rifle from one of the soldiers guarding him. This was a fatal mistake as he immediately received a blow across the head from the stock of the weapon.

The battle seemed almost hopeless, hundreds of Indians appearing from all sides. But at the crucial moment cavalry troops joined the fray and the concerted charge scattered the Indians who took to the hills and did not return. Kelly proceeded on his original mission, to meet Gov. Stevens.

Before leaving the body of Peu-peu-mox-mox, soldiers scalped it and cut off the ears for souvenirs, placing them in a jar of whiskey. Some time later it was discovered the container had been drained. Question — who drank the whiskey off the ears of Chief Peu-peu-mox-mox?

OLD ST. ROSE MISSION cemetery was laid out in separate sections, one for whites, one for Indians. Peu-peu-mox-mox was buried in latter, tall wooden cross placed at spot. After many years frail monument fell to ground, as did other wooden markers, until most identities were lost. Finally, farmer-owners of ground rescued cross, replacing it on new support near monument marking site of white settlers' and priests' graves. Then entire area surrounding two remaining markers was plowed and planted to grain. Markers now stand on skyline plainly visible from stone monument marking site of vanished Frenchtown, beside highway near Waiilatpu.

MEMORIAL MONUMENT
FOR FIVE SOLDIERS

After disaster in White Bird Canyon, the stage for action in the Nez Perce War of 1877 moved to the Clearwater. Here General Howard was in charge of troops, and although his soldiers were hemmed in and separated from the river for a time in hot weather, suffering greatly from thirst, victory was eventually theirs. General Howard commented later "I do not think that I had to exercise more thorough generalship during the Civil War than in that march to the battlefield and the ensuing battle with Joseph and his Indians on the banks of the Clearwater River." Routed Indians fled up the Lolo Pass, making good their escape even though hampered by accompanying old men, squaws and children. Their mounts were urged on unmercifully, forced over rocks and fallen trees until many gave out and were left to die.

Indian fatalities in Battle of the Clearwater were heavy but numbers not exactly determined. White's losses were 40 casualties in dead and wounded. Five of the dead belonged to a company stationed at old Vancouver Barracks (then called Columbia Barracks.) Old cemetery records there show that a "marble monument" was erected to their memory.

ON DAY FOLLOWING battle of Clearwater, burial parties interred thirteen soldiers and 15 warriors. Eight more Indian bodies were found later. Still later when weather had cooled, white soldiers' bodies were exhumed, taken to Walla Walla for permanent burial. Most were unidentifiable, two that were have separate markers.

AMONG THE WILD CAYUSES

THAT BLEAK DAY IN NOVEMBER
Whitman Massacre

The 29th of November, 1847, is a vital one in the history of the Pacific Northwest, a notorious one in the long record of Indian atrocities. This was the day of wanton slaughter at the Marcus Whitman mission at Waiilatpu on the Walla Walla River, an event that had many repercussions and brought about war between the settlers and Cayuse Indians.

One of the motives that triggered the attack was the Indian suspicion that all missionaries, the Whitmans in particular, were attempting to kill the natives by slow poison. The foundation of this belief was laid at Astoria shortly after news of the *Tonquin* disaster reached there. In spite of the friendliness of the Chinooks, as expressed by Chief Concomly, Factor Douglas McDougal was worried. He felt the episode would so embolden and excite the Indians they might attack the fort at Astoria.

The factor called a meeting of chiefs and sub-chiefs and showed them a small corked vial. He told them it was packed with dreaded smallpox and that if he were to pull the cork all tribes would be struck by pestilence. Frightened Indians begged McDougal to leave the cork in the vial, swearing they would always be friends of the white man. The incident occurred in 1813 and word of it spread from tribe to tribe, penetrating deeply and was never forgotten. Every attack of smallpox, measles or venereal disease was attributed to the traders, or later to missionaries.

The Whitman's and others who died at Waiilatpu were victims of their acts of kindness.

Marcus Whitman and wife Narcissa served as doctors to the tribesmen. Naturally results were not always successful, many Indians already near death could not be saved by medication. It was Joe Lewis, mixed blood Delaware, who actually sparked the slaughter. Some time earlier Lewis had gone to the mission in a condition so near death he could hardly crawl. The Whitmans took him in without question and nursed him back to health. Instead of being grateful the half-breed talked of murder to his Indian friends. He told them the Whitmans had no intention of keeping them well but were gradually poisoning them with medicines, planning to exterminate the tribes and gain control of their lands. He reminded Peu-peu-mox-mox, chief of the Walla Wallas, of the fact that his son had gone to Fort Sutter in California to buy cattle for his people and had been wantonly slain there. He recalled to the tribesmen an age-old custom that demanded the slaying of a medicine man who failed to effect a cure.

Little Nancy Osborne had been at the mission just five weeks when the fatal day came. Dr. Whitman hired her father to take charge of the mission so he could spend more time with the Indians. Osborne was to receive $300 a year for two years, paid in either livestock or money, the family to be housed and fed. When they arrived at the mission a measles epidemic was raging, the Osborne baby falling victim and dying as did a six-year-old sister. Mrs. Whitman laid the girl's body on a bench, calling an Indian to explain that the malady was not confined to the natives, that whites were dying too. The brave looked long at the little body, laughing scornfully as he left.

On the 29th of November, Mrs. Osborne went into Narcissa Whitman's room to see Hannah Sager and Helen Meek who were sick with the measles. Two chiefs, Telokite and Tomahas, came to the front door asking for medicine and Dr.

INDIANS RESPONSIBLE for murders of missionaries were rounded up, taken to Oregon City, tried, hanged. Before his execution Tomahas gave his tomahawk to his brother Sonch who gave it to his close friend Stock Whitely as special mark of esteem. Whitely fought whites in past, now joined with them in fighting common enemy, the Snake Indians. He was slain in first battle east of Cascades, his family presenting tomahawk to Donald McKay who in turn gave it to William Logan of The Dalles. Logan donated it to "Sanitary Cause" organization raising funds for medical supplies for Union Army during Civil War. Exhibit of weapon brought $100 and then it was sold to unidentified man who gave it to state "to suggest to coming generations what they escaped." Historic weapon is now on display at Oregon Historical Society.

THIS PHOTO taken from spot once front door of Whitman's Mission House. On hill in background is seen monument to victims. On fatal day Indians stationed braves on summit, charged them with seeing no one escaped. Just beyond rail fence is section of original Oregon Trail, used while mission flourished but after massacre travelers took route farther south. Framing view is venerable locust tree, still leafless in March.

MEANDERING WALLA WALLA RIVER once brought waters in sharp bend close to Mission House, first primitive, smaller residence on bank. Marshy area shown at right marks old river location. Whitman's toddling daughter wandered into stream near or at this point, was drowned. Dry bank also marks place where Nancy Osborne and family hid in thicket overnight to escape after slaughter of others. Tall grass at left remains from summer's growth of rye. Name of mission — Waiilatpu — means "Place of Rye Grass". Snowy range in background is part of Blue Mountains.

Whitman, who was reading by the fire got up to get it. While one Indian was distracting the missionary's attention, the other drew out his pipe tomahawk and smashed it twice into Whitman's skull.

With Osborne's help, Narcissa Whitman carried her mortally wounded husband to a couch. She asked him if she could do anything for him and as he died he said simply, "No". Mrs. Whitman cried out, "My husband is dead and I am left a widow! That Joe Lewis, he has done it all." Then she went to the front of the house where the Osborne family were loosening some boards and secreting themselves under the floor. Nancy Osborne later remembered, "I could see the Indians through the cracks in the boards. The room was full of Indians. They were laughing and talking as if it were a holiday."

A volley of rifle fire came from outside and bullets coming through the window struck Mrs. Whitman twice. As she fell dying, Joe Lewis and other Indians forced their way into the house. Lewis pointed a rifle at Francis Sager, fourteen, and

Nancy's schoolmate, as he cried, "Oh, Joe, please don't shoot me!" The plea went unheeded. Lewis killed the boy.

The slaughter went on until all male members of the mission force in the building were killed — except Osborne under the floor with his family. Two men sick in another house were spared but clubbed to death later when it appeared they would recover. Several others hid in the emigrant house and later slipped away. One was Peter Hall who obtained a canoe and disappeared down the Columbia. He was never heard from and it was thought he became insane from horror.

By ten o'clock all was quiet in the charnel house. The Osborne family emerged and Nancy touched the white forehead of young Francis Sager, but there was no hoped-for warmth there. They crossed the fields in the darkness toward the Walla Walla River, Osborne carrying the others across one at a time. Even Mrs. Osborne, still weak from her near fatal bout with the measles, had to be helped and all hid in the bushes on the bank.

With daylight they saw they were near a trail, Indians passing empty-handed toward the mission and returning with plunder. The Osbornes dared not move, not even the short distance to the river for water, but Osborne fastened a stick to the tin cup Nancy picked up as she left the Whitman house, and managed to poke it into a pool, obtaining a swallow or two each try.

That night he took his small son on his back and made his precarious way to the nearby Fort Walla Walla where he left the boy in the care of a Mr. Stanley and with a horse and friendly Walla Walla, returned to his near-starving family. All were then reunited in the dubious safety of the fort, and subsequently rescued along with the other survivors.

REV. J. B. BROUILLET of St. Anne's Mission on Umatilla River went to Waiilatpu shortly after massacre and found bodies of victims still unburied. He stayed overnight and in morning went to aid of Joseph Stanfield who was trying to bury them himself. Brouillet gathered mission sheets to wrap up bodies and helped Stanfield carry them to graves. All victims but one were buried there, the man killed bringing load of wood being buried where he lay.

Next January Joe Meek and George W. Ebberts of French Prairie, on their way to Washington, D.C., stopped at site, found lightly covered bodies dug up by coyotes, flesh stripped to bone. They dug deeper grave on level spot up slope and reburied skeletal bodies. Some time later Oregon Volunteers appeared on scene and added more soil, placed wagon bed over grave as further protection. Some years following Rev. Eells built farmhouse near site, his young son putting fence around unmarked mound. Present marble slab was laid over "Great Grave" and dedicated in 1887, several women attending being girls who survived slaughter, one, Nancy Osborne.

White marble shaft nearby marks graves of Rev. William Henry Gray and wife. Gray collaborated — and quarreled — with Whitmans and Spauldings, resigning from mission service in 1832, going to live in French Prairie and thus escaping massacre as well as voting for Provisional Government at Champoeg. Small bronze plaque on left side of marker near base is common one denoting graves of signers.

The massacre, besides arousing a nation in reprisal against the Indians, stirred up a storm of religious controversy that has never been settled. The seldom used source of history concerning missionary work of several faiths, *Oregon Missions* by James Bashford, published in 1918, gives an almost hysterically biased report by Rev. Eells on Marcus Whitman from the Methodist viewpoint. He says surviving members of the white families slaughtered in the mission believed to their dying days that Roman Catholic missionaries tolerated if not encouraged the superstitious Indians in the belief of poisoning. He says further that Vicar General Brouillet of the Catholic mission arrived at Waiilatpu just after the massacre, and while bodies lay unburied, the Indians took Brouillet to the house of one of the victims, telling him to make himself at home.

"All night long," Eells writes, "the air was rent with shrieks and groans of the white women with whom the Indians were sating their lust. There was no protest from Father Brouillet against the satanic conduct of the Indians." He continues in this vein to say that next morning while the slain white men still lay all around, Brouillet assembled the Indian children and baptized them in the

GRANITE SHAFT was erected to memory of massacre victims 50 years after catastrophe. Massacre ended Protestant missionary work among Indians in Oregon, led to war on Cayuses by settlers in Willamette River Valley.

MORTAR DR. WHITMAN USED to compound medicines branded by superstitious Cayuses as "death potions". Writer Bernard De Voto often berated authorities for neglect of several historic sites, especially that at Waiilatpu. Oversight has been rectified by Federal government, establishing area as Whitman Mission National Site. Mortar is among many relics displayed in modern museum on grounds.

Catholic faith, afterwards aiding another white man in burying the dead.

Bashford tries to counter this. When Father Brouillet left Waiilatpu, he writes, he met Rev. Spaulding who was on his way to visit the Whitmans, totally unaware of what had happened. Spaulding later wrote of how Brouillet told him what he did at the mission, including his baptizing of the children and aiding in the burial. And Brouillet strongly urged Spaulding to turn back and avoid meeting the fate that befell Whitman. In defending the Catholic side of the argument, Bashford asks, "Would Father Brouillet have told Spaulding of his actions at Waiilatpu if he felt any guilt or sense of wrongdoing? And surely if he had wanted to dispose of Spaulding, the easy way would have been to simply allow events to take their course by allowing him to proceed on to the mission and certain death."

"I WILL FIGHT NO MORE FOREVER"

"Whenever the white man treats the Indian as they treat each other," Chief Joseph once said, "then we shall have no more wars. We shall all be alike — brothers of one father and one mother, with one sky above us and one country around us and one government for all. . . . ."

Hin-Mah-Too-Yah-Lat-Kekt was his Nez Perce name, meaning Thunder Rolling in the Mountains, but the white men called him Chief Joseph — this brilliant, intelligent, spiritually-minded warrior and leader. He wanted peace but accepted war and when he saw it was useless he surrendered. Expecting the government to keep the promises of Gen.

Miles, to return the warriors to Idaho, he saw them broken, his Nez Perce shunted from one reservation to another, suffering with each change.

Finally, with 150 tribesmen, Chief Joseph was sent to the Colville Indian Reservation at Nespelem where he lived out his life in comparative peace and comfort. At his death the wish he once made was granted him. "Let me be a free man, free to travel, free to stop, free to work, free to trade where I choose, free to choose my own brothers, free to follow the religion of my fathers, free to think and talk and act for myself." (From *Here Rolled the Covered Wagons*: Albert and Jane Salisbury).

"HEAR ME, MY CHIEFS," began Chief Joseph in his famed appeal to his people during treaty negotiations with the whites. He lies buried in the Catholic cemetery at Nespelem, Wash., site of Colville Indian Reservation, surrounded by graves of other Indians of the Nez Perce wars. Pointed stakes flanking monument were used at time of burial to display prized possessions of deceased Indians.

PORT TOWNSEND

THE DUKE OF YORK—INDIAN STYLE

It was a case of strong men struggling with the word. The Chimacums were a small, deteriorated tribe of Indians living on the Strait of Juan de Fuca where it opened into Puget Sound but in one respect they had the white settlers buffaloed. Since the whites could not talk like dogs growling and coughing they could not pronounce names like Lahkanim and Quatumalow. So the chief became "King George", two females "Queen Victoria" and "Jenny Lind", and the chief's younger brother the "Duke of York."

When Port Townsend was settled the Duke of York was about forty, short and stocky of stature with large luminous eyes. Born about 1808 of a Skagit father and Clallam mother, both of whom had established some rapport with George Vancouver and other early explorers, the child was named Chetzemoka. He was about fourteen when a large band of predatory northern Indians, supposedly Haidas from the Queen Charlotte Islands, descended on the more peaceable Chimacums at Kuhn's Spit and massacred all but four, bones of the slain lying exposed for years.

Chetzemoka, familiarly Duke of York, was a frequent visitor to the Port Townsend settlement and was fascinated by white men's clothes, expressing a desire to have some like them. To keep on his good side some of the women made him a unique outfit, coat and pants fashioned from a blue blanket. Bright red stripes cut from a petticoat were sewn on arms and legs, the gaudy ensemble topped by a ship's officer's cap. Chetzemoka was so regaled most of the time.

Officers of the brig *Franklin Adams,* in port around 1852, invited the gorgeously caparisoned native to go to San Francisco with them. In the Bay City James G. Swan showed him the attractions — Seal Rocks, Woodward's Gardens, dance halls — and the Indian made the pronouncement in Chinook jargon, "White man powerful, soon big city grow up on Olympic Peninsula too, no use fighting intruders."

Chetzemoka's tribesmen were not disposed to be so friendly although they did not actually wage war. While Chetzemoka was in California they became insolent, often offensive, and some settlers panicked, sending to San Francisco for help. In response the U.S. *Active* was sent north. Selecting a time when many natives were in evidence, the ship fired a salvo of loud, harmless shots and sailed south and this ended outward displays of hostility for a time.

While his young brother was seeing the white man's life in the south, King George, regarded as chief, was making himself obnoxious. Always surly, he drank constantly, would go into a trading post, pick out whatever pleased his fancy and refuse to

GRAVE of "Protector of Port Townsend", Chief Chetzemoka, "Duke of York", located in tranquil Laurel Grove Cemetery, Port Townsend. After his death, comment made by Judge James G. Swan could well have been his epitaph. "The Duke and I were firm friends. He was the truest friend among the Indians the early settlers ever had, and the one who did more than any other to keep his tribes from warring with the whites". Old chief's grave is distinguished from all others by cover of gleaming oyster shells.

pay for it, saying, "you can apply cost of this to small payment on land you take from us." He spoke with some logic but was behaving abominably when Chetzemoka returned.

The two quarreled and King George gathered up his belongings, paddled out into the harbor, boarded a ship and departed. In San Francisco he prospered in the oyster business, married a white woman and bought a schooner. His meanness prevailed however and the crew was reported to have thrown him overboard one stormy night. They later said their Indian captain had been accidentally swept overboard. Chetzemoka was now chief in fact, no one worrying over his brother's fate.

From then on, although his followers often showed signs of unrest, sometimes even planning attacks, the new chief was always able to control them at the cost of his tribal prestige. His position was comparable to that of Seattle's guardian Chief Sealth who also suffered taunts from his own people.

PRINCE OF WALES was younger son of Duke of York, his tribal name Lahkanim. Prince was well liked by population of Port Townsend, known to be honest, upright, industrious in contrast to most members of tribe. Prince's older brother, Duke's first son, was known as General Gaines, died in earliest days of settlement.

GRAVE OF CAPTAIN THOMPSON is lonely insofar as humans are concerned, but gulls soar overhead, cormorants pearch for hours on nearby rotting pilings, their graceful shapes silhouetted against often stormy skies. Spot is near western entrance of Discovery Bay, glimpsed here in background.

WHAT CHEER WAS A DEATH SHIP

The bark *What Cheer*, master Cap. Thompson, wrote Mary Ann Lambert in her book, *From Dungeness Massacre and Other Tales*, cleared San Francisco for Portland Dec. 23, 1856. She went north from the Columbia River, many of the crew dying from smallpox, and all infected clothing and bedding were thrown overboard. Indians on the southern shores of Straits of Juan de Fuca salvaged the garments, were themselves infected and almost the entire village of 400 Ozett Indians was wiped out.

The *What Cheer* drifted on the sands of Deadman's Spit on Discovery Bay, Washington, near the point where the U. S. Quarantine Station would be established. Capt. Thompson presumably lived ashore here for a few years, dying in 1860 and buried in a plot on Deadman's Spit.

The story is told of the Indian, Big Ben, the Grandee, who lived at Washington Harbor, picking up a jacket on the beach and going the same way other smallpox victims went. Because there was so much death in his body, the Indians would not bury it but dragged it into the woods. Wolves set upon the body, contracted the deadly disease and it was many years before any number of them inhabited the woods again.

SAILORS from all over the world were buried in old quarantine station cemetery. Many Chinese were detained in station hospital because of contagious diseases, many dying and bodies taken to quarantine station crematorium.

CAPT. THOMPSON of death ship **What Cheer** is buried on Deadman's Spit, Discovery Bay, Wash., on Straits of Juan de Fuca. Most of crew perished of smallpox and ship drifted on sands. U. S. Quarantine Station was later built nearby. Inscription on weathered cross is hand cut by knife.

THEY BURIED HIM WITHOUT HIS HEAD

Col. Isaac N. Ebey

Prominent among the few settlers on Whidbey Island in Puget Sound in 1857, the Ebey family had a farm on the western side facing the sun setting over the Olympic Mountains. The Ebeys also faced certain dangers in the form of marauding Indians from the north. On August 11 a party of Haidas from the Southeastern Alaska area came down "like a wolf on the fold" and took Ebey's head back with them.

The Haidas were stalwart, intrepid sea hunters with a most advanced Indian culture. They built sea-going canoes of cedar trees, ranged far into the Pacific for sea otters and south to the Columbia River to trade furs and shell money with the Chinooks for slaves and goods that tribe got from eastern ones and white traders. On their way they were not above raiding villages of the Tsimshians and Kwakiutl or fighting white men who were threatening their hereditary waters and lands.

They lost twenty-seven men including a chief in a battle with the U. S. Navy on October 26, 1856, and in retaliation murdered the crews of two sailing ships, the *Blue Wing* and *Ellen Maria,* either sinking or sailing the ships away. Yet revenge was not complete. The Haida code required their taking the head of a chief.

Several canoes slipped along the shore of Whidbey Island, the warriors looking for Dr. J. C. Kellogg who by his good clothes and boat was obviously a *Hyas Tyee,* "big chief." Kellogg proved to be away so the canoes cruised on until a man was sighted working in a hayfield. The Indians signaled friendship and were able to understand enough English to learn the owner of the land was indeed "a great chief." The farm hand had as much as signed Col. Ebey's death warrant.

The Haidas waited until after dark, beached their canoes, approached the Ebey cabin and asked for the Big Chief. When he appeared they killed him instantly, cut off his head while the other Ebeys, with some guests, fled to neighbors. Finding armed resistance, the Haidas took their trophy and slipped northward in the night.

The head was discovered two years later in an Alaskan village by Ebey's friend, Capt. Charles Dodd of Hudson's Bay Co. At great risk of life he secured the skull and took it to Whidbey Island to be buried with the rest of the body. For this act Capt. Dodd was given a vote of thanks by the Territorial Legislature of Washington January 20, 1860.

MONUMENT TO COL. EBEY stands on western side of Whidbey Island at edge of bluff almost directly above water, across ship lane of Puget Sound from Port Townsend.

OLD LOG STRUCTURE is relic of "Blockhouse Era" starting after series of Indian raids in winter of 1856. Citizens were urged not to leave settlements, to build block blockhouses wherever there were three or more families. This survivor of period was built by a man named Davis, stands within boundaries of Sunnyside Cemetery on hill to east of Ebey farm.

CENTRAL SHAFT marks Ebey family plot in old Sunnyside Cemetery, near Prairie Center, Whidbey Island. Decapitated body of Col. Ebey was buried here, head added later when recovered. Also here are Ebey's wife and children who escaped with guests U. S. Marshal George Corliss and wife when Ebey was killed, but slain later by northern Indians.

GNARLED GROWTH DEVELOPED by old Camperdown elm shown in winter photo. Typically, "Scotch elm", **Ulmus glabra**, is upright but variation would sprawl over ground if not grafted on erect sapling. Joint shows clearly here. Tree is comparative rarity, similar one growing in Old City Cemetery in Vancouver, Washington, and was once depicted in newspaper "Believe It or Not" feature. Caption under sketch read — "The tree that grows upside down with its roots in the air."

CRADLE OF NORTHWEST HISTORY

FORT VANCOUVER CEMETERY

A decade after John Jacob Astor established Astoria in 1811, the Hudson's Bay Co. acquired possession of the post, and in 1824 moved company headquarters to the site of the present military reservation, up the Columbia on the Washington shore. Dr. John McLoughlin was made factor with plans to create a great depot that would serve as headquarters for the entire area west of the Rockies. Forty wooden buildings were erected inside a palisade measuring 500 by 750 feet, the whole named Fort Vancouver.

In 1829 the entire establishment was rebuilt closer to the river at a point now occupied by Pearson Army Airport. Commerce to Hawaii was started with the building of a sailing vessel named *Vancouver*. Its first return voyage brought back 300 islanders as laborers at the Fort and they kept quietly by themselves, living in the colony of Kanaka Town not far away.

It was not long before the Hawaiians began to die from white men's diseases and a cemetery was prepared. It was the only burial ground for many years and many of the earliest pioneers were interred here.

WHEN REMAINS OF DEAD buried in section of Post cemetery disturbed by building of freeway, and (supposedly) of those removed from old Fort Vancouver burial ground, some were identified by permanent stone or marble markers, more were not. All were reburied in sequence as they arrived after exhumation, those unidentified marked by common slab inscribed "Unknown". Some 200 of these stones now stand in undulating rows, marking graves of military, civilian pioneers, Kanakas brought from Hawaii.

Fort Vancouver Military Barracks was established on a site encroaching on if not absorbing much of the old fort grounds. And here begins a mystery that has defied persistent research. Robert Clark, historian at Fort Vancouver National Historic Site says any record that may exist as to the actual removal of bodies from the old cemetery would be in charge of Sergeant Beaver of the Military Barracks but he says, "All those records have gone to Never-Never Land. They simply do not exist. But I know enough about the U. S. Army to be certain that when the theater and other buildings were erected on the old graveyard, authorities would have first removed the bodies there". But where? And when? To complicate things further, when Mill Plain Road was run through part of the Military Barracks Cemetery, all remains encountered were moved over out of the right of way. Some graves, such as that of Lt. Watson, who was killed in an affray with Chief Paulina, were marked with durable headstones, and these were moved with the remains, yet the records show only the original date of burial, not of the transfer.

Among those almost certainly buried originally in old Fort Vancouver Cemetery were Esther Short, young John McLoughlin Jr., killed at Fort Stikine, Pierre Pambrun, killed at Fort Walla Walla, George Le Breton and one "Rogers", killed at Oregon City, Lt. Stephen Watson, killed in Central Oregon, and numerous personnel of the fort. It is definitely known that the remains of Esther Short were transferred to the then new City Cemetery. It was hoped that the date could be ascertained, helping to establish time of removal of others, probably occurring in same period.

It develops that all these records were destroyed in a court house fire long ago. It seems that what happened to the old Fort Vancouver Cemetery must remain a mystery, at least officially, authorities assuming those originally buried there now rest in anonymity in the Post Cemetery.

GALLANTRY WAS HIS UNDOING
Pierre Pambrun

On June 12, 1938 the Oregon Chapter of Daughters of 1812 erected a marker near the old, original Fort Vancouver Cemetery. Primarily the monument honored veterans of the War of 1812 buried there. Among them was Pierre Pambrun who distinguished himself in a heroic charge at Plattsburg, N.Y. in which he was wounded.

After the war Pambrun joined the fur traders flocking to the West, eventually becoming an employee of Hudson's Bay Co. He was made factor in charge of Fort Walla Walla in 1832, and there on March 4, 1834 was forced by company policy to refuse supplies to the suffering party of Capt. Benjamin Bonneville, it being the latter's intention to establish a rival fur trading post.

Pambrun was known for his successes with the ladies and gallant behavior toward them. Returning to Walla Walla from a trip to headquarters at Fort Vancouver, he was riding his favorite horse, a skittish mare, and as he approached the Fort buildings he came abreast of a group of women. Taking off his large hat, he made a grandiose flourish in greeting. His mount took fright and bolted, throwing the unprepared Pambrun to the ground, the fall killing him. His body was returned to the old cemetery at Fort Vancouver for burial.

IMPRESSIVE MARBLE MARKER was discovered by accident while photographing "unknown" markers in old Vancouver Barracks Post Cemetery. It is placed at random among small, anonymous stones, some showing in background, indicating grave was probably moved from earlier Post burial ground when Mill Plain highway overran it.

Of interest is sculpture of bird at top. Where many tombstones carry carved doves as emblems of peace, gentle bird would be out of place on fighting man's headstone and rampant eagle was used. Military cemetery is seldom visited by general public, otherwise historic grave would have been discovered earlier.

(See also "Slaughter by the Snakes," page 120.)

Caption on marker:
LIEUT. STEPHEN WATSON,
1st Ogn. Cavalry.
Born in St. Stephens N.B.
MAY 15. 1828.
Killed in battle with the Snake Indians near Crooked River Ogn.
MAY 18. 1864.
Erected to his memory by members of the Regiment

MURDER AT FORT STIKINE

John McLoughlin Jr.

Dr. John McLoughlin, the "White Headed Eagle", Hudson's Bay Co. factor at Fort Vancouver, wrote a startling letter to a friend in 1842. Calmly enough he commented on business and the weather at the Fort then suddenly blurted out "My son has been murdered by the company's servants at the post of Stikine in the Russian Territory (which we rent from them and of which he had charge) on the night of 20-21 April."

Young John, the father explained, had a force of 22 men, that Gov. George Simpson had "improperly" taken away his assistant, that at any post where liquor was dispensed there should always be at least two men in charge, and on hearing of his son's death, he sent a trusted employee to Fort Stikine (now Prince Rupert) to investigate.

It was clear employees at the post were more than a little unhappy with the young factor, complaining he treated them with unwarranted cruelty, unjust punishment by floggings and beatings, that most of these incidents occurred while he was drinking. An Indian woman, whom young John had taken as his "wife" contradicted this latter accusation, testifying she had never seen him take a drink.

An Owyhee (company term for Hawaiian employee) testified that on hearing a shot he looked out the window. "There was my son lying on the ground, melting in a pool of his own gore," wrote Dr. McLoughlin. "One man stood with his heel on the boy's throat while he fired additional shots into his body." Employees testified young John had "flogged one man for sleeping while on guard duty, one for fighting and refusing to desist, one for giving away all his property to an Indian woman, rendering him helpless and necessitating his re-equipping by the company, and four for stealing."

There had obviously been a general plot among all employees to kill the young factor, said McLoughlin, that the affair had come to a head on this particular night because his son had in the evening given the men one and a half gallons of spirits, the letter not explaining the reason.

In concluding his letter McLoughlin defended his son's character. "My son John was intelligent, active, and had the faults of youth, was inconsiderate and thoughtless, but was frank and open, firm and generous. His less desirable traits had seemed to be wearing away." The body was put aboard a ship and taken to the old Fort Vancouver cemetery.

CRADLE OF THE DEEP

ON THEIR LAND LIES VANCOUVER, WASHINGTON

Amos and Esther Short

Amos Short acquired more than a section of land on the Columbia River by default and a well-placed bullet, lost his life soon after at sea and his wife Esther ran the property into riches. When she died her ten children benefited but people who bought the city lots had their titles contested for twenty-five years.

In 1848, not long after evacuation by the British, Fort Vancouver was formally recognized as a part of the United States defense system. No sooner was the area safely under the American flag than a survey party headed by 1845 settler Henry Williamson of Indiana platted a township on the site. The men involved began securing property rights but the news of gold discoveries at Sutter's Mill in California lured Williamson and others to the south putting the new townsite at the mercy of the remaining residents.

Amos Short was one of them, claiming the whole site was his by default in Williamson de-

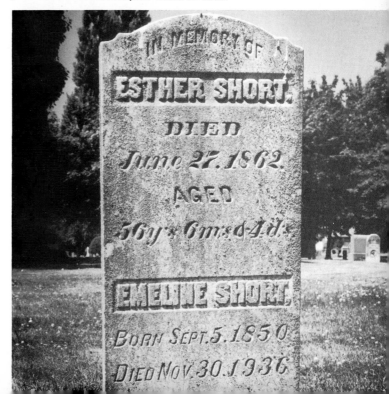

MONUMENT TO Esther Short stands in Vancouver's old City Cemetery. Mrs. Short was first buried in original Fort Vancouver Cemetery, transferred here later. At still later time spinster daughter Hannah Emeline was apparently interred in same grave and additional inscription added on stone.

IN MEMORY OF

ESTHER SHORT,

DIED

June 27. 1862.

AGED

56y & 6m & d 4 d.

EMELINE SHORT,

BORN SEPT. 5. 1850.

DIED NOV 30. 1936

ROCK-BARRICADED INLET where body of Capt. E. N. Beard, master of American bark **Vandalia** was washed in. Spot has been known as Beard's Hollow since wreck of ship, no remains of which were ever found.

serting his claim. Only one contender made difficulty and he was quickly removed from the scene by Short's gun. He was acquitted of murder on the grounds of defense of his home and came into possession of much of the land which Vancouver now occupies. Further establishing his status was his appointment as one of three probate judges of the new Clark County, Oregon Territory, almost immediately becoming Presiding Judge.

At this time San Francisco was booming with an influx of gold seekers. Fresh vegetables with other food was worth about as much as placer yieldings. Short had a bumper crop of potatoes in 1852 and took them to the Bay City, sailing for home with the proceeds on the *Vandalia,* which foundered on the Columbia bar. Last seen by Captain Phillips on the *Grecian,* the *Vandalia* signaled that though wallowing she was not in need of assistance.

Sometime later the wreck of the ship was found near rocky McKenzie Head. Apparently she had fouled on Peacock Spit, nemesis of many ships, her hull filled and was blown on the rocks bottom up. The body of Captain E. N. Beard washed ashore in an inlet later named Beard's Hollow. Three other

bodies drifted in, one of them that of a 14-year-old boy. The others remained unidentified and it was assumed Judge Amos Short was one of the twelve listed as lost. The land he possessed now passed into the hands of his widow Esther and their ten children. Historian Howard Burnham of Clark County Title Co. states that litigation over title to the property made news for twenty-five years.

On October 4, 1853, Esther Short filed notification of her claim to 640 acres extending west from Main Street and from the Columbia River to 26th Street. Legal description gives starting point for survey "a Balm of Gilead tree about 16 inches in diameter on the northern bank of the Columbia about 60 yards below the Salmon House of the Hudson's Bay Co." Legal disposition of Mrs. Short's property gave her half, her ten children ranging in age from 2 to 22 the other half. The astute widow now had the land subdivided, offering most of it for sale. Many who bought lots and larger parcels, developed their property then later found their titles contested, in some cases by relatives of the Esther Short children. When she died in 1862 the widow left her entire estate to her youngest and favorite daughter Hannah Emeline, a cripple who never married.

DEAD MAN'S HOLLOW, just south of Beard's Hollow. On this tiny beach in idyllic cove were found three bodies from *Vandalia,* one that of 14 year old boy, none ever identified.

EARLIEST EXPLORERS to Pacific Coast found some Indians with slanted eyes, red hair and other evidences of foreign blood, likely one result of Japanese or Pacific current which carried ships in distress onto rocky and sandy shores north and south of Columbia River mouth. Probably most early wrecks on Oregon and Washington coasts were Oriental junks or ships of Spanish origin. Throughout history thousands of lives and hundreds of ships were sacrificed to currents and storms over Desdemona Sands, Peacock Spit or other hazards at the river mouth, most of them quickly disintegrating or sinking into sands.

One exception is hulk of full-rigged sailing ship **Intrepid**, one time U. S. naval bark, built in 1903 at Mare Island, Calif., serving many years as training vessel in sail. In 1920 proud ship was cut down for use as barge and in 1954 suffered further ignominy in being towed to Portland to go on block. Storm threatened to carry tugs and tow onto dreaded Peacock Spit and to save them, tugs were cut loose. Gale blew **Intrepid** into pounding surf and beached her north of Long Beach, Wash. Vessel remained upright in grip of sand, serving many years as monument to countless vessels and lives lost in vicinity.

A LITTLE ALCOHOL GOES A LONG WAY ON A FUNERAL CORTEGE

CROSS COUNTRY CORTEGE
William Keil, Willapa, Wash.

It was the day after Christmas, the place the summit of a gently rounded knoll close to the Willapa River and not far from the bay of the same name. With the early winter darkness closed in Indians with flaming torches flanked the gaping hole in the ground. A group of mourners gently lowered a heavy casket into the grave and as the first clods of muddy earth fell upon the lid, the little band broke into choked song—"Ein Jungling, der Sucht sein himmlisch Gluck." Buried at last was the 19-year-old Willie Keil who died 8 months before and 2000 miles away.

Prussia-born William Keil, father of the dead youth, emigrated to New York, worked as a tailor but reverted to his chosen profession of preaching the faith, his inherited Lutheranism. Becoming dissatisfied with these teachings, he changed to that of the Methodists but being an original thinker began to set up a religion of his own which departed from conventional creeds.

Keil and his wife moved to a tiny settlement on newly opened land in western Pennsylvania and lived with the Andrew Giesy family. The elder Giesys had numerous brothers and sisters near them and were the parents of ten sons and four daughters. When he had converted all these souls he had a nucleus for a colony. Many new converts were added but persecution by unbelieving neighbors forced the group to more isolated ground in Missouri where the colony and village of Bethel was founded.

Arrangements were strictly communal, all moneys earned going into a common fund, all needs of members supplied from stores and shops within the community which was almost self-supporting. Marriages were permitted only to "those who think as we think" according to the constitution. All sick or aged would be tenderly cared for. Everybody must work at whatever job suited his capabilities best. Whoever wished to join must contribute all his available cash but was welcome if he had none.

Bethel flourished, gaining in wealth and members but began to experience an increasing unrest. By 1853 the "Oregon Fever" was sweeping the country with the lure of land free for the taking. Would this be the place for Dr. Keil and his followers to expand the colony's holdings and teachings?

A small group of disciples, including Christian Giesy and his wife, set out to explore the new land to find a suitable site, Giesy leading the party. Following the well marked trail to Oregon Territory, he led the people across the Columbia River at The Dalles and eventually arrived in the lushly timbered area around Willapa Bay. Here was

SECTION OF CARVING bordering top of marker in telephoto detail represents artist's conception of what Willie Keil hearse may have looked like. Mules Queen and Kate which hauled hearse across plains were taken to Aurora, pampered for rest of lives.

WASHINGTON STATE PARKS marker stands at foot of knoll on Edward Buell farm.

plenty of material for lumber to be made into furniture by Bethel artisans and deep, rich soil for raising vegetables. Messengers were sent back to Missouri while the men remaining set to work building log shelters for the expected migration of colonists.

Full scale preparations went ahead in Bethel, Dr. Keil's plans calling for departure in the spring of 1855, as soon as grass made sufficient growth for pasturage. His son and namesake, affectionately called Willie, was among the most enthusiastic of the members expecting to go with the first train. For two years Willie had taken special pleasure in training his three-yoke ox team, selecting the calves himself and naming them Buck, Jim, Blackie, Brindle, Jack and Billy. He would have the responsibility of driving them across country to Washington Territory, newly separated from Oregon. Then only a few days before departure,

he fell seriously ill, doctors pronouncing the disease malaria. Willie fell into frequent spells of delirium, shouting to his oxen and brandishing an imaginary whip. During one lucid period he saw his father by the bed and made him promise, no matter what happened, that he would be taken on the big adventure.

Dr. Keil gave orders for the lead wagon to be converted into a plains ambulance equipped with a comfortable bed and pulled by a fine team of mules. During these preparations however Willie died and the wagon became a hearse. His father secured a casket, lined it with lead and in it placed the body of his son, filling it with alcohol or perhaps whiskey produced by the industrious colonists.

At the appointed hour on Wednesday, May 25, 1855, the hearse drawn by Queen and Kate, moved out and was followed by covered wagons, ox teams and mounted riders—the go-ahead signal being

TINY CEMETERY near Willapa, Wash., was dedicated with burial of Willie Keil who died 8 months earlier in Missouri. Next interment was of Christian Giesy, one of advance group who selected location for Dr. Keil's religious colony. He was drowned while crossing Willapa Bay in small boat during storm, his marker next left to that of Willie Keil's.

Dr. William Keil, Willie's father, officiated at funeral, was on his way to new colony site at Aurora, Ore. when news reached him that a Giesy brother, Andrew, had drowned similarly. Hurrying back, Keil learned Andrew's body had not been recovered. Next and 3d grave left is that of Giesy family patriarch, Andrew, in whose Pennsylvania home the religious movement was started.

Fourth and last tall stone at left is for Andrew's wife Mary. Wooden marker nailed to cedar tree is inscribed in fairly clear black letters for Henry Giesy. Huldamay Giesy Buell and husband Edward Buell, own site, found board rotted off, fastened it to tree. It still bears surprisingly vivid wreath design in green.

47

the dirge written for the occasion by Dr. Keil, the title line: "Das Grab ist tief und stille," in English—"The grave is deep and still." The piece would be played and sung at all future funerals for the colony members.

Following the approved route west the train reached a camping place on the banks of the Blue River without difficulty with Indians but was warned there would be trouble. "Arapahoe and Cheyenne warriors are just ahead," the leaders were told, "and they are in defensive fellowship with the Sioux chiefs of the plains—and the Sioux think they own the buffaloes. And beyond are the Utes and Snakes—they have laid aside their internal strife and have united to stop the covered wagons . . . to burn them and kill the white travelers." Dr. Keil told his people that thousands were

turning back. "Shall we do likewise?" The vote was no. They would go on.

Shortly after crossing the divide between the North and South Platte Rivers the leaders of the Keil train sighted a large band of Sioux warriors, painted for action. "Tell the people to sing," the wagonmaster directed, three outriders carrying the word back to the end of the line. All voices broke into—"Freu euch des Lebens" and several other songs in German. They had nearly reached "O du lieber Augustin" when they were almost surrounded by mounted Sioux. But instead of charging forward, the perplexed Indians, in double file on both sides of the train, silently surveyed the hearse and listened to the singing, then quietly moved away. This pattern of charmed progress prevailed all through the hostile Indian country.

On reaching The Dalles and roaring Celilo Falls in the Columbia River, the train transferred to the newly launched steamboat *Fashion* which proceeded downstream past Fort Vancouver and the passengers disembarked on the north shore near the river mouth at the Pacific Ocean. Moving northward by land the colonists reached Willapa Bay and continued upriver to the site of the new Bethel where they met the vanguard party, some of whom had come by way of the Isthmus of Panama.

This was Nov. 1 and with the days short, air raw and rain almost constant, little time was wasted in greetings. Dr. Keil placed his son's casket in a shelter to await burial until after Christmas rituals had been performed. Then a grave was dug on the Giesy farm and Christian joined in the singing of the Keil dirge, helped lower the casket of Willie Keil beside whom he would himself lie 18 months later.

One winter at Willapa convinced the colonists that this was not the place for a permanent headquarters. Rain was incessant and there was no market near for furniture and vegetables. In less than a year Dr. Keil made a down payment of $1,000 on a tract of land embracing two quarter sections a few miles south of Oregon City, Oregon, and near the thriving towns of Champoeg and Butteville. Most of the colony moved there, leaving only a token settlement at Willapa.

HANDSOME MONUMENT to despotic Dr. William Keil, founder of Aurora colony, has thus far escaped desecration by vandals, fate suffered by others in same private cemetery. Inscription in German reflects Prussian origin of patriarch.

"SLIPPER" HILL

AUTHOR OF TRAGEDY
Frederick Homer Balch

"Bitter blasts of wind swept down the Columbia Gorge and the watcher on the high bank crouched lower under the projecting canopy of rock. Down below the water coursed madly, swirling in black eddies ahead of the easterly gale. Men stood at the river's edge chopping ice which clamped a skiff tightly in its jaws. The boat freed, they lifted a blanketed bundle from a sled and laid it gently between the thwarts, taking up oars as the current snatched at the craft with greedy violence."

Such might have been a paragraph in a dramatic account of the moving of the girl's body from the Oregon shore downstream ten miles to the Washington village of Lyle, had Frederick Homer Balch been able to write dispassionately about it. For the pathetic scene described the last journey of his 18-year-old sweetheart, Genevra Whitcomb, at whose funeral he was to conduct the service.

LYLE CEMETERY is adjoined by small plot containing many Indian graves, which without markers have lost all identity. This one is of infant belonging to numerous Cloud family, is comparatively recent. Placing of such knick-knacks as this broken "Bambi" planter on children's graves is common Indian practice. Lily is of enduring plastic, other flowers are "real", commonly called purple grass widows.

ROUGH, WEATHERED GRANITE boulder marks grave of Homer Frederick Balch, guarded by massive oak. Little Lyle cemetery seems uncrowded because most graves were marked by wooden headboards long since rotted away.

He was born near Lebanon, Oregon, December 14, 1861, into a family which moved from settlement to settlement always seeking a place where the mother's health might improve. They remained in one home just east of Portland for several months and 15-year-old Frederick received his only formal schooling. The rest of his education was supplied by his college-graduate father, James A. Balch.

On the north bank of the Columbia near Lyle the Balch family settled in a frontier-style log farmhouse in which a huge stone fireplace supplied heat for cooking and warming. This was where Frederick, an insatiable reader at 16, studied the few books obtainable. He wrote later, "I kept a big pile of pine knots by the fireplace. One of these, when thrown on a bed of coals would blaze into brilliant light that would flood the room, dying down in a twilight glow."

In his late teens Balch got a job as laborer with the Oregon Railroad and Navigation Co. then building a line along the Oregon shore. He put in ten hours with pick and shovel every day, not counting the time spent rowing a boat across river and back. Most of these hours were spent in turmoil with the determination to write a novel. He had long planned that his Indian neighbors would be the subject and the title—*Wallula*.

Once started on the book young Balch had many conversations with the Indians and then worked far into the night before the fireplace, getting up early for the long, arduous row to work. His sympathies and interests were strongly with the natives and his own religious feelings and beliefs were rebellious to custom. His family said he was an infidel but it appeared he was merely rejecting dogma he could not digest.

During this period Frederick Balch became acquainted with Genevra Whitcomb, daughter of a neighbor. Genevra was pretty and witty, Balch handsome and intelligently superior to the neighboring farm boys. On an evening in December 1882 the two attended a revival meeting in the Lyle community schoolhouse. Both responded to the closing appeal of the missionary preacher, walked down the "sawdust trail" together and were converted. To Genevra this act was only a gesture, perhaps to be in accord with her lover since she was already a devout churchgoer. But the experience consumed Balch. Not content to merely embrace the faith, he became home missionary of the Congregational Church, acting first as pastor at Lyle and Goldendale, then as "horseback preacher" for the entire area.

Genevra and the agnosticism of *Wallula* seemed forgotten and then, during one of his stays at home, he carried the piles of manuscript to the fireplace, throwing section after section into the flames until the whole book was burned. The next day he saw Genevra in her home and left her in tears. Soon after this the girl went to The Dalles across the Columbia to continue her schooling but succumbed to an attack of pneumonia during the severe winter.

Plans were made to hold the funeral in Lyle, a grave blasted in the frozen ground up the hill. And the minister? The man who had apparently spurned her. His biographer, Alfred Powers, wrote in 1930: "Frederick Homer Balch preached the funeral sermon for the girl he knew now and would forever know that he loved . . . the girl who had gone from him in estrangement and silence." Balch himself later wrote: "When the lid of the coffin was removed, and I looked upon her dead face . . . it all came back. I knew I was looking for the last time upon the face of the only girl I would ever love."

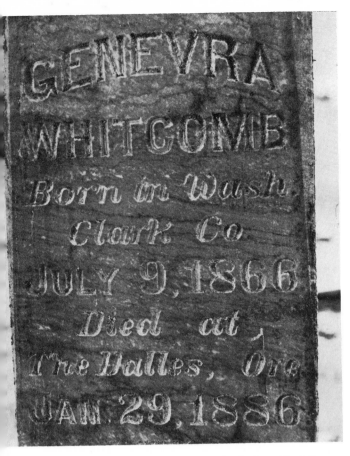

SORROW AND TRAGEDY led to untimely death at 20 of Genevra Whitcomb. Body lies in family plot, side of monument dedicated to her facing north and offering problem for photographer.

After a period of deep depression Balch started another book, planned along the lines of Wallula but having a strong religious theme. Coloma, the hero, would be converted, and the lovely heroine named Genevieve. Not published until many years later, the book was almost autobiographical although Coloma married Genevieve in the end. Balch allowed him to be absorbed by low living in Portland, the experiences in saloons and brothels probably known to the writer by hearsay only.

This novel was laid aside and another begun— *Bridge of the Gods*. This story was to have as its basis the old Indian legend of the former existence of a natural rock bridge across the Columbia River and its later destruction by earthquake. Balch firmly believed in the existence of such a span and its subsequent collapse.

The now generally accepted theory explaining sheer walls and rapids is that about 800 years ago the Columbia flowed uninterruptedly from Celilo Falls to the sea. At that time the falls were sixty feet high, stopping upward migration of salmon, Indian tribes above the falls consequently subsisting on a near starvation diet. In this period Table Mountain extended southward about three-quarters of a mile beyond the present great scarp. The extension, as is the remainder of the mountain, was capped by a layer of Columbia River Basalt, about 1500 feet thick. The whole rested upon the easily eroded Eagle Creek formation. At that time the river flowed in a nearly straight line from the present Stevenson to Beacon Rock.

GENEVRA'S GRAVE is individually marked by this 10-inch footstone. Ground is covered by dried oak leaves remaining from fall.

Finally there came a time near 1250 A.D. when the south end of Table Mountain could no longer sustain itself upon the undermined support of the Eagle Creek formation and collapsed in vast landslide (likely triggered by an earthquake) carrying millions of tons of rock into the channel and even against the opposite shore. The river was dammed long enough to deposit twenty-five feet of silt around the bases of large trees drowned beneath the waters. The stream finally eroded its way southward around and partly through the barrier which continued to hold back enough water to enable salmon to hurdle the then lowered Celilo Falls. Most of the evidences of this cataclysm, thoroughly studied some years ago, are now submerged beneath backed up waters of Bonneville Dam.

The novel was sent to many publishers and rejected so often the author gave up its publication. Then in 1889 it was accepted by A. C. McClurg Co. of Chicago and published in September of the next year. The first printing carried a brown cover with a sketch of an Indian stamped on it. While not a spectacular "best seller", it was later mentioned by the publishers as being a "steady seller". Its success, though moderate, stimulated the young author to plan more books, several on Indian themes.

None of these got beyond the plotting stage. With Balch plagued for some time with tuberculosis and little done for the condition, he became seriously ill in Oakland, California, while studying at the Theological Seminary. He returned to his pastorate at Hood River, Oregon, but was soon forced into Good Samaritan Hospital in Portland. He died there at less than 30 years of age and was buried in Lyle cemetery near the grave of Genevra Whitcomb.

Bridge of the Gods has since gone through a total of 33 printings, being taken over by a Portland firm in 1938 which brought out a "de luxe" edition in 1965. In 1932 the firm printed the first edition of *Genevieve, a Tale of Oregon* which purportedly sheds historical light on the life and love of Frederick Homer Balch. Perhaps the book would have been successful had it been published in the period when written. It appears "quaint" now as it takes its place with other out-of-date efforts.

COLUMBIA RIVER in dramatic view on stormy winter afternoon, Beacon Rock shown in near silhouette. River makes sharp left turn at right to wash base of rock. Upstream is Lyle, home of Frederick Homer Balch, and general locale of his two novels.

BEACON ROCK, WASH., second largest monolith in world, rises almost sheer 900 feet from waters of Columbia River. "Little Beacon Rock" snuggles against base, hidden behind alder trees in foreground. It was site for Lewis and Clark November 2, 1805 and again on return trip, April 8, 1806. In his highly dramatic novel **Genevieve, A Tale of Oregon,** Frederick Balch has Indians climbing main pillar at will, even carrying victims of savage vengeance to be thrown to death on rocks below. Actually Beacon Rock defied all climbing efforts to reach summit until 1901 when banner of Columbia River Steamship Co. was carried up and flown from top as publicity stunt. Now steep switchback trail winds across face to summit.

This unusual view was made from Oregon shore with telephoto lens. Foreshortening almost eliminates width of Columbia, hidden behind trees on island in lower center. True proportions of rock are preserved, "leaning back" effect of usual close-up views avoided.

"BIGGS JUNCTION" — unique Columbia River rock. At Oregon terminus of highway bridge shown in photo of Samuel Hill's grave site is Biggs Junction, grain elevator being visible. Hamlet is at bottom of steep-walled canyon, called in early days "Spanish Hollow", then often used by emigrant parties descending to Columbia.

Recently deposit of unique rock material, thought to be form of jasper and called "Biggs Junction", was uncovered in highway construction. Rush of rock hounds to area threatened undermining of roadway. Hobbyists were stopped from digging but not before tons of "picture rock" had been removed. Flood of December 1964 washed away or buried now rare material. Slab pictured is one cut by author, colors ranging from black-brown to cream-white.

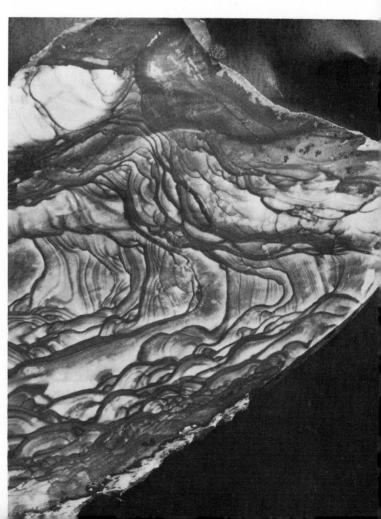

MARYHILL

MONUMENT ON SAMUEL HILL'S GRAVE shown in center foreground. Simple inscription reads: "Samuel Hill — Amid Nature's unrest he sought rest." Left of center is seen picturesque little Maryhill church, at its right what remains of village and in middle distance bridge to Oregon shore of Columbia.

Samuel Hill had enough charm and business acumen to accumulate large fortune but was an impractical visionary. Most of wealth went into such projects as huge pile now called Maryhill Castle on bluffs above Columbia River (see **Ghost Town Treasures**) and replica of England's famed Stonehenge nearby. When he died heirs discovered provision for burial on forbidding, spectacular site just below his "Stonehenge." This view made with aid of wide-angle lens on "Professional Model" Mamiya camera.

HAINE HAINT NO MORE

Vancouver, Wash.

"Chisel me a stone", Arthur Haine told a monument maker, "that will bear two words only— Haine Haint. Don't put any date or anything else on it."

So runs the tale of the Vancouver, Washington eccentric who made hoops from hazel poles and shipped them to England, worked as store clerk and bank employee. He is a legend in the Columbia River city and a vivid memory to a dozen or more residents who knew him around the turn of the century as "Judge". "He was a fine looking man," Richard Schane told this reporter, the complete story appearing in the Vancouver COLUMBIAN Dec. 7, 1965. "He wore a long flowing mustache and was always impeccably dressed. Haine kept two dogs just for the hunting season—their names Pat and Mike. On the first day of the bird season he would dress carefully in his correctly designed hunting outfit, let out his dogs and proceed to the nearest tavern. He then would take a table and order a drink, slowly consuming it while Pat and Mike waited patiently at his side. Haine continued this until closing time when he and the dogs would return home."

Then on Oct. 16, 1905 Arthur Haine wrote his will in a fine, meticulous script. One paragraph read: "My funeral is to be of the cheapest kind and I don't want my body transported but buried near the place where I may die. As I have lived an infidel, I want to be buried as such without any monkey business."

HEADSTONE was inscribed by order of Arthur Haine and placed on grave at his death and funeral in 1907. Originally it read "Haine Haint" as now but on a single line. later friends were shocked at grim levity, ordered stone mason to erase offending word "Haint", carve leaf design in its place. Other friends, aware of Haine's expressed wish, had cutter reinscribe word below.

HEADS ITS PORTLAND!

TOSS OF A COIN, TOWN HAD A NAME
Asa L. Lovejoy

In the year 1842 the only habitation on the site of Portland was the log cabin near the junction of the present S.W. Hood and S.W. Macadam Avenues. William Johnson, sailor off Capt. Couch's brig *Maryland*, built it, found the place too lonely and moved his family to French Prairie, leaving newcomer William Overton in a cabin some distance to the north.

Overton seemed disenchanted with the Oregon country and on a trip to Fort Vancouver told Asa L. Lovejoy he had decided to go to Texas. Maine farmer Lovejoy was looking for land and considered Overton's proposition to sell.

When he accepted the offer the next day he said, "Now you'll be free to head for Texas". But Overton, ever vacillating or wily, replied he wouldn't go to Texas under any circumstances but would sell half his claim to Lovejoy. No sooner had the latter started out to find his new land than Texas again took on the aura of green pastures for Overton. He found a buyer for the other half of his claim in Francis Pettygrove, ex-Maine merchant who came to Oregon with a load of goods with which he opened a store in Oregon City.

The two State-of-Mainers, close neighbors in a massive, dripping forest beside the Willamette River must have had vision to see beyond it for they began to talk about starting a town. All right, what would the settlement be named — after some city in Maine, say Portland for Pettygrove's home, or Boston for Lovejoy's birthplace?

Discussion brought no solution but an 1835 copper penny did. Two flips out of three settled the issue and the collection of log cabins all but afloat in a sea of mud that winter was called Portland.

COMPARATIVELY MODERN MONUMENT replaces original wooden headboard. This one is carved from granite. Design is etched in black, contrasting strongly with gleaming, polished surface.

ONE MORE RIVER TO CROSS

"Uncle Jimmy" Stephens

The Willamette was the last river the pioneer wagon train encountered coming over the Oregon Trail. And where the mountain streams in Idaho and eastern Oregon could be forded or followed to a crossing place, the Willamette was too big, too bold. So James B. Stephens, scorning the makeshift methods people used to get to the west side of the river, built a skiff for families and a flatboat for teams and on Jan. 7, 1853, started a regular ferry service.

Virginia-born Stephens paid $200 to Dr. John McLoughlin for the Hudson's Bay Co. employee house on Portland's east side and later built a home at what is now S. E. 12th and Stephens Street. The settlers called him "Uncle Jimmy" and he set about to serve them by obtaining a charter from the territorial legislature for his new ferry system. Power for the flatboat was supplied by a team of big mules and the driver was Capt. Charles Frusk. He always carried a bucket of rocks to throw at the mules when they stopped or slowed down and after a few trips he needed only to bend over the bucket to get results.

When steam power came in Stephens eventually sold out his ferry business. On one of the final crossings, on Sept. 13, 1859, the last team on board was a fine pair of horses hitched to a wagon loaded with rocks. A sharp blast of the steam whistle so startled the animals they backed the wagon off the apron, pulling them with it, and were drowned.

Stephens developed a fine farm on his property, planting a variety of valuable berries and fruits. Peaches easily brought a dollar each and he made the first cider in the area, possibly in the whole Oregon country, discounting any production from the apples grown from English stock at Fort Vancouver.

In 1852 Colburn Barrell bought part of Stephens' acreage for a farm and when his friend, 20-year-old Crawford Dobbins, died after an explosion on board the steamboat *Gazelle* in 1854, he donated a grave site on the farm, located near a solitary fir tree. Dobson was buried there and Barrell erected a monument. When James Stephens' old father died, he too was buried there and Lone Fir Cemetery came into being. It was then fitting and proper for Uncle Jimmy and his wife to rest forever on what was once part of their own farm.

REVERSE SIDE STEPHENS MARKER photographed at same time as front is less fortunately illuminated but surely epitaph is unmatched anywhere.

STRIKING MONUMENT to "Uncle Jimmy" Stephens and wife Elizabeth. Located in old Lone Fir Cemetery in Portland, Oregon, site was part of Stephens farm. Photographer made special trip to cemetery to make picture of slab marking grave of pioneer Capt. Daniel Wright at just right time of year and moment to catch beam of sunlight on marble, nearly crowded out by giant redwood trees. Absorbing job completed, he looked up from camera to see this beautiful monument shining in same early morning sunshine. One hour later strong shadow covered upper portion.

CAPTAIN DANIEL WRIGHT—

The Daily Oregonian
Thursday Morning
September 18, 1873
Page 3, Column 1

DEATH OF CAPTAIN WRIGHT:—At nine o'clock yesterday morning Captain Daniel Wright quietly and peaceable breathed his last. His death was caused directly from injuries which were sustained last Sunday morning in falling a distance of 25 feet from a pile driver. The terrible shock he received at the time of the fall, and the subsequent deprivation of one of his legs — amputation being regarded by several excellent surgeons as indispensably necessary — proved too much for Captain Wright at his advanced age. He survived the operation sixteen hours.

Deceased is an old resident of Portland. He came to this state about the year 1854 as one of the Government contractors for opening the road from Astoria to Salem. Since then, Captain Wright has resided in the state, and followed the occupation of general contractor.

He was a native of Massachusetts, and in his 58th year. Many years ago he immigrated to California, and was a resident of that state during the mining excitement of 1849-50. During his residence in California, — embracing a period of several years—Captain Wright was engaged in various branches of business, and at one time was a wealthy man.

He was a man of generous impulses, industrious, enterprising and persevering. Now that he has departed this life, his familiar face and well known form will be sadly missed from the walks of the busy world. A tender, loving companion, and many friends survive to mourn his sad and sudden removal from our midst.

Ibid.

Page 2, Column 4

DIED:—On Wednesday morning, September 17, 1873, Captain Daniel Wright, age 58, a native of Massachusetts. The funeral will take place from the residence of John P. Walker, Esq., corner of Montgomery and First Streets, at 2 P. M., today. Friends of the family are respectfully invited.

The Daily Oregonian
Friday Morning
September 19, 1873
Page 3, Column 1

FUNERAL PROCESSION:—The remains of the late Captain Wright were followed yesterday to their final resting place in the Lone Fir Cemetery by a large number of friends. A number of our citizens who had long known the deceased during his residence in Portland, acted as pallbearers and accompanied the body to its place of sepulture. As the procession moved slowly down Front avenue toward the ferry landing, all work was suspended; the sounds of hammer, saws and trowel were suspended for a few moments, and all the workmen, on each side of the street came to the side walk and stood with uncovered heads until the cortege had passed. It was the last respect that could be shown to the memory of a fellow-workman who had forever passed from the sight of men.

PORTLAND'S OLD LONE FIR CEMETERY is full of interesting stones and monuments. This one attracts notice immediately, being surrounded by huge redwood (Sequoia) trees, presumably planted at corners of plot at time of Capt. Wright's burial, Sept. 18, 1873. Wright, while mining in California High Sierra, may have gathered cones with seeds as did others, to take to Oregon. Trees growing from these seeds on his home place would have themselves been of seed bearing age when he was killed. Family may have planted their seeds or saplings at grave.

ORDEAL BY FIRE

Frederick H. Ramsey

Under the headline — PIONEER BURNED TO DEATH — the Portland MORNING OREGONIAN of Friday, January 4, 1895 gave the facts about the death of a notable citizen of the Willamette countryside. "On Wednesday night Frederick H. Ramsey, living alone at the mouth of the Willamette River, opposite Sauvie Island, came to a frightful end, being burned to death in his own home. No one was at hand to render assistance. At 7:30 o'clock last night neighbors of Ramsey living on Sauvie Island discovered the house to be on fire and started to render assistance, but due to the river being full of ice they were unable to cross the stream to the mainland. Yesterday morning they went to the house finding the building in ruins, and in the charred and smoking ruins lay the body of Ramsey. The arms and legs of the old pioneer were burned off, and all that remained was the blackened and burned trunk".

The item went on to state that only six weeks before the house caught on fire. That time the island neighbors were able to reach the burning building, drag out an intoxicated Ramsey and put out the fire. Ramsey, an alcoholic, had been smoking in bed and fallen asleep, and it was to be assumed events had repeated themselves on this fatal occasion. Ramsey came to the St. Johns area, now part of Portland, 44 years before in 1851 from Pennsylvania, acquiring 700 acres of land now occupied by a complex of residences, businesses and port facilities.

Coroner Cornelius located bones of the missing limbs and the remains of a small dog unable to escape the flames. The box in which the pioneer kept $15,000 in notes held against "different parties" in St. Johns was found but fire had destroyed the contents which removed all obligations from "the parties".

The OREGON JOURNAL added color to the story on June 5, 1953: "On the site of the Vanport Flood there's the stone of an Oregon pioneer named Fred H. Ramsey. Vanport students used to visit the spot to eat their noon lunches. . . The grave has a concrete foundation. Originally the tombstone had a large marble ball on top of it but during the Vanport College era it fell off. The ball remained on the ground for a number of years, then somebody rolled it away. The tombstone is still quite a flossy one for a hardy old pioneer who went south one cold night at New Year's."

LONELY GRAVE MARKER stands in small grove of old cedars near the junction of N. Burgard St. and Swift Blvd. in North Portland. Once supporting large marble ball, monument to pioneer who fought Indians in Cayuse War in youth has been deprived of it by vandals. Legend says grave digger, preparing plot for burial of Ramsey's brother, unearthed four skulls, that Ramsay had four Indian wives who were buried beside him. Old news item reports a brother living in Centralia, Washington, but there is no indication he was buried here. Civic groups make periodic projects of clearing grave site of blackberry vines, rubbish, etc., such as one accomplished on Oct. 8, 1964 by members of St. Johns Bachelors, social group of North Portland community.

THE FIGHT THAT NEVER DIES
Virgil W. Earp

"The Fight at the O.K. Corral" has been told in many books, (one of them GHOST TOWN ALBUM), television programs and moving pictures, and will be retold into the next century. The Tombstone classic, occurring on October 27, 1881, comes to light here as the result of information from the Oregon Historical Society that Virgil Earp is buried in Portland. A clipping from the OREGON JOURNAL of August 8, 1958, started a search for the grave and some latter day facts about Virgil.

Tall, gaunt and intrepid, the Earp brothers caused considerable comment when they first arrived in Tombstone, particularly because of Wyatt's reputation as peace officer in Dodge City, Kansas. All the brothers knew what six-shooters were for, but Wyatt had the reputation. Hailing from Lamar, Missouri, the Earps were sons of Nicholas Porter Earp. Virgil seems to have arrived in Yavapai County, Arizona Territory, about 1876, Wyatt about 1879 having resigned his law job in Dodge City a few months earlier.

Virgil was appointed deputy marshal at Prescott, November 27, 1879, sworn in as Tombstone chief of police on October 28, 1880, and again on July 2, 1881. This information from THE JOURNAL OF ARIZONA HISTORY seems to settle the contested status of Virgil at the time of the famous fight, itself the subject of so much controversy.

The long simmering feud between the "cowboy faction" and Tombstone law as represented by the Earps and "Doc" Holliday, reached its boiling point with the fight in the O.K. Corral and was followed rapidly by assassination attempts against John Clum — founder of the TOMBSTONE EPITAPH — and Virgil Earp and by Morgan Earp's murder.

Clum later recalled the incident in these words: "It was a day which suddenly turned chill at noon. I had just gone to my room to change my clothing, when crack, crack, crack, the guns let loose down at the corral. Before I could turn the corner it was all over. The dead and wounded were carried away by friends." In the shotgun and six-shooter carnage, Ike and Bill Clanton, Frank and Tom McLaury, and Billy Claibourne, all of these of the cowboy faction, clashed with Wyatt, Virgil and Morgan Earp, and John "Doc" Holliday for less than one minute on Fremont Street. When the smoke had cleared, Frank and Tom McLaury, and Billy Clanton were dead; Virgil and his brother Morgan were seriously wounded and Doc Holliday grazed by a bullet; Billy Claibourne and Ike Clanton (who had not drawn his gun) had fled the scene of battle. And Wyatt remained unscathed. Later that afternoon Wyatt Earp and Doc Holliday appeared before Judge Wells Spicer (Virgil being hospitalized with his wounds) and all were speedily acquitted; a Cochise County grand jury subsequently refused to issue indictments against the foursome.

Clum summed it all up neatly: "There has been a lot of talk about the justification for it. But I always held that the Earps were officers of the law and I could see no reason why an officer should wait until he was fired upon two or three times before opening up himself."

But the decision did not end the matter. A letter, "written with a stub of pencil held backhand to disguise the handwriting", was received and appeared in the EPITAPH December 14, 1881: "To Wells Spicer — Sir, if you will take my advice you will take your Departure for a more congenial Clime, as I don't think this is healthy for you much longer. As you are liable to get a hole through your coat any moment. If Sons of Bitches as you are allowed to dispense Justice in this Territory, the sooner you Depart from us the better for yourself. . ."

That these were not empty threats was shown on December 18 when Clum, then mayor of Tombstone, was fired upon by unknown assailants but escaped injury. Virgil Earp was ambushed by gunmen near the corner of Fifth and Allen on December 28, receiving near-fatal wounds which crippled him for the rest of his life. And the following March Morgan Earp was slain while playing a game of pool in a saloon. Virgil and his wife accompanied the brother's body to Colton, California, and lived there for a time moving to Goldfield, Nevada, where he died peacefully.

VIRGIL EARP'S GRAVE in Portland's Riverview Cemetery. If it seems strange that Virgil Earp, brother of Wyatt and of Tombstone, Ariz. fame, who died in Goldfield, Nev., should be buried in Portland, Oregon, the reason lies in the simple request by Earp's sister, Mrs. L. D. Bohn, that the body be sent to the city where she lived.

These facts came to public notice in 1958 when Mayor Terry Schrunk of Portland received a letter from Manfred S. Bordasch of Hanover, Germany. This student of western U. S. history had heard Earp was buried in Portland and requested information. Assistant Mayor Howard Traver located grave, had photo taken of stone, sent it and information to Bordasch. Stone is cylindrical, situated in old part of cemetery and shaded by thick-growing variegated English holly.

TRAIL BLAZERS AND ROAD BUILDERS

RESCUER OF THE WHITMAN CAPTIVES
Peter Skene Ogden

Known principally as the man who accomplished the release of the pitiful survivors of the Whitman massacre, held as hostages by the Indians, Peter Skene Ogden was well equipped for the life he led. Most of the French Canadian adventurers going into the almost limitless western wilderness in search of furs had little education but the necessary courage, stamina and "trail sense." Ogden had all these and his attainments as geographer, explorer and peacemaker were many.

But for the Revolutionary War, he would have been an American. At the outbreak of hostilities the loyal royalist Ogdens left New Jersey for Quebec which became the birthplace of Peter in 1794. The relatively wealthy parents sent him to England to prepare for the bar but he gave this up because of "voice trouble." Back in Canada the 24-year-old Peter joined with the North West Company of fur traders and was at once selected as leader of a trapping party to headquarter at Fort George. This was prior to the merger of this group with the Hudson's Bay Company and before Fort George became Astoria. When these events occurred, "man of the hour" Ogden was retained by the expanded concern with headquarters at Fort Vancouver.

In 1825 Chief Factor John McLoughlin, recognizing Ogden's qualities of leadership, placed him at the head of a party of trappers and Indians with families to explore, map and determine fur potentialities of the central Oregon area. Ogden traversed the Crooked, Deschutes, and Snake River areas and compiled the first written record of the country.

Other explorations followed, to Nevada, California, Idaho and Utah which gave his name to the city of Ogden. He traveled about half the year during which he brought in the $25,000 annual fur consignment from Stuart's Lake to Vancouver. The trips required as many as nine boats with sixty voyageurs and the arrival of the *brigade de porteurs* was a great event at the company post. Fort guns would signal the boats as soon as the lookouts sighted them, the boatmen would put on plumed hats and paddle up to the landing singing their traditional songs to the welcomers.

After the "abdication" of McLoughlin and loss of Douglas and others, Ogden became chief factor and held the post for two years when news of the Whitman massacre was received. To avoid a possible full-scale war the Company sent Ogden to the scene in an attempt to secure the release of the 51 survivors. He left for Waiilatpu Dec. 7, 1847 at a time when Willamette Valley settlers were considering the organization of a force to attack the Cayuse Indians in the face of an almost complete lack of funds.

Ogden was shrewd with Indians, having married one and been engaged in many dealings with them. At Fort Walla Walla he called a council of neighboring tribal chiefs and pointed out a number of bitter truths, foremost of which was that if they allowed events to progress to total warfare, all tribes would be wiped out. He offered a clear-cut proposition—to pay a ransom for the captives but not immunity for the captors. The chiefs conferred and offered compromises, then returned to their tents, the pattern repeated time after time while Ogden remained inflexible. The last meeting was on Dec. 28 and on the day following the Cayuses gave in, delivering the survivors to Ogden. In return they received a ransom of blankets, guns, saddles, shirts and tobacco to the total of some $400.

Many stories are told of events transpiring while the survivors were held in captivity. Tragically true was the report that Helen Meek and

Louise Sager died in confinement. The former was the daughter of Joe Meek, a circumstance of no help to the guilty Indians when Meek hanged them at Oregon City after their capture, trial and conviction. One of the hostages, Mary Smith, and Edward Tilaukait, became lovers while in Indian hands and were later married, the union breaking up because of the latter not wishing to give up Indian ways.

A French Canadian named Stanfield asked a Mrs. Hays to marry him but she refused him on the grounds that her husband had been dead so short a time. But she did accept his proposition to occupy the same bed at the emigrant house where they were held captive, propriety being observed by her young son sleeping between them. After they were rescued, this romance too faded out.

As soon as the released captives left Waiilaptu all buildings except the grist mill were burned by the Indians, the hostages arriving at Vancouver after a voyage of six days. They spent one day at the fort and Ogden then took them to Portland where they were turned over to Gov. Abernethy. Peter Ogden retained his post at Fort Vancouver until his retirement to Oregon City. His first wife dead, he married another Indian and left six children at his death.

HANDSOME MONUMENT was placed on grave of explorer Ogden early in October, 1923. Dedication ceremonies were held on the 29th, attended by possibly largest crowd ever gathered in old Mountain View Cemetery, Oregon City. Among those present were members of three sponsoring societies — Oregon State Historical Assn., Oregon Pioneers Assn., Sons and Daughters of Oregon Pioneers Assn.

Among guests of honor were three women who, as little girls, survived Whitman Massacre. One, Mrs. Nancy Osborne Jacobs, 83, was small Nancy Osborne who, with her father, mother and little brother, hid under loose floor boards while hideous slaughter went on above. Another was Mrs. O. M. Denny, 86, who was Gertrude Jane Hall, whose father Peter D. Hall, was forced to flee and leave wife and children behind. Hall was later reported as demented, stealing an Indian canoe and drowning in river rapids. Mrs. E. M. Helm, 87, was little Elizabeth Sager whose brother Francis was shot by Joe Lewis in league with attacking Indians.

PETER SKENE OGDEN
1794 — 1854

BORN AT QUEBEC
DIED AT OREGON CITY
FUR TRADER AND EXPLORER
IN OLD OREGON
ARRIVED COLUMBIA RIVER 1818
CLERK OF NORTH WEST COMPANY
CHIEF FACTOR HUDSON'S BAY
COMPANY AT FORT VANCOUVER
RESCUED SURVIVORS OF
WHITMAN MASSACRE 1847.

HE HACKED OUT THE LOGIE TRAIL ROAD

James Logie of Sauvie Island

There had always been an Indian trail over the Tualatin Hills. It twisted from Champoeg through the fertile plains of the Tualatin Valley over the hills then called Scappoose Mountains, to the rich farm lands of Sauvie Island. When the Scotch couple, James Logie and wife Isabelle, took out a donation land claim on the island, James was irked at the inadequacy of the old trail. Almost single-handedly he undertook to remove some of the kinks and widen passages between trees to make possible wagon travel over the hills.

It is not known how long Indians had inhabited the island before the advent of white men. Lewis and Clark reported it well populated. Floating downstream on November 4, 1805, William Clark wrote, "Several canoes of Indians from the village above came down, dressed for the purpose as I supposed of paying us a friendly visit, they had scarlet & blue blankets, Sailor Jackets, overalls, shirts and hats independent of their usual dress." While Indians of the Continental Divide had never seen white men before, these lower Columbia people displayed many signs of having traded with crews from ships at the river's mouth. The Sauvie Island Indians were very hospitable, inviting the expedition's leaders to eat with them, the invitation gladly accepted. "During the time we were at dinner those fellows stole my pipe Tomahawk which we were smoking with . . . while searching for the Tomahawk one of those Scoundrels stole a cappoe (a long coat with hood) of one of our interpreters, which was found stuffed under the root of a tree near the place where they sat, we became much displeased with these fellows which they discovered and moved off."

Understandably the expedition's leaders were unaware that behind the island was the mouth of a river second in size, in that area, to the Columbia. They missed it on the return also but soon after passing the upper end of the island, they were told of it and returned to explore its course about as far up as the site of present Portland. They called the river Multnomah, the name later changed to Willamette.

The Indian villages on the island and entire lower Columbia Basin were stricken by plague, likely small pox or malaria, in 1831. Later John K. Townsend, Philadelphia physician and naturalist, spent a short time studying the flora and fauna of the island. He wrote, "A gentleman told me that only four years ago as he wandered near what had been an Indian village, he counted no less than sixteen dead men and women, lying unburied and festering in the sun in front of their habitations. Within the houses all were sick, not one had escaped the contagion; upwards of one hundred individuals, men, women and children, were writhing in agony on the floors of their houses, with no one to render them assistance. Some were in the dying struggle, and clenching with the convulsive grasp of death. Their disease-worn companions shrieked and howled in the last sharp agony."

The few able survivors carried out the tradition of placing the dead in canoes elevated on stakes. Braves were so arranged with weapons, women with trinkets. Dr. Townsend discovered one of these canoes on the island containing the well preserved body of a young girl. With scientific curiosity he removed it to his quarters for study. Shortly thereafter the brother of the dead girl found the canoe crypt empty and confronted Townsend with a demand for the body. The doctor handed it over and later wrote, "The poor Indian took the body of his sister upon his shoulders, and as he walked away,

EX-HUDSON'S BAY EMPLOYEE James Logie lies in tiny private cemetery on original Sauvie Island claim. Naturalized daffodils crowd site, about to bloom in early March. Donation land law, passed in 1850, allowed 640 acres to couples after four years residence, half that to single men. Island is 15.1 miles long, 4.55 miles at widest, contains 24,064 acres, much in lakes, remainder in tillable land. In Logie's time and for years thereafter farms were covered by spring floods but now encircling dikes hold freshets back. Immediately behind stone shown here, narrow channel can be seen (through brambles) separating island from mainland on Oregon side, hills beyond traversed by Logie's trail.

HOUSE BUILT BY JAMES F. BYBEE and wife Julia in 1856 still stands, now on Howell farm. Located on highest land of Sauvie Island, site was never flooded, was place of refuge for humans and cattle when spring melting of snows in wide Columbia Basin covered entire flood-plain of river. With 9 rooms, 6 fireplaces, house saw many social gatherings in days when island colony was isolated from world. Giant trees are typical "Oregon oaks" common to valleys and bottom lands, capable of surviving short periods of flooding.

grief got the better of his stoicism, and the sound of his weeping was heard long after he had entered the forest."

The first white settler on Sauvie Island was the born-to-disaster Nathaniel J. Wyeth. Leaving a successful ice business in Boston, Mass., Wyeth took his entire fortune to the raw Oregon country in an attempt to expand it further. Instead he lost almost all of it, in succeeding stages. In the East he organized the Columbia River Fishing and Trading Co., spending $40,000 for supplies and a ship to carry them to Vancouver on the lower Columbia. He went West by land, stopping to lose a few thousand dollars in an ill-fated fur trading venture in the Rockies. In Vancouver he found his ship had foundered near Cape Horn, losing all men and supplies. Almost penniless, Wyeth was deserted by his remaining men.

Undaunted, the ice man went on to Sauvie Island to establish a trading post on its lower or north end at a location called Warrior's Point. It

was here that in 1792 Lt. William Robert Broughton, exploring up river, encountered "twenty-three canoes, each carrying from three to twelve persons all attired in their war garments, and in every other respect prepared for combat." The incident had a peaceful ending however.

Wyeth set up a forge and woodworking plant, and started a farm. The site being submerged in the first spring floods, he started another on a rise of land nearer the center of the island but was still dogged by bad luck. Nearly to the bottom of his resources, he made a trip to Fort Hall to salvage funds invested there which were rapidly diminishing. In his absence some of his Kanaka workers deserted, taking his horses with them. On his return he wrote his wife in Boston, "I hope you will make yourself comfortable and happy. It is only good policy to enjoy ourselves while we can."

Predictably the Sauvie enterprise was a complete failure. Just before he left in 1835 he wrote his wife again, "The season has been very sickly. We have lost, by drowning, disease and warfare seventeen persons to this date and fourteen now sick. Keep up good spirits, my dear wife, for I expect when I come home to stop there, and although I shall be poor, yet we can always live." He did "stop there," engaging in the ice business again and making another success.

By 1838 the Hudson's Bay Co. had established extensive dairy farms on the lush bottom lands of the island with French Canadian Laurent (often erroneously called Jean Baptiste) Sauvie in charge. When he settled on the island Sauvie lived with an Indian woman named Josephta and their son, then six. He then married Josephta and a daughter Catherine was born after the nuptials and baptized at Fort Vancouver as was the son Joseph. Sauvie and family retired to St. Paul where Josephta died he remarried and died at sixty-nine, being buried in the original church cemetery at St. Paul, the grave marker long rotted away.

When Sauvie retired from the island, James and Isabelle Logie were installed in his place, but momentous events were brewing which would change everything. The Logies may have anticipated the eventual removal of the Company, their arrival on the island coming about the time of the Champoeg meetings. With formal establishment of the boundary line at the 49th parallel in 1846, and the end of British occupation of the island, the pair from Scotland took 640 acres as their donation land claim and remained where they were.

Through the years Sauvie Island has been known to white men, its name has been a constant subject of contention. Aboriginal Indians there were of several tribes and each had a name for the space it occupied as well as for the island as a whole. Geographers Lewis and Clark called it Wappato, with their usual variety of spellings, after the edible root serving the Indians as a staple eaten with fish. Then came the names Multnomah, Wyeth and others including Laurent Sauvie which had some continuing use. Colloquially the name was Sauvie's Island. Omar Spencer, author of *The Story of Sauvies Island*, only definitive book on the subject, defends his spelling, saying, "The Board of Geographical Names has said the name should be 'Sauvie' but since the people prefer 'Sauvies' and say 'the Island,' that is what it will be called here," this perpetuating the controversy despite official decision.

SITE OF SECOND FORT WILLIAM, only slightly more permanent than first, at northern end of Sauvie Island. It was washed away in spring floods of Columbia River, second eventually abandoned because of lack of salmon, poor management. Since fir trees can grow only on land seldom or never flooded, these in background could well be successors of those forming forest where Indian boy carried dead sister back to canoe burial place.

AFTER JAMES LOGIE'S DEATH, widow Isabelle married Jonathan Moar, couple continuing to operate farm. She was likely first white woman to live in Sauvie Island, was known as Angel of Mercy, giving aid and care to whites and Indians. She died at 49, is buried with Moar under larger stone at right. First husband, James Logie, buried at left.

THE SQUIRE WAS EUCHRED
George W. Ebberts

George W. Ebberts, called "Squire" from boyhood, was born in Kentucky in 1810. He learned the machinist's trade in the land of Daniel Boone but caught a bad case of wanderlust at an early age and in 1829 went trapping in the Rockies. He served six years with the American Fur Co., then three with Hudson's Bay Co. He worked as blacksmith at the Lapwai Mission, there met and married a Nez Perce Indian girl.

Moving wife and children to French Prairie, near Champoeg, Ebberts became a gentleman farmer with funds given him by well-to-do parents back in Kentucky. After adventurous days trapping, he fancied the placid life—until he met smooth-tongued Joe Meek.

Shortly after the massacre at Waiilatpu, Meek had been selected by Governor Abernethy to go to Washington with a plea for military aid as protection against the expected general outbreak of Indian hostilities. Meek was known to be self-reliant and a persuasive talker. The governor gave him what money he could raise for expenses and Meek asked Ebberts to go with him, knowing the Squire could pay his own way.

Ebberts agreed and just before the two left Meek placed his hand on his heart and swore in the presence of Mrs. Ebberts that her husband would be treated as an equal, sharing with himself in any compensation from the Oregon settlers or U. S. Government.

On the way they came upon a party of Bannocks greatly excited by reports of the Cayuse war. Meek had just enough time to don the Canadian cap and red belt of Hudson's Bay Co. employees, the Indians riding up without firing. To make sure of safety he told them the renowned marksman, Capt. Thomas McKay was coming along a day behind, that he had a large party intending to barter with them. The chief ordered his men to stand back and allow the white men to proceed. They did and reached Fort Hall tired enough to rest, the snow being deep and weather cold, but they feared the Bannocks had discovered the deception by now and would be close behind. After a meal they went on, abandoning horses for snowshoes, and reached St. Joseph, Missouri, in two months, setting a near record. In Washington they were invited to the White House, Meek claiming relationship with the family of President Polk.

During their stay in the capitol, Meek dressed in borrowed finery and was lionized socially while the Squire shone only faintly in reflected glory. Tired of the life and treatment, Ebberts told his partner they should return home now that they had the wheels turning for aid. No, said Joe Meek, he had no intention of leaving his "dear cousins in the White House" so soon and stayed on while the Squire started back alone. He was now without funds as Meek had spent all the money both had, and was forced to work as blacksmith to reach French Prairie by stages.

Through glib talk Meek obtained $7,250 in expense money but gave his companion not a cent of it. "Nevertheless," says an old account, "Meek with his wit, manner and braggadocio of a Falstaff, his great courage and common sense and power of initiative . . . and on account of his kinship with the president, no other man in Oregon could have made the journey and secured government aid with equal speed and success." So Joe Meek got the credit as well as the money. And nothing much is made of the fact that Ebberts was one of the fifty-two who voted for provisional government on that fateful May Day in 1843.

EBBERT OR EBBERTS? All available references spell the name with the "s" but inscription on tombstone omits it. George W. Ebberts is buried in old cemetery of West Union Baptist Church with his many friends in Tualatin Valley.

On right side on monument is marker of Multnomah Chapter D.A.R., reading: "TO ONE OF THOSE PATRIOTS WHO ON MAY 2, 1843 FOUNDED THE PROVISIONAL GOVERNMENT AT CHAMPOEG." Some 30 of the 52 trappers, preachers and farmers are likewise designated, graves of others not located thus far. Some never will be, one signer cut up by Indian attackers, one drowned, body never recovered. Another died of cholera on shipboard, was buried at sea. At least one lies in Old St. Paul cemetery, his wooden headboard long since rotted away.

IN TINY CABIN of David Lenox group of pioneers with Baptist affiliations met to draw up covenant on May 25, 1844. Lenox donated ample land from his claim for church and cemetery. He is credited with having captained first wagon train to Willamette Valley which explains design on monument. Fittingly he is buried in West Union Baptist Church graveyard on land originally his and among such friends as George Ebberts and Caleb Wilcox.

ROSE was most frequently used flower carved on tombstones, proving it "Queen of Flowers" for many years. This one is on grave marker at nearly vanished Bethel, Oregon.

HATTER, TRAPPER, WAGON DRIVER
Caleb Wilkins

Born in Zanesville, Ohio, Caleb Wilkins was trained as a hatter but finding the trade dull, he joined with Wyeth and Bonneville in their premature and disastrous efforts to establish agriculture and business in the Oregon Country in 1832-34. Then with the American Fur Co. he made a lifelong friend of George Ebberts.

The two shared many adventures. In 1835 they were on a hunting and trapping expedition with three other men and in an encounter with Blackfeet Indians were robbed of all horses and equipment. One man was killed and the rest barely got away alive, being forced to tramp back to Fort Hall through deep snow, almost starving on the way.

With the break up of the American Fur Co., three of the employees left stranded and destitute were Wilkins, Robert Newell and Joe Meek. They were at Fort Hall when missionaries Harvey Clark and P. B. Littlejohn gave up trying to get their wagon to Waiilatpu and on June 4, 1839, the ex-trappers were hired to do the driving. Wilkins already had a wagon so a small cavalcade was formed, successfully reaching Waiilatpu — the first wagons to go all the way to the mission. Then the men with their Indian wives and children went on to French Prairie. Wilkins settled on adjacent Tualatin Plains and on the day scheduled for the big meeting at Champoeg, he and his friend Ebberts went together to the river landing town to vote for the Provisional Government.

SHAFT MARKING GRAVE of Caleb Wilkins shown at left stands only a few feet from that of his close friend George Ebberts (not included in photo). These and many others of earliest pioneers in Oregon Country are in yard of West Union Baptist Church shown in background at right.

On May 25, 1844 a few members of Baptist Church met in home of David T. Lenox, pioneer of year earlier where constitution and covenant was drawn up for West Union Baptist Church west of Rockies. Part of covenant reads, ". . . we are thrown together in these wilds of the West. . . agree that we constitute and come into union." Lumber for building measuring 30'x40', was hauled from mills at Milwaukie by ox team. Rafters were cedar poles, joists fir poles, sills hewn from fir logs. Structure was dedicated and first services held on Christmas Day, 1854, congregation dissolving about 1878 which ended regular services.

Historic edifice is first Baptist Church west of the Rockies. It is also said to be first Protestant Church still standing west of the Rockies. (Jacksonville, Oregon, Methodist Church, erected year later, carried plaque stating it is oldest Protestant Church, this error being innocently perpetuated by author in his **Western Ghost Towns.** Publicity because of error caused removal of misleading marker). Venerable West Union Church is almost isolated, standing alone in center of farm lands. Cemetery is quiet and peaceful. On Sunday selected to make photographs, neighborhood was filled with sleek, new cars, tiny church swarming with people, day being that of annual historic meeting and services of Baptist Association. Picture taking was postponed.

LIFE BEGAN AT 14

Thomas McKay

As a boy, when he heard his father had been killed by Indians, Thomas McKay said with certain bravado: "I will yet become known on this coast as an avenger of blood." Yet with all his trading, hunting, adventuring on the Pacific Coast he never sought vengeance upon Indians but instead married two, dying in Scappoose, Oregon, in 1850.

With his father, Alexander McKay, Thomas left New York September 8, 1810 on John Jacob Astor's trading ship TONQUIN, registered to the Pacific Fur Co. The voyage was made to establish a trading post at the mouth of the Columbia River and the story of her fortunes and misfortunes with the settling of Astoria is well known in Pacific Northwest annals.

The 33 colonizers aboard suffered a rough voyage particularly because of the actions of Captain Jonathan Thorn, a "Captain Bligh" type of master whose iron discipline aroused passengers and crew almost to murder and mutiny. The ship reached the Sandwich Islands without bloodshed, replenished its supplies and set sail for Oregon. Outside the Columbia River bar, anxious to land his mutinous crew, Thorn sent out a party in a small boat to take soundings. It was swamped, the crew lost and several more men swept overboard as the ship almost foundered crossing the bar into the river.

After discharging supplies the TONQUIN departed for Vancouver Island in the hopes of picking up cargo, anchoring off the Indian village of Neweetee. When the old chief came on board to barter pelts he attempted to make such a sharp bargain Thorn

MOUNT HOOD, altitude 11,245', looms over Summit Meadows, this photo being made from point about 2,500' higher. Seemingly smooth snowfield at left was determined by Portland mountaineers' club, the Mazamas, to be glacier in 1924 when season of light snow exposed crevasses. It was named Palmer Glacier for Joel Palmer who made sightings from nearby point while trying to find way over mountain's shoulder in 1845.

In center is White River Glacier, once occupying entire canyon to point far below present snout. From this glacier flows wild, silty White River, difficult to cross, regularly tearing out highway bridges. It was at river's crossing that "Woodsides' Sick Train" was forced to camp while waiting for aid and supplies and where Morgan baby was fatally injured. Also here, 35 years later, Perry Vickers was slain by fleeing bandit. Trees are Whitebark Pine, **Pinus albicaulis,** always marking extreme high timberline limits in Cascade Mountains.

had him tossed overboard. On the next day a party of Indians boarded the TONQUIN apparently in a peaceful and forgiving mood but at a sudden signal they fell upon crew and officers, killing all but four whites, Alexander McKay among the dead. An Indian crewman, Lamazee, made his escape with the attackers and during the night three of the captives got away in a boat but were caught and tortured to death.

The following morning, the one crew member remaining, ship's clerk Lewis, walked the decks motioning Indians aboard and about 150 came swarming over the rail from scores of canoes. While they were plundering the vessel, Lewis slipped below decks to the powder magazine and set a blaze under the main storage. The resulting explosion scattered bodies of savages in all directions, killing at least

one hundred. Lamazee, the Indian crew member who was free made his way back to Astoria and told of the tragedy.

The story of Alexander McKay's son Thomas is also colorful history but not covered in popular volumes. He was ill and remained in Astoria when his father sailed north with the TONQUIN. At 14 he was left fatherless, facing an uncertain life with his manly oath of vengeance. Hired as a clerk by the North West Co. when Astor left in 1813, Thomas joined various expeditions, one of them to the Eyakema (Yakima) Valley in 1814 where he hurt his hip and was lamed for life. He retained connections with the North West Co. or Hudson's Bay Co. with which it merged in 1821.

Dr. John McLoughlin, physician for the North West Co. at Fort William, Ontario, married Mar-

BODIES OF THOMAS McKAY and two others lie in tiny clearing in grove of "scrub oaks." One of the other graves is probably that of McKay's third wife, Isabelle. Site is on private farm land, once McKay's, just north of Scappoose, Ore. Columbia County Historical Society once started movement to mark and fence graves properly but difficulties in purchase of property including site and access lane postponed project. It has been restarted by Byron L. Larson, Americana-conscious Portlander. Secretary Pearl Becker, guiding Larson and this reporter to virtually unknown and entirely unmarked site in late summer of 1965, vowed Society would this time establish proper marking of historic grave. In photo actual site is slightly north (near camera tripod) of rotting stump seen here at right of random stone.

garet McKay, widow of Alexander and mother of Thomas. When the newly appointed factor of the Columbia department moved to Fort Vancouver, mother and son were reunited.

Then began an era of long forays for young Mc-Kay — to the Fraser, Willamette, Umpqua, Klamath and other rivers. A chronicle of the trips states: "The effective gun of Mr. McKay brought down enough game to make unnecessary the eating of too many horses." He built a grist mill on the Willamette for his company in 1836 and dabbled in real estate, buying and selling several claims.

When McKay settled on his farm near Scappoose, his wife was a former Chinook princess, daughter of the famous Chief Concomly, whom he had married prior to 1824. At her death McKay took another squaw, this one from the Snake country with no claims to royalty. She also died and on December 31, 1838, he married Isabelle Montour, the ceremony performed by Father Blanchet in the old St. James Church in Vancouver.

Of Thomas McKay it was said by contemporaries: "The contour of his frame and features is Scotch, his manners . . . strongly tinctured with Indian". Such observations were possibly accurate since his mother was the daughter of a Swiss fur trader and a squaw of the Cree nation. Thomas McKay was said by his daughter to be "tall, dark and tremendously powerful".

After the Whitman Massacre in 1847 McKay stirred himself from the role of gentleman farmer to become captain of a military group which took part in the Cayuse War under Col. Gilliam. Following the detachment's one brush with the enemy the OREGON SPECTATOR reported on April 6, 1848: "The arrival on this day of Capt. Thomas McKay with the remains of Col. Gilliam . . . has cast a general gloom over this city".

In one incident of the war, Chief War Eagle who claimed he could swallow any bullet the white man could fire at him, brazenly rode out to face lined up troops. A little dog belonging to the soldiers ran out to meet him. War Eagle killed the pet and was promptly shot through the head by Captain McKay, the Indian dying immediately.

Although he too was wounded slightly in the Cayuse affair, McKay heard the alluring cry of "Gold!" in 1848 and departed for California. Possibly because of ill health he returned to Scappoose the next year. THE SPECTATOR of May 2, 1850 reported: "Mr. G. Groom has been appointed administrator of the estate of Thomas McKay, deceased."

A GIGANTIC WHITE SKELETON

TH FACTOR WAS THE FATHER
McLoughlin, Oregon City, Ore.

"I pointed the flashlight down into the yawning hole. The beam shone on a crumbling, glass-covered casket, revealing the gigantic white skeleton of a man. The size alone identified it as being the mortal remains of Dr. John McLoughlin."

So said Father Laidlaw who in 1948 was placed in charge of moving the bodies of the "White Headed Eagle" and his wife Margaret. The old St. John's Catholic Church where the McLoughlins were originally buried was about to be razed to make way for a new supermarket.

Much has been written about the life of this giant often called "The Father of Oregon". Installed by Hudson's Bay Co. as factor of the trading post at Vancouver, Oregon Territory (now Washington State), McLoughlin was adjured to be stern to "American immigrants who might stop at the post to beg for supplies." The British had apprehensions about the increasing number of settlers in the Willamette Valley and they were well founded for eventually enough Americans did take up farms in sufficient numbers to bring the land under the American flag. Had the big, snowy-thatched man at Vancouver been a tough "company man", American settlers would have been discouraged from coming west to this area for many years. But McLoughlin was his own man and could not refuse the ragged, near-starved settlers who had come the hard way over the Oregon Trail. He fed them immediately, provided supplies to tide them over, gave them wheat to plant and loaned many substantial sums of money, most of it never repaid.

Foreseeing his eventual separation from the Company, McLoughlin laid claim to part of the site later occupied by Oregon City, shortly after the first cabin was built there in 1829. When Methodist missionaries began encroaching on his property, held only by squatters rights, McLoughlin had the town platted and named, thus establishing the first legally planned community west of the Rocky Mountains. The man selected for the platting was Sidney Walter Moss who came in with the first immigration in 1842. His qualifications? He owned a pocket compass.

When Dr. McLoughlin left Vancouver he made his home in Oregon City for the balance of his life, dying at 73 in 1857. Poet Edwin Markham, author of "Man with the Hoe", remembered him as "six-feet-six, handsome and impressive." He also recollected the doctor's funeral. "I was taken into the cathedral at Oregon City where the good man was lying in state . . . some strong man lifted me on his shoulder that I might look down on the face of the great dead . . . it was my first encounter with death." Markham was 5 at the time. Dr. McLoughlin was placed in a "zinc or lead" casket with a glass top and buried under the floor of the old St. John's Church. Laid with him later was the body of his wife Margaret, the half-Cree Indian widow of Alexander McKay who was lost on Astor's ship *Tonquin*.

Years later the church was expanded and while the graves remained indoors, the original marble slabs were placed in the outside wall some distance away. By 1948 the church became dangerously decrepit as well as inadequate and it was scheduled for removal, a new edifice planned for the northeast corner of Fifth and Washington Streets where the McLoughlin remains were to be reinterred. But the new owners wanted the old church property vacated quickly so grave removal plans were set ahead. Father Laidlaw hired a crew of workmen to locate and open the old graves and when they were unable to find the exact spot he called in experienced grave diggers from Mountain View Cemetery.

When they telephoned an urgent summons, Laidlaw hurried to the empty church and verified the discovery of Dr. McLoughlin's coffin. The adjoining one of Mrs. McLoughlin was soon located, the wood almost completely decomposed.

DR. JOHN McLOUGHLIN and wife Margaret now rest in crypts where bodies were placed after removal from original graves under floor of old St. John's Catholic Church in Oregon City. Small marble slabs set in pavement served as footstones for original graves. Present location of graves is at Fifth and Washington Streets in section high on bluffs above Willamette River falls. Old section of city was at falls where power for early projects — sawmill, grist mill, etc. — was available. McLoughlin's original home was there also.

Since neither casket would stand the strain of removal, the priest had two cedar boxes constructed and placed beside the old containers. The bones were transferred one by one to lie in the same position they had all the years. The cedar boxes were then placed in standard caskets and reburied with proper ceremonies at the corner where the new church was to be built. But when the time came for the actual building, the city refused to issue a permit for this site because of zoning developments and the new St. John's Catholic Church was erected several blocks southwest.

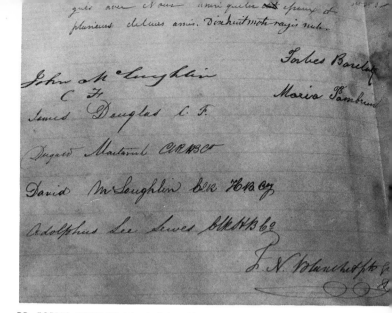

DR. FORBES BARCLAY joined McLoughlin at Fort Vancouver as medical officer. He married Maria Pambrum while still stationed there as this entry in old church record book shows. Among those serving as witnesses shown by signatures were McLoughlin (C.F. indicating Chief Factor); James Douglas, assistant factor who took over post when McLoughlin left Company and moved to Oregon City; David McLoughlin, factor's son and clerk of Hudson's Bay Co. He later joined Indian relatives in Idaho, was found and brought back as old man to be featured at Lewis and Clark Exposition in Portland in 1905, after which he again disappeared.

STONE BOOK, usually signifying Bible, is sometimes seen in old graveyards. This one marks resting place of wife of Dr. Barclay, attending physician to Dr. John McLoughlin, Hudson's Bay factor at Fort Vancouver, and is next to "broken column" on his grave. Fraser Lake, given as Mrs. Barclay's birthplace is on present provincial highway between Prince George and Prince Rupert, British Columbia. Mainland part of province was originally called New Caledonia.

DR. BARCLAY'S GRAVE in Mountain View Cemetery is marked by symbolic "broken column". Of all McLoughlin's associates at Fort Vancouver he was only one to follow him to Oregon City, serving as McLoughlin's personal physician as well as having general practice. He died honored as city's most beloved doctor, reverse side of monument bears legend: "Erected in honour of Forbes Barclay M.D. by the Citizens of Oregon City 1875." Trees in background are characteristic of Pacific Northwest — Douglas firs.

PIONEER CATTLE MAN OF CHAMPOEG
Ewing Young

The man whose death set in motion the effort to secure the Oregon Country for the United States, is buried 200 feet from where he died in the first house built on the west side of the Willamette River, opposite the settlement of Champoeg. This was the end of a stalwart pioneer, a restless, aggressive man of principle, who fought for what he considered his rights on the raw frontier.

Ewing Young was born on the banks of the Holston River in Knox County, Tennessee about 1810. As a young man he went on a trading expedition to Santa Fe, New Mexico. The Mexican traders there put the Americans to such a disadvantage that Young asserted his leadership, assembled about 50 of his countrymen and took possession of the town and quieted the Mexicans for a time. But Young was a restless man, as well as an enterprising one, and decided to secure a farm in the "Wallamet" region. On the way in Southern California he found a man with like ambitions — Hall Jackson Kelley.

Young was driving many horses and cattle with him, Kelley adding his stock to the string as well as those of several Mexicans who had joined the party. Unknown to the white men, the Mexicans had stolen their cattle and were anxious to get clear of the area. The cavalcade progressed northward safely until it reached a river in Southern Oregon where considerable supplies were lost to thieving Indians, the Mexicans decamping. Young and Kelley named the river "Les Coquinas", meaning "The Rogues", the name later shortened to Rogue.

Arriving at French Prairie on the Willamette River, Young found Mexican authorities had advised the Hudson's Bay agents that he was in possession of stolen stock. Young went immediately to Factor John McLoughlin at Fort Vancouver to explain the circumstances and secure supplies. But McLoughlin had also heard of the theft and did not extend his customary hospitality, turning Young away without even seeing him.

Undeterred, the trader managed to establish a stock farm and start a whiskey distillery. For the latter he went to Wyeth Island (later Sauvie Island, named for a French Canadian employee of the Hudson's Bay Co.) and obtained a caldron which had been used for pickling salmon from the abandoned plant of Nathaniel Wyeth at Ft. William. Soon after setting up his equipment, Young received a visit from William Slacum, emissary of the Jason Lee Methodist Mission (later Salem) and allowed himself to be talked out of the project, agreeing with the missionary that spirituous liquors would be a bad influence in the new settlement. When Hudson's Bay authorities heard of this, they conditionally forgave Young for what they conceded might be mistaken accusations on the part of the Mexican government. And Slacum offered Young $150 to go to California to try to clear himself of the charges.

Young's rude house was built opposite to Champoeg on the west side of the Willamette on land appropriated in the free and easy fashion of the times and constituted almost the entire Chehalem valley. He erected a sawmill, his cattle and horses multiplied and he became a rich man by local standards. Eventually he was cleared of charges of complicity in the stolen stock affair and became an influential man in the community.

On February 10, 1841 Young became ill and confined to his bed, death coming five days later. Employee Sidney Smith was with him at the time and later wrote: "It was a most dreadful scene. He raved and fought imaginary foes, his eyes would glare, his hair rise upon his head and it was almost impossible for one man to keep him in bed."

The funeral was held on February 17, burial close to his cabin. Even at the funeral there was talk about the disposal of the extensive land holdings, stock and money. There were no known heirs. Young had taken or married an Indian woman at Taos, New Mexico, and had a son by her. Both were abandoned but the French Prairie settlers

WOODEN PLAQUE ON STONE MONUMENT beside State Highway 240 — 3.2 miles Northwest of Newberg on South Valley Road. Oak tree on grave of Ewing Young is visible from this point, accessible by dirt road starting a few hundred feet south of marker. Plank bridge across little Chehalem Creek would seem unsafe for cars.

BRONZE MARKER fastened to oak tree growing on Young's grave.

were unaware of all this and there was no government to inherit the estate by escheat. After the services, an informal meeting was presided over by Rev. Jason Lee to look into what might be done to establish some sort of government to safeguard the settlers in just such an emergency as this one. It was the first of several gatherings leading up to the historic one at Champoeg, May 2, 1843.

The later-established Provisional government appropriated Ewing's estate amounting to $3,734.26, with the proviso that it would be available to any heirs who might later appear. The funds were used to build a wooden jail, this burning soon afterward.

Then an heir to Young's estate did appear, Joaquin Young, product of Ewing's dalliance at Taos, N.M. Joaquin proved his identity and collected the money due him.

SYMMETRICAL SPECIMENT OF "OREGON OAK" — Quercus garryana — was planted on unmarked grave of Ewing Young as sprouted acorn by Miss Bayley, fiancee of Sidney Smith, employee of Young. Several other oaks stand in neighborhood, one surrounded by bee hives whose denizens attacked this photographer with a vengeance.

OREGON CITY ORDEAL

George Le Breton

Le Breton had no chance with the girl and even less with the cocksure Molalla Cockstock and his war party riding up and down the street inviting battle. When his single bullet missed, Le Breton dropped the pistol and charged recklessly. It was the end of his short, happy if frustrated, life in Oregon — and of Cockstock's.

In his four years in Oregon George Le Breton seemed to impress people with his good looks and charm, was said to be man of rare intelligence, pleasing manners and one accustomed to good society. In "The Falls" or Oregon City his good points were recognized and he was elected as clerk of courts and public recorder. His efforts to win a Catholic girl were not so successful. He allied himself with the church in St. Paul as apostate but the gesture was fruitless and he "gradually withdrew from the church," according to historian Bancroft.

At this time Dr. Elijah White, formerly associated with the Methodist Mission as sub-agent, was in deep trouble because of methods used in handling his charges. Already outraged by the influx of settlers and angered by White's manhandling eight Indian prisoners taken April 1, 1843, the tribesmen were seething with unrest. White warned settlers near Oregon City to be prepared with good muskets and a hundred rounds of ammunition each. Trouble brewed for a year with no outbreak of violence but some loss of livestock in Indian raids.

Then early the next year the Molalla troublemaker, sub-chief Cockstock, broke several windows in Dr. White's house. Unsuccessful in apprehending the Indian, he offered $100 for his capture. On March 4, 1844, the jittery citizens of Oregon City were thrown into a panic when Cockstock rode into

MONUMENTS dating from around turn of century or before frequently show examples of near lost art, transfer of photographic portrait to enduring china plaque. Generally about 3" x 4" in size, they are impervious to all ravages of time, though always at the mercy of vandals. Employee of Blaesing Granite Co., Portland, when asked about portraits said: "This was very popular years ago. There were half a dozen firms making them here on the Pacific Coast. You provided the picture, no matter what of — we turned out a plaque which we could cement to the stone. Now we have calls for only a few a year, mostly for Jewish cemeteries where the stone is still placed upright with English inscription on one side, Hebrew on other." Ceramic supply house reported having ready-made "decals" with floral, fruit, and other designs for firing on to china plates or other vitreous surfaces. No explanation was given as to how design or portrait is made, stating art is now family secret confined to two firms in the East.

CHINA PORTRAIT here is combined with sculptured lamb as symbol of innocence once much used for memorials to infants, small children. In old cemeteries in or near population centers these small sculptures often show damage, lamb's head broken off in most cases. The above perfect examples of vitreous portrait and lamb sculpture are on stone in remote, secluded burial ground in Columbia Gorge few miles from Lyle, Wash.

town leading a band of warriors painted and armed for battle. They saw nobody ready for it and it was later believed Cockstock's appearance in broad daylight was meant in conciliation or was a move to clear charges against him.

The Indians crossed the river, turned and came back. Groups of white men, wits now gathered, having had time to get their muskets, marched to the landing to meet them. Firing broke out on both sides. George Le Breton discharged his one-shot pistol at Cockstock but missed and rushed at him unarmed. The Indian fired at him point blank and Le Breton's hand was shattered, a ball lodging in his elbow, another in his arm. Flaunting his pain, he came to grips with the chief and the two fell to the ground, Le Breton crying out that he was being killed with a knife. A mulatto ran up and rammed his rifle barrel into Cockstock's head.

The noise and confusion were "frightful", according to a local account, yet two men, Wilson and Rogers, continued to "work quietly at their jobs nearby" but Rogers was wounded by flying arrows.

Young Le Breton and Rogers were taken to Fort Vancouver where there was a doctor. The canoe trip took ten hours and Le Breton was then beyond help, dying in three days from "the horrid disaster". The report adds, "Mr. Rogers lived but one day longer".

Since Le Breton was one of those voting at Champoeg during his short stay in the Willamette Valley, the D.A.R. in later years made a thorough but unsuccessful search for his grave that it might be properly marked with their customary bronze plaque. It would seem certain he was buried in the only cemetery available at the time, the Fort Vancouver plot. Considering Le Breton's short tenure in Oregon and lack of local family ties, no permanent marker would likely have been placed on his grave and a common wooden headboard would long since have disappeared, as the records did.

BODY BODY WHO HAS THE BODY?

Lewis and Clark spent the winter of 1804-5 among the Mandan Indians, having constructed a "fort" on the Missouri River in what would be North Dakota. The winter was typical of the area, snows deep and temperatures often plunging far below zero.

Many of the entries in the Capt. Lewis journals at this time were concerned with the weather, with frost-bitten feet and ice-locked boats. But on Monday, February 11, he wrote, "About five o'clock this evening one of the wives of Charbono was delivered of a fine boy. It is worthy of remark that this was the first child which this woman had boarn and as is common in such cases her labour was tedious and the pain violent; Mr. Jessome informed me that he frequently administered a small portion of the rattle of the rattlesnake, which he assured me had never failed to produce the deaired effect, that of hastening the birth of the child; having the rattle of a snake by me I gave it to him and he administered two rings of it to the woman broken into small pices with the fingers and added a small quantity of water. Whether this medicine was truly the cause or not I shall not undertake to determine, but I was informed that she had not taken it more than ten minutes before she brought forth."

The "Charbono" referred to was Touissant Charbonneau, engaged as interpreter mainly for the difficult Minnataree language. The new mother was Sacajawea, (variously spelled, pronounced and translated), a Shoshone woman, married or allied to Charbonneau.

Sacajawea, who later proved to be indispensable to the success of the expedition, was almost lost to it on March 12 when the flightly Charbonneau, in a fit of pique, "resigned". The captains had no choice but to let him go, his service bound only by verbal terms. The interpreter took his wife, new baby and such supplies as he was allotted, and grumpily moved across the river. Then he changed his mind, petitioned the leaders to take him back "agreeably to the terms we had proposed and doe everything we wished him to doe @c, @c". His change of heart was fortunate for on several occasions when hostile Indian scouts saw the expedition included a woman, they concluded the party meant no harm.

When the explorers reached the area native to the Shoshone woman she was able to guide them by the best routes. On actual contact with her people she was invaluable as interpreter and in securing horses necessary to travel over the Continental Divide. And when game was scarce or non-existent she searched out roots and plants for food. Lewis wrote, "When we halted for dinner the squaw busied herself in searching for the wild artichokes which the mice collect and deposit in huge hoards. This operation she perform by penetrating the earth with a sharp stick." And on any and all chores, Sacajawea's papoose rode securely on her back.

The next winter was spent in a cheerless camp on the Oregon coast where it rained and stormed monotonously. Clothing made of skins taken from animals eaten never dried out, rotting on backs. Food was scarce and often spoiled, and while others complained, Sacajawea did not, attending to her tasks which included nursing Jean Baptiste, now almost a year old and thriving lustily.

The two captains and entire party were eager to start on the return journey to St. Louis but it was decided to wait until April to give the deep mountain snows a chance to melt. On March 18, 1806, the expedition started up the Columbia, found much snow but with the aid of Sacajawea's Shoshones who served as guides, the present site of Lolo, Montana, was reached by the end of June.

In the Mandan village where Jean Baptiste was born it was clear not all the party wished to go on to the "big city" and among those spurning even the rudest civilization was the party's old reliable John Colter. He asked the leaders to excuse him so he could join two trappers heading up the Missouri. Clark wrote on August 15, "The offer was very advantageous to him, his services could be dispensed with from this down and we are disposed to be of service to any of our party who had performed their duty as well as Colter has done." So he headed back toward the wilderness, soon discovering the wonders of Yellowstone Park. Eventually he did go to St. Louis where his stories of spouting geysers and burning mountains were laughed at.

Shortly after this the Indian chiefs who were

... OREGON?

to accompany the party to meet the "Great White Father" in Washington, D.C. changed their minds. Since the only need for Charbonneau's service was as interpreter for the chiefs, he would go when they did. Wrote Clark on August 17, "Seattled with Charbono for his services as an interpreter the price of a horse and Lodge purchased of him for public service in all amounting to 500 $ 33 1/3 cents."

Actual separation from Charbonneau was a painful contemplation for Clark because with him would go Sacajawea and little Jean Baptiste. The journals show Clark growing very much attached to the child, many times in the dugout canoe holding him in his lap and fondly referring to him as "My boy, Pomp" — the boy's nickname from the Shoshone word for chief. One of the landmarks on the route was called "Pompey's Pillar" by Clark in honor of little Pomp.

Before departure of the family Clark broached the subject of adopting Jean Baptiste, something he had long considered. He wrote, "I offered to take his little son a butiful promising child who is 10 months old to which they both himself @ wife were willing provided the child had been weaned. They observed that in one year the child would be sufficiently old to leave his mother @ he would take him to me if I would be so friendly as to raise the child for him in such a manner as I thought proper, to which I agreed @c."

Until recently it was assumed Jean Baptiste lived out his days on the Wind River Reservation in Wyoming, that he was buried thereabouts in 1885. Government records list the residency there of one "Pa-tez Charbonneau". Presumably Sacajawea is buried there. The records say "The

wife of Charbonneau, the guide" is but he was known to have had three wives. However new light has been shed on events concerning the son, most of it supplied by Dr. Leroy Hafen in his book *Mountain Men and the Fur Trade.*

Clark had doubts about Charbonneau's promise to send the boy when weaned because of the man's vacillating nature. He wrote him a letter on August 20, 1806, entrusting it to a party of traders bound upstream. It read, "Charbono — Your present situation with the Indians gives me some concern. I wish now I had advised you to come with me to Illinois where it most probably would have been in my power to put you on some way to do something for yourself. You have long been with me and have conducted yourself in such a manner as to gain my friendship; your woman who accompanied you on that long, dangerous and fatiguing route to the Pacific Ocean and back, deserved a greater reward for her attention and services on

SACAJAWEA, done in bronze by Helen Cooper in 1905, stands on eminence in Portland's Washington Park, Statue is impressive, fitting monument to heroic Indian woman important to success of Lewis and Clark expedition, particularly near and in her home country of Shoshones. Sculptress took "poetic license" according to some experts in Indian lore. American Indians, Shoshones specifically, strapped papoose to board which was strapped to mother's back so baby faced backward. Also, say those informed, mother would of necessity bend forward, the better to support burden.

OLD PHOTO OF INSKIP station was copied from post card owned by Mrs. C. Wm. Moore, writer-historian of Vale, Ore. Built primarily as stage stop on road from California to Silver City, Idaho, structure was often utilized as fort where early settlers took refuge from Indian attacks. Ruins still stand on Ruby ranch near Danner west of Jordan Valley, old timers claiming doors bore bullet holes. It was here Jean Baptiste Charbonneau was taken ill with pneumonia and died. Some say he fell victim to disease due to wetting received in fall while crossing Owyhee River.

that route than we had in our powers to give her at the Mandans. As to your little son (my boy Pomp) you well know my fondness for him and my anxiety to take him and raise him as my own child. I once more tell you if you will bring your son Baptiste to me, I will educate and treat him as my own child. . . Wishing you and your family great success, and with anxious expectation of seeing my little dancing boy, Baptiste, I shall remain your friend, William Clark."

The parents did shortly take the boy to Capt. Clark at St. Louis and for the next several years while Charbonneau frequently took various trail jobs as interpreter or guide, Jean Baptiste and his mother remained under the care of the "Redheaded Captain." As the boy grew he was tutored by a succession of Catholic priests, nuns and Baptist ministers and apparently took some trips with his own father. Hugh Munroe reported seeing the 11-year-old Jean Baptiste among the Mandans and said the elder Charbonneau had just gambled away the fine horse given his son by Clark.

In a trader's village on the Kansas River Jean Baptiste, at 18, met 25-year-old German Prince Paul of Wurttemburg who was on an expedition of "scientific interests" and planning a trip back to Europe. The two became close friends and in St. Louis the Prince obtained the consent of Clark to take young Charbonneau with him. They sailed on the brig *Smyrna* for Le Havre on November 21, 1823, and arrived February 14 of the next year.

For the next six years the young half-breed lived with the Prince in a castle thirty miles from Stuttgart, Germany. He learned the German language to supplement his now fluent French and English, mingled with Europe's bluebloods, studied horses, guns and hunting. Then the two returned to America and went their separate ways.

Prepared to accept any of several proffered jobs in diplomacy and other "civilized positions", Jean Baptiste instead secured a "passport" from Clark to ascend the Missouri with a party sent out by the American Fur Co. This was the start of a 15 year period in which he lived as a mountain man in the Rockies and Oregon. He joined briefly with Joe Meek in 1832, with Jim Bridger the next year and in 1834 was camped near where Capt. Wyeth had stopped. Indians raided Charbonneau's tent and Wyeth wrote, "The Indians got seven horses, all there were. Charbonneau pursued them on foot but got his gun wet crossing a little stream and only snapped twice."

During 1839-40 Jean Baptiste was with a party led by Louis Vasquez and Andrew Sublette, a member writing, while camped on the South Platte August 6, 1839, . . ." Besides the main company there were two half-breeds employed as hunters. One of these was a son of Capt. Clarke, the great western traveler and companion of Lewis. He had traveled in Europe during seven years."

In 1842 John C. Fremont was on his first tour of western exploration and reported, "Arrived at Chabonard's camp on an island in the Platte . . . Mr. Chabonard was in service of Bent and St. Vrain's company . . . Mr. Chabonard treated us hospitably." A little later Rufus Sage came upon the same camp and noted, "Under the direction of a half-breed named Chabonard, who proved to be a gentleman of superior information . . . he had acquired a classical education . . . having visited most of the important places in England, France and Germany, he knew how to turn his experience to good advantage. There was a humor and shrewdness in his conversation . . . he at once insinuated himself into the good graces of his listeners."

William Clark Kennery, nephew of the explorer, made comment certainly identifying Jean Baptiste as "My boy, Pomp". He said, "One of the drivers was the son of an old trapper named Charbonneau and Sacajawea, the brave Indian woman who had guided Lewis and Clark on their perilous journey through the wilderness." William Boggs, son of Missouri's Governor E. W. Boggs, wrote, ". . . Charbenau, an educated half-breed. His father was a French Canadian and his mother said to be a Blackfoot Indian squaw . . . he wore his hair long, so that it hung down to his shoulders. It was said that Charbenau was the best man on foot on the Plains or in the Rocky Mountains."

Then came the Mexican War. St. George Cooke and his Mormon Battalion marched from Santa Fe to San Diego in 1846, Jean Baptiste hired to guide them across the New Mexico and Arizona deserts, some 700 miles. An entry kept by one of the officers exposes a facet of the guide's nature. "Nov. 1846 — Since dark Charboneaux has come in; his mule gave out, he said, he stopped for it to rest and feed up for half an hour; when going to saddle it, it kicked him and ran off; he followed it a number of miles, and finally he shot it; partly, I suppose in anger, and partly to get his saddle and pistols which he brought on to camp."

The military taking over in San Diego, Charbonneau was released and sent to nearby San Luis Rey as Alcalde. There he became implicated in an insurgent move. A line from his long rebutting statement is given here as it identifies him in California and establishes the proper spelling of his name: "I, John B. Charbonneau of St. Louis, state of Missouri, came to California in the service of the U. S. as guide for the Mormon Battalion." He resigned July 24, 1848, finding his Indian blood precluded fair judgment.

FIVE UNMARKED GRAVES in Inskip area. One is that of Jean Baptiste Charbonneau, according to local legend and several newspaper obituaries. Others buried here are two unidentified soldiers, two unknown children. Spot is on county road property, bulldozers about to level area several years ago when stopped by nearby rancher S. K. Skinner, pictured here. (Photo by Mrs. C. Wm. Moore, Vale, Ore.)

Charbonneau next turned up in the gold fields. James Beckwith's diary reports, "At Murderer's Bar on the middle fork of the American River I found my old friend Chapineau housekeeping, staid with him until the rainy season set in." An 1860 census report from Placer County lists "J. B. Charbonneau . . male . . from Missouri . . address P. O. Secret Ravine." (Secret Ravine was ten miles from Auburn). Shortly after this he was reported working as clerk in the Orlean Hotel, Auburn.

An obituary in the *Placer Herald,* Auburn, California, July 7, 1866, draws the final curtain. "J. B. Charbonneau — Death of a California Pioneer — A letter announcing the death of J. B. Charbonneau who left the country some weeks ago with two companions for Montana Territory. This letter is from one of the party who says, 'Mr. C. was taken sick with mountain fever on the Owyhee, and died after a short illness'. . . . he had remained here with little intermission until his departure for the new gold fields of Montana, which strangely enough was the scene of his birth . . . his father was a French Canadian and his mother a half-breed of the Crow tribe . . . as a young man he went to Europe . . . at breaking out of the Mexican War was engaged as guide and came to California . . . he determined to return to the scene of his youth, but the weight of years was too much for him, and he now sleeps alone by the bright waters of the Owyhee."

The *Owyhee Avalanche,* Ruby City (later moved to Silver City) Idaho, gave another obituary on June 2, 1866. "At Inskip Ranch, Cow Creek, in Jordan Valley, J. B. Charbonneau, aged 63 years, of pneumonia. Was born at St. Louis Mo., one of the oldest trappers and pioneers; piloted the Mormon Brigade . . . resided Placer County, was on route to Montana."

MY BOY POMP

What really happened to Sacajawea's papoose? Until recently it was generally believed the boy lived to an advanced age on the Shoshone Wind River Reservation, that he died there and was buried beside her. Now this is questioned and supporters of each theory offer what would seem to be uncontrovertible proof.

Researching in the 1920s for her book *Sacajawea,* historian Grace Hebard found all information on the wanderings of Jean Baptiste Charbonneau substantially the same as given here. The point of difference is at San Diego, California. Refuting the story of Charbonneau's going to the gold fields from there, Miss Hebard contends, "From 1852 to 1855 Baptiste was with his mother's

DRAWING FOR ANOTHER STATUE of Sacajawea, commissioned in 1905. Considered a good likeness of the Indian girl, it shows her papoose, Baptiste, riding in conventional position of Shoshones. Photo from **Sacajawea** by Grace Hebard.

tribe, Shoshones, in Bridger Valley and on the Shoshone Reservation in Wyoming."

There are many differing descriptions of the physical attributes and mental attainments of the Baptiste who lived at Auburn, California, in the 1850s and '60s and those of the Baptiste on the reservation during that period, assuming there were two of them. The first was described by many trappers, guides and others as being light colored "for an Indian", of medium height, graceful in movement, fluent in several languages, and agreeable in nature. One of those who felt Baptiste was a personable youth was Prince Paul, the German aristocrat, who befriended the half-breed. Years after he had taken Baptiste to Europe, Paul again traveled in America's West and as guest of John Sutter at Sutter's Fort he wrote in his journal, "It is not alone the men of the Hock Nation, who are in the employ of Mr. Sutter as farm laborers, but also red men of such nations as the Juba, the Koshi . . . even a few of the Shoshones or Snake Indians. One of these was a fine young lad, quite intelligent, who reminded me strangely and somewhat sadly, of the B. Charbonneau who followed me to Europe, and whose mother was of the tribe of the Shoshones."

The Baptiste of the reservation was differently described by Mrs. James Patten who lived at the reservation agency. "He was a man of little importance in his tribe, about 5' 6" in height, quite dark, stocky build, about 200 pounds, thick lips, his mouth drawn well down at the corners. . . He acknowledged Sacajawea as his mother but seemed

. . . OR WYOMING?

to take but a passing interest in her." Another old timer said of Baptiste, "He was small, complexion as dark as any full-blooded Indian." Another said, "Baptiste was a treacherous man, because he liked his firewater and used it often."

The Baptiste of the gold fields seems not to have married but the one of the north had three wives and many children. One was Barbara Myers who said in an interview, "Baptiste, my father, did not always live with Bazil (his brother) . . . often spoke to me of being across the big waters into another country toward the rising sun and how funny the white people were over in that country . . . he saw many curious people and often spoke of that period in his life . . . he spoke several languages." This one interview would seem almost conclusive in identfying Baptiste and all but cancelling out the other discrepancies.

Sacajawea arrived at the reservation after a hectic career. Her marriage to the Lewis and Clark guide, Charbonneau, withstood his taking a second wife, another Shoshone girl, but when the Frenchman took a third from another tribe, the long-suffering Sacajawea left his crowded cabin. She then married several times, outliving each husband. She arrived at the Shoshone Reservation in Wind River Valley in 1871, along with Bazil, his wives, Baptiste and his three wives. She did not talk much to other Indians about her trip with Lewis and Clark. Understandably, her part in guiding the whites on an expedition that led to the ultimate crushing of her people would not add to her popularity. In an unguarded moment she described a huge fish she saw on the beach beside the big waters of the Pacific and was branded a liar. The "fish" was, of course, the whale washed up on the beach near Fort Clatsop, an incident well documented by Lewis and Clark.

Sacajawea never suffered a major illness but on the morning of April 9, 1884, at the age of 100, she failed to awaken. She was removed from her teepee, wrapped in sewn hides and buried in the reservation cemetery. A small lettered board marked her grave

PHOTO OF THREE HISTORIC GRAVES, likely made in 1920s, in Wind River Reservation cemetery, Wyoming. In center is that of Sacajawea, monument now replaced by modern marker. At right is grave of her adopted son, Bazil. At left is monument to "Baptiste Charbonneau," reputedly the papoose born to her on Lewis and Clark Expedition. Stone marker is memorial only, actual bones lying in lost, unmarked grave in nearby mountains. Dr. John Roberts (shown here) performed last rites of church for Sacajawea. Photo courtesy John Standish, Portland.

REPRODUCTION FROM PAINTING by Molhausen in Stuttgart, Germany, purports to show conference between Prince Paul and group of Shoshone Indians. Included is Jean Baptiste Charbonneau, facing Paul (in dark clothing) and holding long pipe. In spite of many romantic discrepancies, such as huge trees in area of meeting somewhere on Missouri River above St. Louis, some details are interesting and possibly true to fact. Charbonneau is shown wearing bauble suspended from chain or thong around his neck. Could this be medal given his father by Lewis and Clark, detail dictated to painter Molhausen by Paul? Photo from **Sacajawea** by Grace Hebard.

and when it deteriorated it was replaced by a rock without inscription. Later, H. E. Wadsworth, Shoshone agent, erected a cement monument with the help of the Indians. Still later, the Hon. Timothy Burke of Cheyenne donated a bronze plaque to be placed on the monument. All these have been supplanted by a modern marker erected by the Wyoming State Historical Society.

Baptiste followed his mother in death a year later. Several Indians took his body to a deep gully near the reservation, letting it down to the bottom on ropes. They threw several rocks down on the body in token burial, one crushing the skull. Years later, in a belated attempt to discover his identity, a search party was led to the site to ascertain if Baptiste did wear the medal given his father by Lewis and Clark, as reported by the Indians. Searchers found a slide of boulders had covered the bones, concealing the grave of the last survivor of the Lewis and Clark Expedition, if this was the same Baptiste.

Bazil died in 1886. He was the orphaned son of Sacajawea's sister, adopted by her while with

Lewis and Clark, the incident recorded only in the Biddle Edition of the Lewis and Clark Journals. Bazil did not see his adopted mother again until he was a grown man when he joined her on the reservation. He was an outgoing, popular type described as tall, well built, affable, contrasting in every way to his younger brother.

Bazil's body was likewise taken into the hills, but on a winter day when the ground was frozen deeply. A small niche was hacked out of the side-hill to await thawing and sliding earth to cover the grave. And again a search party was sent to determine if papers reportedly buried with the body were still intact. It had been said Lewis and Clark gave Sacajawea papers and letters of recommendation, these being treasured and passed on to Bazil who carried them in a billfold or leather packet. Bazil's son located the grave and gave permission for disinterment. The leather case was there under Bazil's head but the papers had deteriorated to the point where nothing could be read. Not long after this episode, the body was removed to a grave beside that of his adopted mother.

A SIOUX WOMAN PUT
THE WHITES TO SHAME

Madame Marie Dorion

Only tolerated at first as the Sioux wife of a French halfbreed interpreter, Marie Dorion became the vital spark to the feeble leadership of the Wilson Price Hunt party, Astor's overland expedition to the Columbia River. Her raw courage and survival sense pulled the white men up short and helped get them to Astoria.

In 1810 John Jacob Astor sent two expeditions to the Pacific Coast to set up a permanent trading post at the mouth of the Columbia—the *Tonquin* by sea, the other overland. Astor's choice of Jonathan Thorn to head the sea voyage and Hunt to lead the journey across country have been branded by history as tragic mistakes.

Hunt lacked nothing in initiative, honesty or bravery but he had little judgment, no qualities of leadership with no conception of the difficulties and dangers ahead. All these weaknesses were more than compensated for in the person of Marie Dorion.

Organized in Montreal, the Hunt party went along the Ottawa River, across the Great Lakes to the head of Lake Huron, thence to St. Louis and a short distance up the Missouri River. During the winter camp here Hunt learned the Sioux were on the war path and was warned to be wary of

them. Heeding this was the main reason for the hiring as interpreter, Pierre Dorion, son of the man who served in the same capacity for Lewis and Clark. Yet Dorion was almost left behind. Hunt was displeased when told the man's wife and two children were to be brought along but since Dorion was half Sioux and Marie full-blooded Sioux, it seemed expedient to take them. In the face of later treacheries and inadequacies of other members Marie Dorion proved to be as indispensable as had Sacajawea on the earlier Lewis and Clark Expedition.

In 1811 the ice broke up earlier than usual and a start was made in April, all going well for a while. There was news of atrocities committed by Sioux tribes and bad reports about the Blackfeet whose anger toward white men was attributed to the lingering bitterness over Captain Lewis killing two of the tribe.

One morning the party saw Indians on a bluff some distance away, yelling and gesticulating. Not understanding the meaning of it, Dorion was sent ahead to talk to them. He brought back the intelligence that a tremendous war party of Sioux was gathered a short distance upstream. Faced with the problem of retreating or advancing, it was decided to keep on, the swivel gun and howitzer fired as it approached the Sioux. Possibly intimidated by the loud reverberations, the Indians made signs for

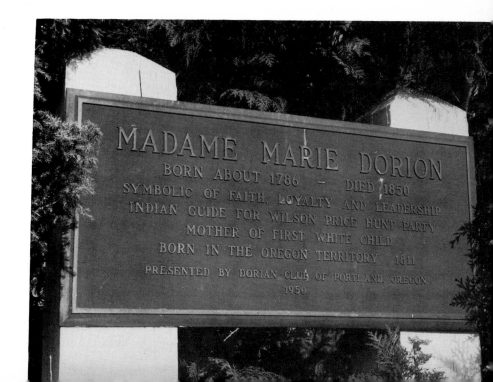

MEMORY OF COURAGEOUS IN-DIAN WOMAN was honored by plaque placed by Dorion Society June 5, 1950. It is located at once busy, now quiet crossroads in St. Louis, Oregon, at corner of St. Louis Church grounds.

"First white child born in Oregon" had full-blooded Sioux woman as mother, French-Sioux Pierre Dorion as father. Long persisting rumors hold members of Lewis and Clark Expedition few years prior to that of Hunt party left living mementos along trail who would have more white blood and more right to distinction.

MADAME MARIE DORION
BORN ABOUT 1786 — DIED 1850
SYMBOLIC OF FAITH, LOYALTY AND LEADERSHIP
INDIAN GUIDE FOR WILSON PRICE HUNT PARTY
MOTHER OF FIRST WHITE CHILD
BORN IN THE OREGON TERRITORY 1811
PRESENTED BY DORIAN CLUB OF PORTLAND, OREGON
1950

friendship and a meeting was held, the peace pipe passed. Hunt promised not to sell any ammunition to enemies of the Sioux and to turn sharply west. The Sioux in turn professed continued friendship and although both sides were wary, the affair passed off smoothly enough. It was the last such emergency that did.

The Missouri Fur Company's boat, with its personnel led by Manuel Lisa, caught up with the Hunt party near an Arikara Indian village and a quarrel developed. Several of Hunt's best men had worked for Lisa and still felt bitter animosity for grievances suffered then. The fighting spread to the leaders but a duel was averted and an armed truce arranged as a matter of policy for travelers in a wild land. Yet the enmity continued.

After many other difficulties, most of them involving Indians and personnel, the company came in sight of snow-capped mountains, the Tetons. Had Hunt taken the advice of men who had been over the divide he would have used the Tetons as a pointer, and in crossing a single ridge would have been on the water-shed of the Columbia. Instead the leader took a southerly detour that led to the headwaters of the Green River and thence to the north fork of the Colorado. The serious mistake plunged them into trouble and more trouble. They eventually entered the Snake River at least 600 miles above the point where Lewis and Clark embarked and encountered many such obstacles as Shoshone Falls. It was in October they left their horses with the Shoshones and took to canoes, another serious mistake. Until now a pack animal had been used by the Dorions, father and mother walking ahead and leading the horse on which were the packs and two children. With canoes all had to carry heavy packs on long portages, Dorions included. It had been evident for some time that Marie Dorion was pregnant but she continued to carry her share of the load.

By the first week in December the party was in an exhausted and starving condition. In a last extremity the men came upon a tribe of friendly Indians from whom they obtained a horse, slaughtering and eating much of it on the spot. Farther along the remainder was almost exhausted when Dorion managed to get hold of another old horse but stubbornly insisted on keeping it for his wife to ride.

At last Hunt and others turned away from the turbulent, canyon-bound Snake, going up what would later be called Burnt River. By December 30, 1811, it was snowing harder than in any storm previously encountered. Everyone was near starvation and freezing for lack of clothing, most of it long worn out. On this day Pierre Dorion stated his wife had been overtaken by labor pains and it was decided he and his little family would remain behind. As the main party pushed ahead a child was born in a snowy bivouac near where the village of North Powder now lies.

ST. LOUIS CHURCH, also itself venerable, is third on site. Original log structure was erected in 1845 by Jesuit missionary, Rev. Aloysius Verecuysee. Church was named for Saint Louis, King of France. Marie Dorion died Sept. 5, 1850, was buried next day under floor of church.

Structure was later removed, more modern edifice erected on site but farther to rear. Mme. Dorion, who had, according to descendants, been buried "under the altar", was now under the middle of the church. This building burned to ground, was in turn replaced by present structure placed still farther back, leaving Dorion remains under vestibule, shown at extreme right of photo. This is disputed by some, especially Daughters of 1812, who in 1936 placed bronze marker on pillar within church proper as being grave site.

Next day the Hunt party emerged in a beautiful, bowl-shaped valley, the Grande Ronde, delighted to find Shoshones camped there. Though not overly supplied themselves, the Indians divided what food they had and the white men ate their first good meal in many weeks. In the midst of what amounted to be a celebration, the Dorions joined the festivities, Pierre leading the old horse. Mounted on it was Marie, cradling the new baby in her arms with the next older slung beside her, the little boy Baptiste walking beside them.

After a short rest Hunt's party pressed on along the winding Grande Ronde River to the summit of the Blue Mountains, then down again to eventually reach the Umatilla River flowing into the Columbia. From there on the going was easier, the company reaching Astoria in February of 1812. The original Hunt expedition had been split into sections, some members dying of hardships and buried along the way. Even Marie Dorion's new baby died in less than a week after birth.

The Dorions rested at Astoria until the next summer when Pierre was hired as guide for a trapping party headed by John Reed who had been a member of the Hunt expedition. As a matter of course Marie Dorion again set out for the wilderness, taking the little boys—Baptiste who was forgetting the miseries of the western trip and Paul

SEARCH FOR LOCATION of grave of Indian woman scout was carried on during late 1920s by group of interested historians including writer Robert J. Hendricks, E. M. Croisan and others. First essential clue came from J. Willard Gay, great-grandson of Mme. Dorion. Story of interment under altar of St. Louis church had been passed down to him and led to search through records.

This reporter found precious record books containing much of early Oregon history had long since been placed in vaults of Diocese Chancery in Portland. Father Laidlaw allowed photography of brittle yellow page in 1850 volume of St. Louis records. Entry near bottom beginning "Le six Septembre, dix huit" etc. translates to "Marie Iowa, wife of John Toupin. The sixth of September, 1850 we undersigned cure of St. Louis have inhumed in the church of this parish Marie Iowa, wife of John Toupin, who died last night, aged 100 years. Witnesses Luke Gagnon, Joseph Dallart, B. Delorme." If Marie Iowa Dorion was 100 at death she would have been 60 or older when her several children were born. Birth year as given on plaque, "about 1786", seems more likely.

too young to remember—back up the Columbia to the Umatilla and over the Blues.

Near Boise the group built a winter shelter and their troubles began. One man, Landry, fell from his horse and was injured fatally. One named Turcott caught some unknown disease and died. Another, Delauncy, lost his mind and wandered into the path of hostile Indians and was killed. The worst tragedy of all for Marie was a raid on the camp in which Pierre was killed by Indians. She was able to save one wounded man, Le Clerc, by getting him on a horse and tying his feet together under the horse's belly. He died in the night and Marie set out alone with her two boys on a 500 mile trip to the nearest habitation, the mission settlement at Wallula on the Columbia.

She knew the way well, this being the third time over the ground. Her supplies, meager to start with, soon dwindled to the vanishing point. Her horse found little or no grass, snow covering all forage save tree twigs. They proved insufficient for the animal and it died just as the little group reached a point near the spot where Marie had buried her baby earlier. Now, at least, she had ample horse meat, smoking it and using the hide for shelter. She carried a buffalo robe to wrap around herself and boys at night and was able to spend about two months here with temperatures dropping below zero at intervals.

The snow was still deep when the meat ran low so she wrapped it and the horse hide in the robe, threw the pack on her shoulder, took a child in each hand and started through the snow. Traveling as far as she could by day, doling out as much meat as could be spared, she crawled under the robe with the children at night. The snow was glaring white and after several days of little or no progress she knew she was snow blind and was forced to rest until she recovered.

As was inevitable the meat ran out before the trio could make the Columbia and little Paul gave out first. In her own weakened condition Marie could not carry the boy but only push him along. When he fell to the ground and could not go on, with Baptiste barely shuffling along, she bundled both in the robe and went on alone. She made better progress but spent the night in near freezing condition. The next day she reached the mission on the Columbia and told the people there about her children who were soon brought in.

Marie and her sons lived near the mission for several years, then she married a man named Venier who stayed only long enough to father a daughter. She married again, Indian style, this time to a John Jean Baptiste Toupin. Years later when the boys were grown, Toupin took his wife to the Willamette Valley and shyly presenting themselves to Father Blanchet at St. Paul, the couple requested he marry them properly in the eyes of the Catholic Church. Baptiste married a French-Indian girl and continued to live in Oregon. Paul reverted to inherited Indian ways, wandering away with a band of natives.

DECAYING HOUSE dated from early days of prosperity in St. Louis when village was farm center, hop growing area. Reputed to be haunted, once proud building, a mansion in those parts, was shunned by all (except this photographer who made series of photos inside and out in 1955). Building was shaded by large cedar trees, stood isolated in field south of church. When research and photos were made for this story old home had disappeared entirely together with trees. Town of St. Louis had postoffice from Oct. 26, 1860 to summer of 1901 when it was moved to Gervais.

TRAMP PRINTER OF GERVAIS

Medare Goddard Foisy

It was printed on a single sheet of rough paper used for cigarette rolling, the size slightly larger than foolscap, and the press that printed it was a wooden, hand-operated Ramage. But it was a bona fide newspaper, CALIFORNIAN, one of the first on the Pacific Coast, and cost *un real*, one bit or 12½ cents. The man who printed it in the Spanish town of Monterey, California, dominated by its Presidio and Mission, was a Quebec Frenchman, an early adherent to the principle that the greenest pastures were beyond the fence — tramp printer Medare Goddard Foisy.

The printing urge struck Foisy in early youth and he deserted home and his father's leather business in Quebec where he was born in 1816. Educated in parochial schools he acquired an ambition to be a printer and a taste for the open road. Both were satisfied temporarily when he migrated to Rev. Spalding's Mission at Lapwai in the Oregon Country of the New West and printed spelling books and tracts. The press he used was one of the first on the Pacific Coast, coming from Oahu in the Sandwich Islands via Vancouver and Walla Walla.

Medare Foisy's wanderlust allowed him only a year at Lapwai. He moved to French Prairie on the Willamette River where he became a member of the legislative committee of Champoeg County, later Marion. Then he wandered again, south to Monterey and was appointed Alcalde under Fremont and worked as printer of the CALIFORNIAN, its first issue August 15, 1846.

As the lure of the wide open spaces succumbed to love, Medare Foisy returned to French Prairie, married Marianne Delore Vaudel and lived in this area until his death on June 11, 1879.

OLD GRAVESTONE presents at least two questions. Did he spell his name "Medere" as inscribed, or "Medare" as text references show it? Was the first newspaper on the Pacific Coast, with which he is credited as printing, produced on the little press at Lapwai where Foisy worked in 1844 printing "school books, portions of the New Testament and hymns, all in the Nez Perce language"? It seems the first newspaper per se west of the Rockies was **Oregon Spectator**, its first issue printed at Oregon City Feb. 5, 1846 by Col. William T'Vault, presumably a one-man project. Henry Lee and George L. Curry followed T'Vault on the paper and by the time they left Foisy was living elsewhere. **Californian**, first newspaper in California, starting five months later than the **Oregon Spectator**, did employ Foisy for a time.

WEEPING WILLOW AND CLASPED HANDS, two frequently used headstone symbols — these in old cemetery in Dallas, Oregon.

REBEL MATHIEU FOUND
A PATRIOTIC CAUSE

Francois Xavier Mathieu

A leader in the movement to bring French Prairie, Oregon, under American government control, Francois Xavier Mathieu found the role a natural one. Brought up in Terrebonne, Canada, he had participated in the agitation and rebellion for equal rights for all Canadians almost at the cost of his neck. Fleeing to New York State, then to Milwaukee and St. Louis, he joined the American Fur Co. in 1839.

He was assigned a territory in the Yellowstone country with headquarters at Laramie. But with Indians getting liquor easily and molesting immigrants, Mathieu took a job as guide for a wagon train heading for the Oregon country. Having learned how to get along with the redskins around Laramie, young Francois was able to dodge serious difficulties with them along the route.

His responsibilities ended when the train dispersed in the Willamette Valley area known as French Prairie because of so many French fur traders turned farmers. Mathieu quickly made friends with Etienne Lucier, one of the rough mountain men who had deserted the Hudson's Bay Co. to raise wheat. The two formed a close relationship that influenced the famous decision at Champoeg, center of the French Prairie farm country.

After several "Wolf Meetings" held by the settlers following the death of Ewing Young, plans were made to "consider the propriety of taking measures for the civil and military protection of the colony." A formal meeting for this purpose was set for May 2, 1843 at Champoeg where there was space enough for a large assembly of wagons.

At the appointed time British sympathizers, largely from the Hudson's Bay Co., French-Canadians and Americans assembled in a large warehouse. When the time came to call a vote as to who would align with the English and who with the Americans, no one could be individually heard or understood. The meeting adjourned to the outdoors where loud-voiced, outspoken Joe Meek, another defector from the fur trade, shouted: "Who's for a divide?" . . . then: "All for the report of the committee and an organization, follow me."

This meant lining up on the American side, the British present not wishing for any organization other than the Hudson's Bay Co. Mathieu, whose American sympathies had been formed in Canada, he said later, moved over with Meek and persuaded Etienne Lucier to go along. The votes of these two clinched the matter of forming a governmental organization under United States regulation.

Mathieu later started a general merchandise store in nearby Butteville, which it is believed he platted and perhaps founded. His store stood at the corner of Butte Avenue and Front Street, the property running down to the Willamette River. His customers were traders, trappers, settlers and Indians, the latter usually paying for staples in beaver skins, buckskin, salt salmon, wheat, shingles and saw logs.

PLAQUE AT SITE of old burial ground once surrounding original log building dedicated as Saint Paul Mission by Archbishop Francis Norbert Blanchet in 1839. Many early pioneers of French Prairie area were buried here, all markers long since vanished. Joseph Gervais is one. He worked for establishment of government, at least one of first meetings was held at his home, where also first school in Oregon was taught by Solomon Smith and wife.

Another pioneer buried here is Etienne Lucier, one of those several French trappers arriving as part of Wilson Price Hunt party which in 1812 established John Jacob Astor's trading post at the mouth of Columbia River, now city of Astoria. Leaving company, Lucier first settled in cabin on east bank of Willamette at present site of Portland, making him its first resident. Finding forest there too dense for farming he moved to French Prairie where he figured prominently in establishment of government.

Louis La Bonte, also interred here, was Hudson's Bay employee. Wishing to plant his own acres on fertile French Prairie, he petitioned factor Dr. John McLoughlin for "leave of absence". Request was denied, McLoughlin explaining he had been advised by authorities no employees could establish themselves among Americans south of Columbia. La Bonte then traveled to Montreal at own expense, quit company, returning to Fort Vancouver in 1830 to take up portion of land near Champoeg. Asked how large his farm would be, he replied: "Begin in the morning on a cayuse horse. Go west 'till the sun is high, then go south 'till it is in the west, then back to the river. That is my manor." Another pioneer buried here is Michael La Framboise also employed by Hudson's Bay. He was sent by McLoughlin each year to Yerba Buena, Mexico, now San Francisco, Calif., to establish southern branch of company. La Framboise then made trips annually for purchase of furs trapped along Sacramento River, project flourishing until gold discovery in 1849 when prejudices of natives and incoming miners forced company's withdrawal. Many more bodies here are unknown or unlisted, among latter is one of the members of Lewis and Clark expedition of 1805 — Francois Rivet, Sept. 27, 1852.

OLD ROSE CHAPEAU DE NAPOLEON — The roses and other shrubs pioneers planted on graves of loved ones were the more available varieties, those in vogue or carried in covered wagons from homes in the east. Often set out were moss roses or variations such as the one shown here, classed among crested roses, named Chapeau de Napolean — the fringed buds being somewhat three-sided to give rise to the name. The original was found growing on an old convent wall near Fribourg. Author photographed this specimen in his own collection of "antique" roses.

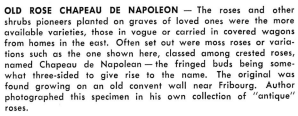

BUTTEVILLE'S EPISCOPAL CHURCH, built in 1860 near Mathieu's store, found its building funds exhausted before bell could be bought. Pastor, Rev. St. Michael Fachkler, was said to have consoled congregation with: "God will provide in his own time." When the great flood of 1861 destroyed the sister church at Champoeg, bell in its steeple was washed downstream, landing close to Butteville. Of no further use in vanished Champoeg, bell was happily installed on Butteville church.

Later the structure was destroyed by fire, bell again salvaged for use by Butteville Congregational Church. Small structure was not stout enough to support it, so bell was mounted on belfry in front. Long time church member says "That bell has rung for church services every Sunday morning since then."

IN 1901 site of historic meeting at Champoeg, embracing 107 acres, was designated as a State Park. Last survivor of those men voting for provisional government, Francois Xavier Mathieu, pointed out spot on road once grandly called Boulevard Napoleon, where outdoor meeting was held 58 years earlier. Old photo shows Mathieu standing proudly beside completed stone marker at dedication ceremonies. His name and that of friend Etienne Lucier are inscribed on near side, other names appearing on other sides. Photo courtesy Champoeg Museum.

ELABORATE WROUGHT IRON CROSS is beautiful example of art in St. Paul Cemetery but lacks any legible identification.

TUALATIN PLAINS PRESBYTERIAN CHURCH is one of the most beautiful pioneer structures in Oregon. Church was organized Nov. 16, 1873 in schoolhouse close to present building which was dedicated in 1878. Charter members all came from same area near Glasgow, Scotland, explaining affectionate term "Old Scotch Church." Many pioneers are buried in old graveyard surrounding edifice, including "Teller of Tall Tales" Joe Meek.

TALL SHAFT MARKS graves of Joe Meek family, patriarch's resting place left one of four markers. Joseph L. Meek, born in Virginia in 1810, headed west at 18, joined Sublette's hunting party in St. Louis to begin career of hunting and trapping. "Settling" on French Prairie, wanderer stayed long enough to figure in establishment of government, later often recalling how he called on those at Champoeg meeting to line up beside him if they wanted a government under the U. S. He also claimed to have induced hesitating Lucier and Mathieu to join him. After long and exciting service to his country, having survived many battles including several in Yakima War in 1855, Meek died quietly on his farm in Willamette Valley. When freeway threatened grave, remains were removed to cemetery of "Scotch Church" on Tualatin Plains.

ABOUT 1842 ROBERT NEWELL, later of Champoeg fame, built a grist mill on this little stream called Champoeg Creek. Beside the mill he built the first house for himself and Indian wife, Kitty, sister of Joe Meek's wife. Newell was devoted to his mate, making trip home from session of state legislature on hearing of her illness. When she died he buried her near the home. Although mill, house and grave were on shelf slightly above creek, its winter torrents in heavy rains washed away all traces of them. Location is just above sharp kink in creek about third of distance between highway and Willamette River, gravesite covered by blackberry vines.

INSCRIPTION ON STONE in front of impressive white wooden cross standing squarely in center of St. Paul's Church Cemetery (not original one which surrounded first log mission) reads: "Pray for the soul of Most Rev. F. N. Blanchet, First Archbishop of Oregon City and Pioneer of the Cross in the N. W." Born Sept. 3, 1795 in Saint Riviere du Sud, Canada, Francis Norbert Blanchet and brother Magloise, later Bishop of Diocese of Walla Walla, (subsequently Nisqually and now Seattle), attended parish schools nearby.

On Saturday, Nov. 24, 1838 Rev. Blanchet arrived at Fort Vancouver after a six-month trip from Montreal, at the request of Dr. John McLoughlin. His purpose was to establish missions in the raw, new country, but was strictly enjoined from activity south of the Columbia, "that area being subject to controversy between England and the U.S." However, in 1839 he visited and dedicated log church a few miles from Champoeg, naming the mission for St. Paul.

Nearby first unit of impressive St. Paul's Church was built by Rev. Blanchet in 1846, first brick church in Oregon. Before immigration days life at St. Paul was "idyllic" according to one old settler. Catholic dominance, supreme while population consisted of original French Canadians, was weakened as Protestant settlers arrived. Strength was further shaken when California gold fever drained away almost all male adults of community. Rev. Blanchet died in Portland June 18, 1883. He consistently opposed establishment of "foreign" government, denying use of church space for "Wolf Meetings." Brother Magloise is buried before altar in St. James Cathedral in Vancouver, Wash.

HE CAN'T PADDLE HIS OWN CANOE

CURIOUS CASE OF CONCOMLY'S CRANIUM
Chief Concomly

Many Indian chiefs were not true leaders or had no tribal right to the title but Chinook Chief Concomly was not one of them. By all standards he ruled his empire by right and might. Described by early explorers as "short but extremely well built, naked except for a kilt-like skirt from waist to midway down his thighs," they agreed he had but one eye and that his hair, cut short, was dark brown.

Lewis and Clark met him at his lodge near Point Ellice on the north shore of the Columbia River near its mouth and presented him with a medal and flag. Concomly had wives from every tribe under his leadership and from others farther away. With dozens of children and numerous slaves to take care of them, his establishment was a village in itself. At least three of his daughters were taken to wife by men at the Astoria, Oregon, trading post.

In 1813 factor Duncan McDougall heard rumors that Britain was at war with the United States and felt that his position could be jeopardized should the post go over to England. Possibly hoping to be assured the friendliness of Chief Concomly in any case, he proposed marriage with yet another princess and her father willingly sent one over to Astoria.

The girl's handmaidens prepared her for the wedding by painting her with red clay and annoint-ing her with rancid fish oil. An old account says, "by dint however of copious ablutions she was freed from all adventitious tint and fragrance, and entered into the nuptial state the cleanest princess that had ever been known of the somewhat unctious tribe of the Chinooks."

In the face of rumors that British men-of-war were converging in Pacific waters, the post was sold to British Northwest Fur Co., under conditions reflecting on McDougall's loyalty. News of the British take-over caused Concomly to appear in a bluster at the post covered with war paint, flying the American flag of Lewis and Clark, and ready to do battle with the entire British navy as represented by the sloop *Raccoon* which appeared in the harbor. He boarded it, was persuaded to change his loyalties to England and presented with an old laced coat, cocked hat, sword and British flag. The next day he came sailing across the Columbia in full uniform and flying the Union Jack. Further, he helped persuade the authorities to retain his son-in-law Duncan McDougall as factor of the now British-owned post called Fort George.

In 1830 a "plague" struck the Chinook tribe, the dead lying unburied on the beaches, many lodges empty and whole villages decimated. Among the victims was the great chief, proven powerless against this unseen enemy, but his body worthy of proper care. On Point Ellice overlooking the Columbia the few survivors erected a war canoe on

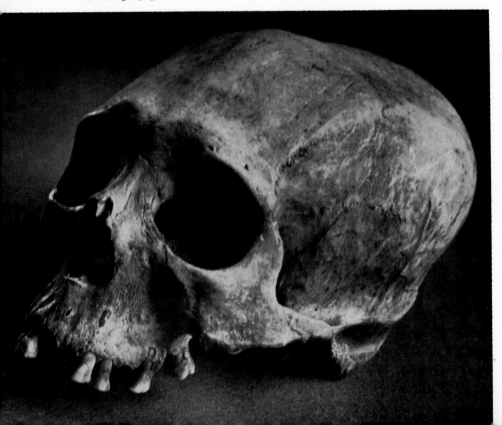

SIDE VIEW of Chief Concomly's skull shows extreme flattening at top and back, tribal custom among Chinook nobles. Fame of prime example of "art" was such as to lure Dr. Gairdner to carry out dangerous purloining of head from chief's grave.

stilts about five feet high and in it the eminent chieftain was laid with all the pomp and ceremony the few mourners could muster. Another canoe was turned bottom up to protect the body of Concomly from the incessant rains.

Up river at Fort Vancouver the plague was felt to a somewhat lesser degree and factor John McLoughlin sent to England for medical aid. Three medical men responded, among them Dr. Meredith Gairdner. The young doctor agreed to go out to the wilderness only on condition he have complete freedom to roam the country, examining and classifying the flora and fauna in accordance with his real interests.

On one of his trips to the coast Gairdner heard stories about the great Chief Concomly and one point fascinated him—the Chinook custom of flattening and pointing the skulls of their infants', especially those of the wealthy and importance. Concomly's was an outstanding example of the art, they said, his skull being flatter than any other.

Back at the post Gairdner was absorbed by a desire to get the chief's skull and ship it to England as a medical curiosity. This would be difficult and dangerous in face of the Indians' strong aversion to having their graves disturbed. He heard one story of a group of doctors opening a grave to remove a skeleton, being discovered by the Indians and chased back to the ship, barely escaping with their lives. As time went on Dr. Gairdner's incipient tubercular condition gave him trouble and he was resolved to try a change of climate and work out a scheme. If he shipped to the Sandwich Islands what was to prevent him from slipping ashore when the vessel anchored at Astoria for supplies, find the chief's grave, retrieve the head and get back aboard? Putting the plan into action, he sailed.

Ashore at Astoria he got safely to where the burial canoes had rested and found they had been removed. A search revealed the fact that the body was carried into nearby woods and buried in the earth. Gairdner set to work digging, the frenzied effort exerting a strain on his limited strength but he uncovered the plank box and found the skeleton. The head was quite well preserved, features recognizable, skin and hair almost intact, skull as flat as predicted. The doctor twisted and pulled at it until he had a hemorrhaging attack but finally got it loose. He placed it in a metal box and was able to get back to the ship safely.

From Honolulu he sent the prized relic to his friend Dr. John Richardson of Scotland, who turned it over to the Royal Naval Hospital. After examination—during which period Dr. Gairdner died, in 1836—the skull became an exhibit in the museum at Haslar, Gosport, near Portsmouth. After being on display several months the head became what was guardedly labeled "offensive" and despite generous dousings of mercury chloride it was removed to the laboratory and all soft, organic matter removed. Then it was returned to the case where it remained for 117 years, except for the occasion of a German air raid in 1941 when the museum received a direct bomb hit and the display case was thrown to the floor. When the skull was discovered the jaw could not be found.

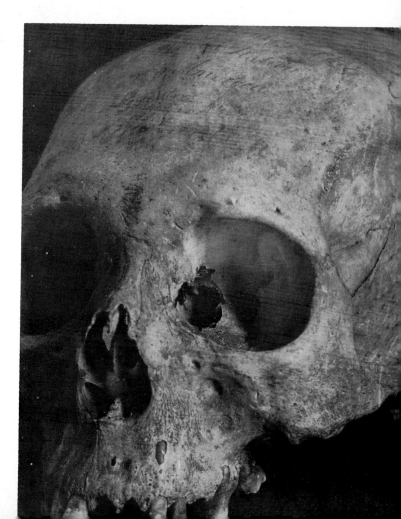

FRONTAL VIEW OF CONCOMLY SKULL shows bone breakage as evidence of eye being destroyed, likely by arrow. Photo made in dim light of Clatsop County Museum shows some of inscription on top of skull, lettering so faded as to be undecipherable or even unnoticeable in direct observation. Further research reveals that inscription also stirred curiosity of staff of Smithsonian Institution. They deciphered it in special lighting, filters. It read "Museum Haslar. Skull of Concomly, Chief of the Chinook Nation, N.W. America, presented by Richardson." (parts of some words are invisible under any light, are here conjectural.)

Capt. William Clark wrote in his journal an item dated Nov. 20, 1805: "Found many Chinooks with Capt. Lewis of whom there were two chiefs **Com com mo ly** & **Chil-lar-la-will** to whom we gave medals and to one a flag. . ." He tells of the beautiful robe made of two otter skins and worn by one of the chiefs and of how it was purchased with a belt of blue "beeds", up to now worn and treasured by Sacajawea, but makes no mention of fact Concomly had but one eye.

In 1952 Burnby Bell of the Clatsop County Museum at Astoria learned the history of Concomly's skull and wrote the English museum, requesting it be returned to Astoria. Eventually it was sent over and placed on view but the curiosity was to travel more. The Smithsonian Institution in Washington, D. C. wanted it for examination and photographs and Bell accommodated those authorities.

On its return, plans were formulated for a gala celebration of Astoria's sesquicentennial to start April 12, 1961. Near the towering monument called the Astor Column would be built a full-sized concrete replica of a Chinook war canoe and in or under it would be interred the Concomly skull. Col. John Astor, Baron of Heber—great, great grandson of the city's founder, John Jacob Astor—would attend to dedicate the memorial.

When plans were publicized a hue and cry went up from descendants of the chief. It was not good, they said, that this part of his remains be subjected to cheap display for the curious. They asked to be allowed to bury the skull with the rest of the body at Point Ellice, a suitable monument erected there. Museum officials remained silent, unwilling to give up the "bone of contention" unless forced to do so.

A conclave of some hundred Chinooks was held near Skamokawa, an old Indian village on the lower Columbia, and tribal members came to an agreement welcome to all parties. Vandals, they said, would be tempted to dig up the skull so let it remain safely under lock and key in the Clatsop County Museum.

And there the famous flat-topped skull of Chief Concomly remains. The concrete canoe was erected, the city did hold its celebration and Col. John Astor did attend all without Concomly's skull. The magazine *Pacific Discovery*, in its May-June issue of 1950, related the story of the skull, its abduction and recovery, in a story headed—"Curious Case of the Concomly Cranium."

VERY EARLY DRAWING of Chief Concomly's grave is signed by "A. T. Agate". Conforming to usual Indian practice, varying with different tribes, bodies were placed in some sort of open receptacle until decomposition had removed flesh, bones then buried or entombed. Grave pictured here was second resting place of chief, burial somewhat premature, relatives having hurried body out of open war canoe where it was first placed, for fear of such molestation as Dr. Gairdner's scientific raid. Photo courtesy Oregon Historical Society

INDIAN WAR CANOE — concrete replica of one holding remains of Chief Concomly, erected according to plans but Chinook descendants of the chief refused to permit skull to be placed in cement memorial or even under huge boulder. Replica is well done, front forming same design shown in old artist's sketch of original. Site is summit of high hill near Astoria, Oregon, near "Astor Column". In background is mighty Columbia as it enters Pacific Ocean. Part of newly constructed bridge spanning river can be seen and in far distance, center, is Point Ellice, Wash., original place of chief's burial.

GOLD IS WHERE WHO FOUND IT?

COULD HISTORY BE WRONG?

Capt. Charles Bennett

Nothing less than startling is the inscription on a tall, square-column monument in the Old Pioneer (I.O.O.F.) Cemetery at Salem, Oregon. The carved words give Capt. Charles Bennett the credit for discovering gold in California's Sierra, completely ignoring well-documented facts that James Marshall had that distinction.

Both men were Oregonians in that this was the area they came to from the East. Both went to California after a short time in the Willamette Valley having heard John Augustus Sutter needed good help at his Sierra operations. Sutter employed many Digger Indians as laborers at Sutter's Fort and in the foothills at Coloma but for overseers he wanted several aggressive Americans. Bennett and Marshall were hired at Coloma where a mill was being built.

James Marshall's diary is definite about who found the gold, Bennett having left no record to contradict it. Wrote Marshall:

"Toward the end of August, 1847, General Sutter and I formed a co-partnership to build and run a sawmill upon a site selected by myself, now known as Coloma . . . The first work done was the building of a double log cabin about half a mile from the mill-site . . . I went to the fort to superintend the construction of the mill-irons, leaving orders to cut a narrow ditch where the race was to be made." On Marshall's return he found the ditch was being cut but at a tremendous disadvantage, the men working downsteam, the cut filling with water as fast as they exposed it. It may have been this blunder that caused the famous first nugget to come to light, although eventual discovery was inevitable.

"Upon my return in January, 1848 I immediately changed the course of things, and on the 19th day of January, 1848 discovered the gold near the lower end of the race about two hundred yards below the mill. William Scott was the second man to see the metal. He was at work on a carpenter bench near the mill and I showed the gold to him."

Marshall then called several other men, Alexander Stephens, James Brown, Henry Bigler, William Johnston among them to see what he had found. "P. L. Weimar and Charles Bennett were at the double log cabin a half mile distant."

From this account it would seem that Bennett was one of the last at the mill site to see the gold. Weimar's wife, Jenny, left an account that gets her husband in on the first discovery. "Marshall took Weimar down to see what had been done while he was away. The water was entirely shut off and as they walked along talking about the work, just ahead of them, lying on the rough muddy rock lay something bright like gold. They both saw it, but Marshall was the first to pick it up." There may be still other variations that give Bennett the credit.

In November of 1855 Bennett was back in Oregon as captain in the Yakima War and on the 12th, with another company of soldiers, he set out for Walla Walla where he met his death. The party engaged a large band of Indians about two miles from Waiilatpu on the farm of a French Canadian settler named LaRoche, met a withering fire as they advanced and were driven back. Reorganizing, they advanced again, driving the hostiles up a canyon to a large farm building into which the Indians had fled.

The troops dismounted and attempted to take the place on foot. It was then Capt. Bennett and a man from another company were killed. A howitzer was brought up but it exploded at the first shot, badly wounding Capt. Wilson in command of the other company. The blast however routed the Indians and LaRoche's house was turned into a hospital for the wounded. Capt. Bennett's body was returned to Salem for burial.

UNIQUE STONE CROSS in Mountain View Cemetery at Oregon City, Oregon. Style is botonee, though with truncated arms. Dark background of old Irish yew emphasizes whiteness of stone.

ANNA M. HEIN
GEB. 18. AUG. 1818,
GEST. 30, DEC. 1899

CARVED DESIGN on monument to Capt. Bennett must remain secret except to members of Masonic order. Salem, Oregon has two interesting old cemeteries — Jason Lee, named in honor of the missionary, and the one usually referred to as Odd Fellows Cemetery although a sign beside the gate reads "Old Pioneer Cemetery". Burials there date back to earliest days in Oregon Territory, many marked by monuments of various natures, emblazoned with epitaphs and capsule biographies in fashion of days long gone.

CAPT. CHAS. BENNETT
the discoverer of gold in Cal
fellin defense of his
Country at Walla Walla

HE COULD NOT WIN FOR LOSING

John Pollard Gaines, Salem Ore.

Ardent patriot that he was, as the legend on his tombstone declares, John Pollard Gaines was a man of misfortune in his personal and political life. His three years as governor of Oregon territory were charged with tragedy, frustration and failure.

In 1850 he sailed for Oregon with his wife, son Richard and two beautiful daughters. The voyage on the U. S. store ship *Supply* started happily enough but both girls contracted yellow fever and died before the arrival in San Francisco. The three Gaines remaining went on to Salem, Oregon, and settled there. An enthusiastic horsewoman, Mrs. Gaines bought a fine riding horse but took a bad fall almost the first time in the saddle and was killed. Within a few months the boy Richard died, apparently from some lingering remnant of the fever.

At least one reference, *Governor of Oregon* by Geo. Turnbull says Gov. Gaines was born in Kentucky, not Virginia as carved on the tombstone. He did serve in both the War of 1812 and Mexican War. He was a staunch Whig supporter of President Zachary Taylor and regarded his appointment as governor by Taylor as a high honor, lessened somewhat when he learned Abraham Lincoln had first been offered the post. (At first agreeable, Lincoln declined when his wife emphatically refused to go to such a wild, far-off country).

While a man of high personal integrity, handsome and full of good intentions, Gaines was unfortunately pompous and austere. His legislature was Democratic and its members had acquired Western manners. Gaines was a Whig, an effete Easterner and in constant conflict with them. When he advocated moving the seat of the state government back to Oregon City, fiery Asahel Bush, strongly partisan editor of the Salem *Oregon Statesman* attacked him physically. (Ironically the two lie buried only a few feet apart). Gaines stood almost alone in his opinions, the most friendly and powerful supporter during his tenure being the Portland *Oregonian* and its Whig editor, T. J. Dryer.

During the Rogue River Indian uprising Gaines wrote to President Fillmore who succeeded Taylor, for troops to fight the natives. Instead of complying, Fillmore authorized Gaines to go to the Rogue River area and recruit a military company. On the ground Gaines found every man already in active service, none available even for an escort. He was forced to delay his return home until hostilities had cooled enough to allow him some safety.

After his term as governor expired, Gaines ran for Congress and suffered a severe defeat at the hands of General Lane. Yet in spite of this and all the adverse events associated with his move to Oregon Territory, he chose to remain in Salem after retiring and at his death at 62 was buried in the Old Pioneer (I.O.O.F.) Cemetery there.

LARGE, IMPOSING MONUMENT to Gov. Gaines bears almost complete biography, omitting grief and frustrations. Tall slab stands near grave of arch enemy Asahel Bush and that of Capt. Charles Bennett, killed in Indian wars.

MEN OF THE OLD MOUNTAINS

OREGON'S FIRST MOUNTAIN ROAD BUILDER

Samuel Kimbrough Barlow

Sam Barlow knew well enough how urgent the need was for a road over the Cascade Mountains. He and his party nearly starved to death attempting to get their wagons over those heavily forested ramparts, the only range of mountains in the west without a natural pass.

Barlow was captain of his wagon train, "all the way", as he later related. He had the acumen to turn down the services of Stephen Meek who led the ill-fated "Lost Wagon Party" through endless labyrinths of desert and mountains in central Oregon. "Stephen Meek," Sam said, "was only after the money and a white wife."

The starting point of the Barlow party was near the old homestead not far from Peoria, Illinois, the date March 30, 1845. Reasonably uneventful was the journey as far as The Dalles on the Columbia River. Barlow had his flock remain there while he went ahead to reconnoiter, since he had decided to take them over the mountains instead of trusting to the treacherous rapids in the river. He traveled with one or two others to Tygh Valley and made up his mind the dangers of the mountain passages had been overdrawn, returning to the wagon train to bring it up the valley for another rest halt.

The leaders now felt so optimistic with their progress they decided to make capital of it and improve the track as they went along. After all, the going was easy and later they would charge other immigrants a toll for the use of the road.

At first everything was in their favor. The summer was almost ended, brush and trees on the eastern slope of the mountains so dry they could easily be set on fire to clear large areas. Nobody worried about the lateness of the season until at higher altitudes snow began to fall and tree growth changed from pine to fir in forests so dense they were almost impenetrable.

As the train neared the summit at around 4,500 feet it was apparent the easy going was over. Even at the highest point "boggy swamps" were encountered miring down horses and wagons. It is assumed these "swamps" were the alpine glades now known as Summit Meadows. By this time it was snowing hard and the party was into even heavier timber,

veritable walls of it. They found passages the Indians had cut in the logs or around the windfalls with obsidian or bone tools to get their ponies through. But the Barlow men found them too narrow for their cattle which had to be herded around or the passages laboriously widened. Wagons were repeatedly taken apart, boxes, wheels, cargo dragged over or through the tangle. And it snowed and snowed.

Yet somehow the summit was passed and the wagons went down grade more easily — at first until there were pitches too steep to attempt. At this point everybody was bone tired, cold and hungry, food supply nearing exhaustion. Even the horses could find nothing to eat with grasses buried deep in snow. There were "laurels" as the pioneers called the rhododendrons native to the western slope of the Cascades. Where the Barlow party ground to a dead stop the growth of these shrubs is extensive, giving the name "Laurel Hill" to the spot which was long afterward dreaded by immigrants. The first morning after entering this area one of the horses was found dead, another sick from browsing on the rhododendrons.

The loss of indispensable animals seemed the last straw. Everybody was half-frozen, with empty stomachs and hope was fading fast. Barlow later wrote: "Men's hearts died within them and women cried." But one did not — light-hearted Mrs. Gaines. "Cheer up, everybody", she said, "we won't starve. If the horses die we can eat them. Why, Henry, your old dog is as fat as butter. We could live on him for a week."

And a plan grew out of desperation. A shelter was constructed to house the main party while Barlow and J. M. Bacon descended to the Willamette Valley to get help. At the age of 79 Sam Barlow still remembered: "We went down Laurel Hill like shot off a shovel". On the banks of what must have been the Sandy River the men camped to eat their last meal — four biscuits, made out of the last handful of flour. Barlow went for wood when the biscuits were about ready and returned to find them gone. Bacon shame-facedly explained: "The biscuits are lost. They fell in the river and floated away". Barlow dropped the wood and kicked it away. "Fell down your throat and landed in your belly, you mean!" But on December 24, 1845, the men got to Oregon City in a starving condition. As soon as he could Barlow organized a rescue party and returned to the snowbound bivouac with food and supplies.

Later in Oregon City he applied to the territorial legislature for a charter permitting him to build a toll road over the mountains. This was granted and as soon as snow began to melt in spring he took a crew of 40 men and began construction. Proceeding eastward a rough road was hacked out to the summit to connect with the already completed eastern section. While work was under way the OREGON SPECTATOR made an appeal to the settlers in the valley for funds to aid the project. Response was less than overwhelming, some $30 being subscribed.

For two years after completion Barlow personally collected tolls. He reported in the fall of 1846 after traffic ceased for the winter that: "During the summer 145 wagons, 1559 horses, mules and horned cattle and one drive of sheep passed through the gates." Turning farmer, Barlow leased the road to Phillip Foster and Joseph Young who confined their efforts to collecting tolls and the road became almost impassable through lack of maintenance.

In spite of this condition the Barlow Road was better than the evil turbulence of the Columbia and remained in limited use by immigrants until the building of the railroad which followed the river level through the Columbia Gorge. Since then the eastern section of the old Barlow Road has fallen into complete disuse, traveled on only by such rare visitors as this photographer while searching for the graves of Jarvis Briggs and his son Newton, their murder occurring near the eastern gate. From the summit in a westerly direction Barlow's old route is still evident as it parallels and crosses the modern highway in some sections.

SHAFT MARKS GRAVE of Samuel Kimbrough Barlow and his wife Susanna Lee, whom he married in Marion County, Indiana. Mrs. Barlow is especially honored by plaque placed at side of marker by D.A.R. Grandfathers of both served in Revolutionary War, Sam's receiving fatal wounds. He bought home property in community, later called Barlow—between Aurora and Canby, Ore.—in 1850 from Thomas McKay, whose story is related elsewhere in this book. As Sam aged he turned property over to son William who came from Indiana home with parents in 1845 when 23 years old. When railroad was built through home place in 1870, the line named community around farm for William, not Sam as is generally supposed. Grave in old Barlow Pioneer Cemetery is overgrown with weeds and scraggly lilac bushes.

GOOD SAMARITAN OF THE MOUNTAIN

Perry Vickers

He said his name was Perry Vickers and he needed a job . . . an emigrant with no wagon or belongings. Then he told the guardian of the mountain pass he was a fugitive from Washington Territory authorities, that he had escaped from them by swimming the Columbia River still fettered by leg irons.

The scene was on the south slope of Mount Hood, well below timberline, near a beautiful alpine meadow, then called Summit Prairie. The green, open swale was a most welcome sight to pioneer travelers after their bitter struggles over the Cascade summit. Although there was more rough going ahead, the peaceful meadows offered temporary respite.

They were faced with a rough track over the mountains, hacked out and maintained by Samuel Kimbrough Barlow who called it the Barlow Road. He charged a stiff toll for the privilege of getting the wagons mired in it and for hauling them out by ropes hitched to the trees. One of Barlow's employees who saw to it nobody got over free was Stephen Coalman, the man who heard Perry Vickers' story in the 1860s and was impressed with the man's sincerity and evident good breeding. It further developed that the two were members of the same fraternity.

Vickers was hired to help maintain the road and soon accumulated enough confidence and money to build a small hotel for emigrants at Summit Meadows. He also established a trading post which prospered in spite of his generosity in giving supplies to those who had no money to pay. Another venture was cutting and drying the ample crop of grass on the meadow and selling it to travelers for their horses. When wagons broke down or emigrants were in distress he rode for miles to render aid. One of the families he helped to his inn was that of W. L. Barclay. His tiny infant had fallen ill and with no doctors of medicines available all Vickers could do was make the family comfortable. When the baby passed away he made a coffin and helped the parents bury it under a tree near the inn.

Vickers loved Mount Hood looming directly above the meadow and spent much time exploring the area. He lauded it in poetry which, according to another mountain lover Fred H. McNeil, author

of *Wy'East the Mountain*: "Verse in the most classic rhymes swinging along somewhat in the style of Tennyson." After making several ascents of Mount Hood, Vickers guided others to the summit for a price of $25 a head.

In the early 70s various Portland groups were agitating for "an illumination of red fire to be set off on the summit of Mount Hood, thereby fittingly celebrating the glorious Fourth of July", as the press had it. The ventures failed for several years and two reasons were advanced by those against it. The huge amount of red fire necessary would be too expensive, they said, considering the small chance of getting it on the peak and igniting it on schedule. Also, if it were ignited, a man would have to remain there overnight and it was well known temperatures on the height plunged to such frightful depths, even in summer, no man could survive them.

Vickers scorned such contentions, took blankets, telescope, provisions, thermometer and "magnesium wire" to the summit, and at 9:30 P.M. began burning the magnesium. His friends at Summit Meadows stayed up all night watching the ten different displays as the white glare flashed over the snows. When Vickers came down he said a close watch of his thermometer, between firings of the flares, had never dropped lower than 28 degrees. A successful "illumination of the mountain" was staged 15 years later but Vickers had long since met an untimely death and could not share in any glory.

In 1882 a man named Steele stole a shotgun in Gresham to the west of the mountain and fled east over the pass, a posse in close pursuit. Always ready to help, Vickers joined it and was told that if and when the posse caught up with Steele, every man was to remain under cover until the thief was surrounded. At the White River crossing, Vickers was the first to see the culprit huddled beside his fire and his eagerness overcame his memory and judgment. He charged forward and in dismounting received a blast from the shotgun. He was able to fire his revolver at Steele before falling to the ground but the fugitive got away.

Vickers was carried into Cornelius Gray's crude hotel at the crossing and was able to say he knew he was dying and wished his body to be placed beside that of the little baby he helped bury the year before. His friends cut a tree at the "Springs", now called "Swim", and made a rough coffin, burying Vickers beside the Barclay baby.

Perry Vickers had never made an effort to legalize his ownership of Summit House or the land and after his death another "squatter" moved in and enlarged it. This was Horace Capbell, known as "King David" because of religious eccentricities. At the rear of the inn he built a large structure shaped like an Indian teepee with a smoke hole at the top which was a landmark for fifty years.

Aside from the graves in the tiny cemetery, nothing remains of all this. There is a nearby level spot with a few rotting crumbs of wood but while the site seems the obvious one, none can say exactly where Summit House stood. There were rumors that Vickers buried large sums of money and for some years "treasure seekers" prowled and dug, getting nothing more than exercise.

SYMPATHIZING WITH GRIEVING PARENTS, Perry Vickers carved crude inscription on native stone, set marker against base of mountain hemlock tree that must have been large even then. At left of Baby Barclay grave is that of Vickers, himself. Again left is another grave marked with rock similar to one serving as monument to Vickers, but lacking even faintest trace of identification. Group of three is surrounded by tottering picket fence.

PERRY VICKERS' RESTING PLACE marked by this stone, the center one of three enclosed in tiny picket square at edge of Summit Meadows. Inscription is almost illegible in low, diffused light in dense stand of mountain hemlock trees.

"BOOTEE" HILL

CASCADE CASUALTY
THE MORGAN BABY

The death of the infant Morgan, injured at the White River crossing, was another cruel blow at the misfortune-plagued wagon train of Jacob Woodsides, called along the trail — "Woodsides' Sick Train".

The wagons left Springfield, Illinois, in the spring of 1847 and just before they reached Independence Rock, Wyoming, Rachel Morgan died of food poisoning. She left an infant daughter and three other small children to be cared for by the bewildered husband, Daniel Morgan.

Months later, when the train reached The Dalles in the Oregon Country, it had suffered many other disasters but the four children were all well. The decision was made to take the pass route over the south flank of Mount Hood rather than trust to the rapids of the Columbia River. At White River camp was made to consider how to get across the foaming, glacier-fed torrent. Through carelessness the tail gate of one of the big covered wagons was swung down violently, striking the head of the Morgan baby placed on a blanket in the wagon's shade.

This seemed to be the final blow under the stress of being short of supplies and probably lost in the mountains. It was decided to send a scout ahead to Oregon City while the party waited at the crossing. When aid arrived three weeks later the baby was still alive. Jacob Caplinger, who headed the relief train, declared the wagons would bump and jostle too much for the injured baby, so he carried her in his arms as he rode horseback. One diary kept by a member of the party recounts: "Each time the babe would cry out we could see tears stream down the rugged Caplinger's face."

When the train reached Summit Meadows the train made camp and rested a day. Here the Morgan baby died. She was buried beneath a "huge house-shaped rock" and the hard luck train moved on to face the uncertain future.

BABY MORGAN'S BODY was placed beneath this huge boulder in 1847 — stone deposited by long-vanished glacier once extending down from prehistoric Mount Hood.

CLOSE-UP OF PLAQUE on Morgan baby's grave. Jacob Caplinger mentioned was man who carried ailing infant in his arms from White River crossing to save her from jolts of covered wagon.

THIS MARKS THE GRAVE
OF
BABY MORGAN
INFANT DAUGHTER OF
DANIEL AND RACHEL WOODSIDES MORGAN
BORN NEAR INDEPENDENCE ROCK, JUNE, 1847
WHERE HER MOTHER DIED, JUNE 21, 1847.
THE BABY DIED AS A RESULT OF AN ACCIDENT AND
WAS BURIED HERE AT SUMMIT MEADOWS OCT. 24, 1847.
BURIAL WITNESSED BY
JACOB AND SARAH WOODSIDES CAPLINGER.
"SWEETLY RESTS OUR BABY DEAR
ALL THE LABOR CEASES HERE
FAR FROM HOME THOUGH LAID TO SLEEP
LOVING HEARTS THY MEMORY KEEP."
DEDICATED BY DESCENDANT RELATIVES, AUG. 20, 1957.

A DEATH—NOT A FARM—WAS RECORDED

James A. McKnight

A second-generation pioneer, one of the McKnight boys reversed the "Go West" trend and went east over the mountain to find land on which he could farm near Bend, in Oregon's "High Desert" country. There were several other boys in his party, one a younger brother — James. There is no record of the farm being history, but a death was — the accidental shooting of James McKnight.

The McKnight family of Sand Ridge, near Brownsville, Oregon, was headed by the father, J. W., a prosperous farmer of the Willamette Valley, whose sons had like ambitions. They borrowed a team and wagon from their father, loaded it with camping gear and drove over the old freight route.

This was a well-traveled road from the Lebanon area in the Willamette running east over the rugged Cascade Range toward Bend. The route passed just north of the spectacular Three Sisters, dormant volcanic peaks, penetrating the extensive lava beds around them. The road was tortuous on both sides of the mountains, on the western side threading through very dense timber. Along the route however there was one natural clearing, an alpine meadow, termed a "prairie" by pioneers from the Middle West. The twenty acres of open space is, in summer, bisected by a sparkling stream, ground covered with a carpet of lush grass and alpine flora.

It was here the McKnight boys camped the night of October 17, 1871. They were returning home after the summer along the Deschutes River and finding early snow in the highest part of the pass, dropped to the 4000-foot "prairie" where the ground was clear.

Bossing the job of making camp, the older brother needed something from the wagon and called to James to bring it. When the younger boy reached into the box for it he accidentally knocked down the rifle which had carelessly been left loaded and standing against the side of the wagon. The weapon was discharged, sending a bullet through the boy's body. He fell to the ground, fatally wounded. The body was wrapped in blankets and as daylight came, the other boys sadly broke camp and headed down the road toward home.

The funeral for James McKnight was held in Sand Ridge and the boy buried in the old cemetery there. The mother suffered severe shock over the incident, brooding for months. Somewhat consoled by the next spring, she commissioned a marble slab about 19 by 40 inches to be inscribed with an eight stanza "poem" supposedly written by her. Then the family made a trip to the "Big Prairie" and erected the stone, planting two alpine fir saplings on either side of the marker.

The area became known as "Tombstone Prairie" and in later years no reason was evident. To survey it for National Forest land, C. C. Olsen, a member of the Willamette National Forest crew, carried his transit between two large alpine firs near the edge of the open space. Catching his toe on a concealed object, Olsen stumbled and somewhat irritated, gave the "rock" a sharp kick, exposing a gleam of white marble instead of the natural dark basaltic rock. The surveyor scraped off several inches of forest duff and uncovered the long forgotten memorial slab with its poetic inscription.

CLOSE-UP OF VERSES James' mother caused to be inscribed on stone. Part of last stanza was lost when stone was re-erected in cement after lying covered on forest floor many years.

PIONEER SAND RIDGE CEMETERY, near almost vanished town of that name, contains grave of James Alvin McKnight who was accidentally shot. Young man's memorial stone stands in alpine meadow in Cascade Mountains seen in background. Original grave marker was replaced by modern stone located just to the rear of camera position.

WHITE MARBLE SLAB marks spot where James A. McKnight was killed. Part of alpine meadow, first called "Big Prairie", later "Tombstone Prairie", shows in background. At placing of marker two Alpine firs, prevailing trees of area, were planted beside stone. Now, almost 100 years later, they have become two large stumps, trunks on ground. Trees were cut down in 1957 by U. S. Forest Service when found to be dying.

MYSTERY OF THE GATE CREEK MURDER
Jarvis Briggs and son Newton

Night was coming on when two men in 1861, one about sixty, the other an eighteen-year-old, approached the eastern portal of the Barlow Road. A gate barred the way to the roughly hacked out route over the south flank of Mount Hood on the way to the Willamette Valley and beside it was the small cabin of the toll collector.

The older man, Jarvis Briggs, knocked on the door and told the gate man he and his son Newton had come from the newly discovered mines at Canyon City, Oregon. They were carrying about $13,000 in gold nuggets they had panned in Canyon Creek, were very tired and worried about the safety of their hard-won gold. Could they please stay with the toll collector over night? No, the gate keeper said — he wasn't running a hotel. They could camp on the small island in nearby Gate Creek. And that is what the Jarvis pair did, making what would be their last camp.

When he told his story to authorities the gate man said he heard shots late that night. Next morning he went to the island and found the two bodies, thinking them killed by Indians. He buried them in one grave on the spot. No, he did not know anything about any money the men were supposed to be carrying. "If they had any money", he said, "the Indians must have taken it."

This is the account Edward Disbrow heard when he settled on a ranch of several hundred acres in Smock Prairie in 1911. One of the few ranchers in the sparsely populated area today, he gave these details of the murders to this photographer when guiding him to the grave. There are other versions of the Jarvis affair, one in the WEEKLY OREGONIAN of August 17, 1861:

MURDER OF TWO MEN.—We are indebted to Mr. Kilbourne, of Tracy & Co.'s Express, for the following particulars:
"Two men arrived at The Dalles on Sunday from the Willamette Valley, who report finding the bodies of two men in the creek at Barlow's Gate, one-half mile from Armitage's trading post, the day before, supposed to have been murdered—one a gray haired man between 50 and 60 years of age—the other between 15 and 20—their tents and some clothes were found near by as though they had camped. It is believed they were on their return from the mines where they had been with cattle. The pockets of the old man were turned inside out, and a cut on his body which appeared to have been done in cutting off a money belt. A wound in the side showed he had been shot."

The Daily Oregonian had this to say on August 22:

"The persons murdered at Barlow's Gate, on the Cascade mountains, prove to be Mr. Jarvis Briggs and his son, Newton Briggs, of Lane County. The murders were committed by Indians. These Indians and others, who have lately committed murders, are all likely to be taken, through the vigilance of Capt. Whittlesey, and Messrs. Logan and Dennison."

Two days later the weekly edition had a follow up story:

THE MURDERS ON THE CASCADES AND IN TYGH VALLEY.—Dalles, August 20, 1861. Editor, Oregonian: (Excerpts taken from this article.) "- - - - the publication of the following summary of the verdicts of the Coroner's Jury, may advertise the friends of the deceased of their fate. The old and young man found together were supposed to be residents of the Willamette Valley.

GRAVE OF JARVIS BRIGGS is almost lost on tiny island in Gate Creek, surrounded by placid waters of many beaver dams, access by trail and foot log. Hearing this grave was "somewhere in the area," Byron L. Larson, Dr. David Mason and this photographer searched out location with help of local rancher Edward Disbrow. Latter said daughter of Jarvis Briggs had found grave about 1911, placed on it fruit jar containing data. Returning home to New York state she had marble marker cut, then about 1918 brought it out and placed it on site. U. S. Forest Service Recreation Area marker at near edge of monument indicates grave will be properly protected and direction sign placed on road about ½ mile distant, when funds become available.

"At the inquisition held over the bodies found at Barlow's Gate, the Jury found: 'That the persons came to their death by violence, on or about the 1st of August, or last of July, 1861. The bodies were so much decayed that no very satisfactory description was given of the wounds or bodies. The under jaw of the older body was broken in several places, and the neck bone was broken, or cut. The body appeared to be stabbed or cut in several places. The right side of the under jaw of the younger body was broken either by a pistol or gun ball, or from a blow from some blunt instrument. The skull was broken in one place, and a wound on the chin.

"In the vicinity of the bodies, in the creek, were found a small tent, made of white drilling, a brown coat, flour sack with some flour in it, a paper of tea, salt, frying pan, two hats, one light brown beaver, the other a black wool. There was blood on both the hats and on the tent.

"By Whose Hands the Violence Was Done, We the Jurors, Cannot Determine.
Geo. B. Curry, Acting Coroner"

FEW PIONEER CABINS still persist on Smock Prairie, level area above banks of Gate Creek. Here is detail of one built of Ponderosa pine, prevailing tree of area, bark still clinging, grain at log ends accentuated by many years of weathering.

OVERALL VIEW of Briggs' grave shows small opening in tangle of growing fir and pine trees, and down logs on island.

"SHOW ME THE GRAVE OF THE WOMAN"

THEY FOUND THE GRAVE . . . BUT NO BLUE BUCKET MINE

Sarah Chambers

The grave of the pioneer woman, Sarah Chambers, has been shrouded in controversy, its very location clouded in doubt for years. Even today many contend the real location is elsewhere, that the gravestone found is not genuine. Questioned too is Mrs. Chambers given name . . . was it Sarah, Sarepta or Sarilda? The inscription on the stone reads simply "Mrs. S. Chambers" which is of little help beyond the initial S. The varying opinions have been due, not so much to interest in this relatively obscure emigrant woman, as to a persistent rumor that the place where she was buried is the clue to the location of a fabulous deposit of placer gold. "Show me the grave of the woman," said those who were supposed to know, "and I'll show you the mine." The mine, mythical or not, later became known as the Lost Blue Bucket Mine.

The uncontested fact is Mrs. Chambers was among the members of a group of six wagon trains, originally traveling separately but gathered at Fort Boise in August of 1845 with a common problem. The trains had been four and five months crossing the plains, enduring many hardships, and now the leaders were trying to make decisions about reaching the Willamette Valley by a better route than the established one. Stephen Meek, brother of the famous and reliable mountain man, Joe Meek, declared he could guide the trains over a vastly improved cut-off for five dollars a wagon. Most of the wagon masters refused to trade known dangers for unknown ones but many went along with Steve Meek's proposal and would bitterly regret their choice.

Included in the latter group were the wagons of Nahum King and family which numbered several sons and daughters. One daughter was Sarah, wife of young Rowland Chambers. Her brother John King, his wife and two children had elected to take the tried and true route down the Columbia River and all lost their lives when their raft overturned. Tragedy also struck their father's party when Sarah died and was buried beside the trail.

In the most commonly told version of the story, two days' travel west from the grave brought the wagons to a stream where camp was made for the night. Several children unhooked a little blue bucket from under one of the wagons, took it to the creek and found some pretty yellow stones which almost filled the bucket. Called to supper, they rehung it under the wagon where it swung for the remainder of the trip. At trail's end in the Willamette, the bucket was taken out and the contents recognized as gold nuggets.

Historical fact seems to leave off with the burial of Mrs. Chambers. The party could hardly have traveled west from the burial site since their wagons emerged on Crane Prairie after the two days men-

LONG HIDDEN GRAVE of Sarah Chambers was thought to be essential clue to location of Blue Bucket Mine. Prospectors even set up "false" graves to mislead others in search for gold. One such mound was opened, failed to reveal bones. Genuine grave was also opened and human bones found, presumably those of unfortunate 22-year-old pioneer wife.

tioned which would have meant an abrupt turn south. There are about twenty-five versions of the finding of the nuggets, if they were ever found, only one having any corroborating evidence. This was related by John Herren years after the arrival of the party. He said he had been with the train when he was twenty-one years old, that his nephew Dan had found the nuggets in some muddy prints of cattle he was tracking. Other pioneer reminiscences include stories to the same effect and on Herren's death in 1907 the Portland OREGONIAN reported he had found the gold on the Meek Cut-Off trip. Certain it is that the lost train suffered hardships, losing and burying at least 28 members besides Mrs. Chambers before arriving at The Dalles October 7. Wagonmaster Samuel Parker wrote later: "I will just say that tongue and pen will both fall short when they go to tell the suffering the party went through." He did not mention the finding of any gold. Far more important was

the discovery of a good spring after many days with no water.

The earliest expeditions attempting to scour the area west of the Chambers grave were routed by Indians but during the Nez Perce War of 1877 a scout under General Howard, aware of the Blue Bucket tale, discovered what seemed to him to be the grave in question. Later he gave the location to an old prospector, Duncan Teter. Teter went to the Malheur area and found the grave, then fruitlessly searched the country "two days westward" for the gold. Then he heard a story that others had located both grave and gold, and removed the marker to keep it hidden. Teter went back to the grave — and found no bones in it.

About the same time a Malheur County cattleman, H. B. Reaves, became interested in the project and traced old wagon ruts deeply imbedded in the nearly barren soil. On the North Fork of the Malheur River he came upon the stone with the

CHAMBERS GRAVE was located by following combination of many clues most important was start at Beulah. Beulah proved to have vanished except for farmhouse, was once small town, most was flooded by Agency Dam. Dam was built in '80s partly by forced Indian labor. Work was disagreeable to savages who revolted, pillaged and burned neighboring farm houses. Troops were sent in to subdue natives, accomplished job by wholesale slaughter, wiping out entire tribe. More enduring landmarks near grave are lake formed by dam and very prominent, 6800 feet high Castle Rock, in plain sight from dirt road leading past site.

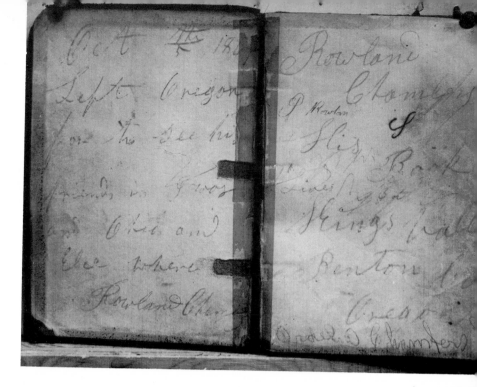

END PAPERS OF BIBLE belonging to Rowland Chambers, widower of Sarah. It seems to have been carried on wonderings of lost emigrants, possibly was read at funeral service for Sarah. Chambers first trip back to old home some 30 years later was important enough to record—"Oct. 5th 186? Left Oregon for to see his friends in Ioway and Ohio and Elce Where Rowland Chambers." Earlier signature at right shows maarked similarity of C to same letter carved on stone marker on Sarah Chambers' gravestone, lending credence to belief that Rowland carved stone himself at time of burial, although at least two people claim to have seen wooden headboard on grave at later dates.

crudely lettered inscription — "Mrs. S. Chambers September 3 1845." To make sure this one was really a grave, Reaves dug into the mound and found actual human bones. Then he made a thorough search of the area west by two days' travel and failed to find any nuggets.

In 1950 the authenticity of this grave was established by Walter Meacham, executive secretary of The Old Oregon Trail, Inc. who independently traced the wagon tracks and located Mrs. Chambers' grave. He photographed the stone marker and searched pioneer records, proving that Mrs. S. Chambers, wife of Rowland Chambers, had indeed been buried beside the trail, date of death being later corroborated by family records. Nahum King, Rowland Chambers and others of the train had settled in what later was known as King's Valley, adjacent to the Willamette Valley, where some descendants still live. (See GHOST TOWN SHADOWS)

This reporter made his search and photographed the grave stone in the summer of 1965, and since the details of the inscription were quite distinct, he presented a print to the Oregon Historical Society which was in need of such a picture. Almost immediately the photograph came to the attention of Lowell E. Tiller of Portland who with Keith Clark is assembling a history of the wagon train in question. He supplied information for this book not generally known. As to the Sarah — Sarepta — Sarilda conflict, his digging has revealed that "Sarah King, daughter of Nahum and Sarepta

King, born July 25, 1823, became the wife of Rowland Chambers and died Sept. 3, 1845."

Concerning the history of the stone, Mr. Tiller discovered a document in possession of the Oregon Historical Society headed: "The Lost Immigrants", written by Maurice Fitzgerald Turner, former sergeant, Troop K, 1st U.S. Cavalry. This is not dated but in part Mr. Turner writes: "I have known that section of the country intimately since 1874. . . Twenty years later after these experiences I have seen their traces. . . At the foot of the bluff flowed the North Fork of the Malheur River and close to its banks, before departing, they laid to rest a Mrs. Chambers who died since their arrival in the little valley, placing a hewed board which was inscribed in well cut letters her name, age and date of demise. This board was still there in place a few years ago and probably is there yet."

Mr. Tiller quotes from an interview with C. A. Sweet in the MORNING DEMOCRAT of Nov. 18, 1924. "On this bench I found the grave of Mrs. Chambers who was buried Sept. 28, 1845. I saw the grave in 1881. . . . . When I was there there was a juniper tree beside the grave and at that time the grave was enclosed with a five foot rail fence which had been put up by Sam Parrish, Indian Agent at the Malheur Agency. After he had gone sheepherders used the rails around the grave for campfires."

If the present stone marker was not placed there at the time of Sarah Chambers' death it is nevertheless very old. Unexplained is the similarity between some of the letters inscribed on it and those on the end papers of the Bible once carried by the bereaved husband, Rowland Chambers.

To safeguard the stone from theft or vandalism it was embedded in a slab of concrete by Mr. L. K. Bullock of nearby Vale, Oregon, about 1954. The location is about 100 feet above the dirt road along the North Fork of Malheur River near Beulah Res-ervoir. Beulah, now nearly vanished, is north of Juntura on U.S. 20. Local inquiry should be made at Juntura, there being no marker or sign in area to indicate location. At the time of this photographer's successful search there was an old stock water-ing trough, carved from a log, lying at the edge of the road close to the grave.

LOOKING EAST ACROSS TYGH VALLEY in central Oregon named for Tygh Indians, once inhabiting fertile area. Oregon's ill-fated "Lost Wagon Train" probably took route along Tygh Ridge (left, out of photo), 1500 feet above valley floor, although in one of many stories of gold nuggets, member of wagon train John Herren said his nephew Dan picked up nuggets along creek which meanders among trees, center left.

OLD PHOTO shows "Barbecue—Burial of Old Chief Joseph." (Photo courtesy Oregon Historical Society).

GRAVE OF OLD CHIEF JOSEPH at foot of Wallowa Lake in Oregon's mountains of same name. Under Old Chief Joseph's leadership Nez Perce made homes in Wallowa and along Imnaha River, an area famous for ruggedly beautiful scenery. Old Chief was tall, handsome, well built, son of Cayuse chief and Nez Perce woman. Young Chief Joseph succeeded him. Father was involved in signing of treaties of 1855 and 1863, agreed to first, refused second. He said: "No man owns any part of the earth; no man can sell what he does not own". Resisting efforts of Rev. Spalding to persuade him to sign, he chided missionary for what he felt was unwarranted interference. "It is your business to talk about spirit matters and not to talk to us about parting with our land,' he said. When elder Joseph lay dying in his lodge, he called son to him, saying: "My spirit is going very soon to see the great spirit chief . . . you are now the chief of our people. They look to you to guide them. A few more years and the white man will be all around you. This country holds your father's body. Never give up the graves to any man." Joseph was first buried near Lostine, later removed to this site in heart of ancient tribal home.

REQUIEM FOR A RENEGADE
Chief Paulina

He was a ragged outlaw, leading a hungry band of raiders across the wind-swept cattle lands, yet there were those who thought Paulina was a good Indian. But not the Central Oregon ranchers. They were "belly sick" of losing steers to the bad bunch and getting only stray shots at the skinny rumps of the Indian's cayuses fading into the canyon shadows.

"Attila of the Sagelands" he was called by Phil Brogan, historian of Bend, Oregon, in his *East of the Cascades*, but by all accounts Paulina was a chief by tribute or respect rather than by tribal succession. He and his followers swooped down on the luckless herds until the ranchers cried for help and Col. C. S. Drew's soldiers arrived ready for action. Paulina and company were ready too, properly painted for battle, but when they saw the howitzer bumping along behind the uniformed detachment, they prudently retired to the sandy gullies.

The outlaw band then held back from the settlements to harass miners along trails to and from gold fields of the John Day area. One such ambush was discovered by J. W. P. Huntington, the Indians

PRECIPITOUS RED-TINTED CLIFFS line Trout Creek in area now called Paulina Basin. Photo was made while jeep and driver took breather, almost immediately diving over brink through sage and juniper to turn left at bottom to reach actual site of slaying of Paulina.

attempting to take the white party's guns. The fracas ended with three tribesmen killed by bullets, their women and children taken captive as hostages. One proved to be Paulina's wife.

This was nothing to deter the chief. Paulina soon moved in on Fort Klamath in an attempt to murder the entire garrison. He failed to do so and lost fourteen braves. This was the start of a long series of raids, pursuits and narrow escapes on the part of soldiers and Indians, Paulina always managing to out-maneuver the U.S. Army. His tactics were generally to conceal his band behind convenient rocks near the trail which his scouts said a detachment of soldiers would be taking. As they rode by the warriors would fall upon them without warning, many times mutilating the bodies. After three years of these cat-and-mouse skirmishes, it was Paulina's lot to be shot and killed by a non-military man.

The man was Howard Maupin, veteran of the Mexican War under Zachary Taylor. He also was attracted to the trails of Canyon City-bound miners, having taken the job of caretaker for the stage station established by Henry Wheeler at the first site of Antelope, about two miles east of the present location. At the time he was the only resident of the area and had good reason to fear Paulina's raids.

In the dead of night the renegade raided the Andrew Clarno ranch some distance east. As the band crossed the route of the stage line he was spotted by the stage driver, James N. Clark, who whipped the team on to the Antelope stop where Maupin was alerted. Clark, Maupin, William Ragan and John Atterbury quickly formed a posse and set out on the plain trail left by Clarno's cattle and Indian ponies.

On a grassy slope shelving into a steeply walled canyon cradling Trout Creek there was a free-flowing spring, later called "Middle Spring". Paulina and his followers had made camp beside it, built a fire and were preparing beef steaks for breakfast. The insulting gesture was its savory odor and may have aided Maupin's party in pinpointing the location of the camp, for they burst upon the savages so suddenly the renegades scattered in utter confusion, not even picking up their weapons.

Most of them escaped although some versions of the story have several Indians killed on the opposite wall of the canyon as they attempted to scale it. Certain it is that Paulina was trapped in front of a rough chunk of lava 15 to 20 feet high. Maupin brought him down with a single rifle shot, crippling

CANYON WALL IN BACKGROUND here is now called Paulina Bluff though few other than local ranchers have seen it or know location. It was at this spot in front of rough chunk of long-cooled lava that Chief Paulina met death. After Maupin removed scalp, body was deserted bones bleaching in several summer suns. Then suddenly it mysteriously disappeared. Presumably members of his band were emboldened by time to gather bones, for what disposition it is not known. Two rocky mounds on opposite sides of canyon, toward left where slope is less steep, are said to be graves of Indians killed in surprise raid and buried there.

him with a bullet in the hip. There is some controversy as to who actually killed the downed Indian, most stories crediting Howard Maupin, a few saying Jim Clark, stage driver, delivered the coup de grace. One writer divides the credit. It seems Paulina, lying on the ground, picked up handfuls of dust which he sprinkled on his bowed head. Maupin raised his rifle but Clark stopped him, saying: "That old so-and-so stole some of my cattle once. Let me finish him off." He did but it was Maupin who carefully scalped the dead chief and for years afterward he kept the grisly relic nailed above his door.

VETERAN RANCHER AARON HALE who owns 3000 acres in vicinity including this site, drove photographer to this spot by jeep, over rocks, through sage brush, often leaning precariously on steep slopes. No road or even trail leads to spot. After safe return to Aaron's home near Ashwood he confessed to doubt about herding jeep over such terrain in future. "I decided you should know the location and now that you do I never expect to go there again."

WHITE MARBLE SHAFT stands over grave of Howard Maupin near his last home site, ranch near enough to Paulina Basin to sight some cliffs at edge. Close by are rotting remains of ranch buildings, one of which carried scalp of Paulina over door for many years.

WIND-CARVED ROCKS crowning pinnacle of "The Island" have always seemed to this photographer to resemble group of prophets, bearded and robed. Formation cleaved junction of Metolius and Deschutes Rivers, just below additionally joining Crooked River. Base of spectacular, fossil-filled rocky promontory is now washed by waters formed by Round Butte Dam. Below is town of Maupin, named for early stage station keeper, rancher and ferry operator Howard Maupin. For a number of years he carried passeners heading for Willamette Valley across Deschutes River.

MAGNIFICENT MONUMENT. View looks west toward snowy Cascade Mountains, in foreground Smith Rocks standing on plains just east of village of Terrebonne — collection of towers, minarets, domes of varicolored rhyolite. Precipitous formations rising above Crooked River have been targets for pinnacle-aspiring mountaineers for many years. One grotesque rock column resembling bust of monkey placed on narrow pedestal was not successfully climbed until Oct. 23, 1960. Those making first ascent of Monkey Face were Vivian Staender, Davis Bohn and James Fraser of Portland-based mountaineers' club, the Mazamas, who required such aids as pitons and ropes to reach dizzying perch at top.
Considerably earlier, about 1863, a company of soldiers was camped near spectacular formation between forays against troublesome Indians. One soldier named Smith, possibly with ideas of gaining summit of one spire, stepped on loose rock which rolled out from under him. He slipped from ledge, was killed in fall. Rock formation was given his name.

SNAKES IN THE GRASS

SLAUGHTER BY THE SNAKES
Lt. Stephen Watson 1

Adventurous Stephen Watson, 5' 10" tall grey eyed and brown haired, left his birthplace in New Brunswick to seek gold in the newly discovered fields out of Yreka, California. Not uncovering any El Dorado there, he went on to Jacksonville, Oregon, where he was also unsuccessful. At 23 he took out a donation land claim just north of nearby Medford. Then came the call for volunteers to fight the Indians at that time harassing travel between The Dalles and roistering gold crazy Canyon City, Oregon. Watson enlisted with the rank of Second Lieutenant at Jacksonville.

Chief among thorns in the flesh of gold-seekers was the renegade Snake Indian "Chief" Paulina. In early 1864 an expedition under Captain John M. Drake was sent after him. With Drake was young Watson. On the night of May 17 the company was camped at what would be Camp Maury. Friendly Warm Springs Indian scouts under their chief Stock Whitley fanned out, soon discovering Paulina's camp at the foot of a bluff about 15 miles from Camp Maury. The Indians were dancing and singing in a noisy fashion later believed part of a definite plan to attract the soldiers into a battle at a defensive site of their own choosing.

Early in the morning a detachment of 26 men was sent to the scene. This was under the command of Lt. McCall. Aiding him was another group of 13 under command of Lt. Watson. "Surprised" in their camp the Snakes readily assumed position behind the rocky fort they had built at the foot of the cliff. As Watson rashly charged up he received a blast directly in his face. He was able to cry out "Pour it into them, boys", then fell with his horse which also was shot. Reporting these details later was the Indian Stock Whitley who had formed a deep attachment for the Lieutenant. Seeing that his friend was killed, Whitley made an attempt to drag the body to cover to save it from inevitable mutilation. He was unsuccessful in this, receiving severe wounds himself. Two other soldiers, Bennett Kennedy and James Harkinson were killed in the same initial fusillade that killed Watson. McCall sent messengers back to Camp Maury to get help.

Captain John Drake later wrote that he and his men responded "at a plunging trot over the rough terrain three hours after the messenger has left." His men found the bodies of the soldiers stripped and horribly mutilated. One of the Indian scouts was disemboweled and scalped. The dead and the wounded who could ride were returned to Camp Maury on horseback, one or two had to be carried. The Indian Stock Whitely lived for a time, but later died of the wounds received in his attempt to rescue Watson's body.

The Thursday, May 19 entry in Drake's journal reads ". . . the day was consumed in the necessary preparations for the burial of our fallen comrades. Their graves were dug side by side on a small knoll south of the camp in the edge of the timber and the three bodies buried with appropriate honors."

Drake's subordinate, Lt. Noble, was assigned the duty of burial, reporting the dreary task in more detail. "Poor Watson all feel deeply @ regret much his loss . . . I little thought I would have to dig his grave and command his funeral escort. We had him and his men who were killed prepared and dressed as neatly as possible, and neatly rolled in their U. S. Blankets, for we had no lumber to make coffins for them. Lt. W. was dressed in his blue uniform Jacket (Shoulder Straps on it — @ grey pants — I took some of his hair . . . a chapter read from the Bible by Capt. Drake."

Camp Maury proved to be unsuitable as permanent quarters, as did a Camp Watson established some time later. Still later that fall another camp also named for the lieutenant was established on Fort Creek about five miles west of the present Antone. Log cabins were erected under extreme difficulty, there being no carpenter or tools available. Scurvy threatened and an expedition was sent to Fort Vancouver to bring back vegetables, one soldier, William Lord, dying of the disease before its return. Two years after the battle with Paulina the volunteer troops were disbanded, Camp Watson being taken over by the regular Army.

Some time after this change, the bodies of those volunteers buried at Camp Maury were removed to Camp Watson. The two privates were buried near several others who had died during occupancy of Camp Watson. The remains of Watson were loaded on a wagon serving as caisson and taken to The Dalles. There the cortege was met by soldiers who lined up double file to salute the body. Watson was placed on a boat and taken down the Columbia River to Fort Vancouver, where he was buried.

Confusingly, name of the original Camp Watson remained exactly that, the "new" Camp Watson is on some military maps as Old Camp Watson.

ROW OF MARBLE STONES mark graves of those who died among junipers and sagebrush in battle with Paulina's Indians, Privates James Harkinson, Co. B., First Oregon Cavalry and Bennett Kennedy, Co. B., First Oregon Cavalry. Also graves of those who died at Camp Watson later, John Donnelly, Co. I, U. S. Cavalry; Thomas Ryan, Co. I, U. S. Cavalry; William B. Lord, Co. I., U. S. Cavalry; Matthew Fitzsimmons, Co. G., First Oregon Cavalry. At right, out of view is separate marker for Lt. Watson. In background is seen wooden enclosure of civilian grave, which with others constitute adjoining civilian cemetery. At lower right is seen fallen flagpole, erected for ceremony in 1932 dedicating new marble markers.
Memorial Division of War Dept., Washington, D.C., states standard Army headstone for Lt. Stephen Watson was shipped August 7, 1927 in compliance with request by Mrs. H. D. Putnam of Prineville, Oregon. Officials suggest Mrs. Putnam was unaware body of Watson had been taken to Vancouver, a fact also established by War Dept. records.

In any event, the camp was entirely abandoned as a military unit May 24, 1869. A civilian "town" had grown up on the site, there were blacksmith shops, saw mill, barns, stores and houses. The place didn't last long after departure of the Army, wooden structures fell into decay, heavy objects such as army wagons sank deep into what the soldiers had called "miry ground". The flat meadow used as parade ground grew up in pine trees and sage brush. The wooden headboards on the soldiers, and later civilians' graves rotted away.

Then in about 1930 the combined American Legion Posts of Mitchell, Prineville, John Day, Prairie City, Canyon City and Fossil started a movement to properly mark the graves. Their efforts were successful, and late in June of 1932 a gathering of more than 300 stood beside the graves of the soldiers in the pine woods. Each grave was surmounted by a gleaming white marble tombstone, provided and inscribed by the U. S. Army.

In the middle of the solemn dedication ceremonies an old man later identified as Martin Lucas of Canyon City spoke up. He said it was untrue that Watson was killed in action by Indians, that he had died in a fall from his horse on the way into camp. Lucas, then 89, had served in the Civil War and was transferred to Camp Watson in 1866. It was generally conceded, however, that the written Journals of Drake and others, the description of his death by Chief Stock Whitley, and the story in Bancroft's History of Oregon. Vol. 2, corroborate the earlier version.

The lonely graves are still decorated on Memorial Days by Mr. Ned Norton of Mitchell. It is this fact that led us to Mr. Norton who gave information leading to our successful search of the history of the graves.

BEARDLESS HERO OF BALER BAY
Arthur Venville

Apprentice Seaman Arthur Venville was in the crew of the gunboat *Yorktown* at anchor in April of 1899 in Baler Bay, Luzon, Philippine Islands, the ship's mission to attempt rescue of some 500 Spanish prisoners. A launch with 16 men led by Lt. Com. Gilmore was sent to reconnoiter along the shore.

"As we approached the beach," wrote the officer in his diary, "we were met by a hail of gunfire. The volley killed or wounded many of our party, the deck soon being covered with blood. Burning to return fire I could not effectively do so, being armed only with a short range pistol. I grabbed up a rifle from the dead hands of one of our men, but found it jammed and useless. Then young Venville spoke up and said:

" 'Mr. Gilmore, I think I can fix it,' and started working on it. At that moment there came another volley of fire from the shore, Venville receiving a wound in the flesh of his neck. 'Mr. Gilmore,' he said, 'I've been hit,' but kept on working on the gun. Then another bullet hit him in the side of his chest, the bullet emerged at the armpit. He said, 'Mr. Gilmore, I've been hit again,' but never stopped trying to repair the rifle.

"Another bullet then creased his head, taking off part of the ear, the consequent heavy flow of blood running into his eyes when he bent his head to his work. Taking a handkerchief from his pocket he wiped some of the blood away so he could see what he was doing. As he stood up to hand me the repaired gun another bullet hit him, this time passing through the ankle. This time he fell, but not before managing to hand me the weapon, saying 'Mr. Gilmore, I've been hit again, but your rifle is fixed.' The beardless boy had never been under fire before."

In the southeast corner of the old Milwaukie (Oregon) Pioneer Cemetery stands a shaft of marble, gleaming white as if newly placed. On the side facing the walkway the stone is inscribed: "The body of D.G.A. Venville was found 12 miles from Baler and was laid to rest here Dec. 15, 1901." The left side reveals another legend: "In loving memory of D.G.A. Venville born Jan. 8, 1881. Who was wounded and captured with Lieut. Gilmore of the U. S. Navy on April 12, 1899 at Baler, Luzon, P. I. and was treacherously murdered by order of Novicio, an insurgent Gen'l some time after Feb. 12, 1900. We know not where his body lies. But his spirit is with God."

Behind these sentiments lies a story full of hope, despair and ultimate tragedy for a boy in the remote Philippine Islands and for his mother and sister at home in Sellwood, Oregon, now a part of Portland.

Arthur Venville was born in Dudley, England, coming to the United States with his parents as a baby, his father dying while the family was enroute to Oregon. The mother remarried and in June of 1899 she, as Mrs. Harry Mash, with her husband and young Arthur settled in Sellwood. The boy attended grade school there and at 17 enlisted in the navy at Mare Island, Calif. The war with Spain broke out shortly after this and the youthful apprentice seaman shipped out on the *Yorktown*.

In a letter to Mrs. Mash written by William Rynders, a friend of her son who was captured with him upon the landing of the party at Baler Bay it was learned the heroic defense by Gilmore and his men was in vain, that all were captured by insurgents.

Wrote Rynders:

"We were landed some distance up the river, all of us walking except Arthur who had received a bad wound in his foot. He was carried by his comrades who took turns at the job. We were marched about a mile and a half to a dirty old church. We could not get away or get any medical attention and some of us died of wounds. We were fed a little rice and water by the native women around there. Several days later the insurgents came to take us to a prison camp at San Jose. Before we were forced to leave Arthur, who still could not walk, we had a chance to say goodby to him. I feel I must tell you that there were tears in his eyes. It was the last time we were ever to see him."

A priest however did see him. Rescued soon after the above episode, the priest reported: "We were imprisoned in a hut along with several others including a youthful American sailor who had been shot in the foot. The wound at first not attended at all and then only being dressed with leaves was slow in healing. The boy could barely place his foot to the ground. He was very likeable and cheerful in spite of the difficulties he found himself in. He soon won all our hearts by his fortitude, but one morning when we woke up he was gone. We were told on inquiring that he had 'gone fishing'."

In reality he had been moved out to still another prison, this one near headquarters of General Gutierrez. The wife of the general was in the habit of helping feed the prisoners in the compound and was soon attracted to Venville by his manners and handsome appearance, and saw to it that he had special favors in better food and lodgings. This bit of information leaked back to the United States where it was distorted to seem that Senora Gutierrez had spirited the boy away to the mountains, hiding out with him there. Soon a man purporting to be a novelist called on Mrs. Mash in Sellwood, attempting to get details on the life of Arthur who would be the central figure of a novel about the "love life" of an American prisoner and the wife of an insurgent general. The episode was only one to plague the grieving mother.

The Arthur Venville story also came to the attention of William A. Shump in charge of rescue operations of the American forces now occupying the area. When he reached the scene at San Jose he learned that news of impending occupation had preceded his arrival, also that Arthur Venville, at last able to walk had been marched away and killed.

Back in America, the story of Venville's heroism and subsequent capture gained wide attention. The papers said that possibly a large sum of money might tempt the insurgents to release him unharmed. A movement was started to raise such a fund, at one point progress being reported on August 18, 1900 in a newspaper story: "RAISING A RANSOM—NEARLY $100 CONTRIBUTED FOR ARTHUR VENVILLE. MONEY WILL BE SENT TO GENERAL MACARTHUR WHO WILL PUBLISH REWARD THROUGHOUT LUZON. If this brave boy still lives he cannot receive a higher service than rescue from his savage captors. Lt. Woods is confident that within another day or two will see the full amount collected. The sum of $250 is deemed necessary to offer a suitable reward."

Before the money could be offered in the effort to save Venville news came that he had been executed, the location of his body unknown. The cash raised was used to pay for a marble shaft to be placed in the cemetery as a memorial. On September 23 services were held in Sellwood Presbyterian Church, a portrait of Venville serving instead of his body. Then followed further prayers at the newly erected shaft in the cemetery. The marker, previously covered by a drape was unveiled, then

MARBLE SHAFT honors memory of 17-year-old Arthur Venville, wounded, taken captive and later executed by insurgents in Philippine Islands. Inscriptions on two sides of monument seem to be in conflict but unraveling of mystery revealed story of heroism in 1900, details occupying front pages of newspapers for weeks and drawing sympathy of entire nation.

again almost concealed by flowers placed around it.

Meanwhile, Captain Shump was unremitting in his efforts to locate the spot where Venville might have been buried. At last, some eight months after the killing he found a native who was willing to point out the direction taken by the execution party. As soon as expert native trackers were put on the trail it became evident that Arthur, as he was forced to limp along, had managed to leave small marks along the way—scuffed ground, broken twigs and ripped ferns. These signs led to a mound of earth barely settled in spite of tropical rains. A little digging revealed the remains of Venville, the method of his slaying all too obvious, the head being buried with the decapitated body.

Mrs. Ellen Martin, custodian of the Milwaukie cemetery, clearly remembers attending the Arthur Venville funeral as a little girl. "All the school children of Milwaukie were there," she said, "but I don't know why." She provided the name of John Smith of Portland who had voluntarily done some clearing work in the cemetery, renovating the Venville plot because he too had attended the funeral. As a small boy one aspect of the funeral seemed a very curious one—instead of the conventional coffin, the pall bearers carried to the grave a small steel box.

All that was left of Arthur Venville was contained in that box which had been shipped to San Francisco and Portland. At the mortuary a cortege was formed which went to Sellwood where it was met by a firing squad. Funeral services were held in St. John's Episcopal Church, the only structure capable of accommodating the large crowd of mourners. Then the long procession went to the grave opened at the foot of the previously erected monument. As the first earth was dropped on the box in the grave a volley of shots was fired over it. Then came taps and the end of the Arthur Venville story.

FLORAL WREATH here is cast in zinc, plate bolted to marble headstone — in pioneer cemetery near Independence, Oregon. Modern hybrid roses and lilies have no place here, small cabbage roses and Madonna lilies being typical of period, about 1885.

ARTISTICALLY CARVED bouquet of Calla "lilies", cabbage roses, lilies of the valley, forget-me-nots, tulips and Madonna lilies on stone in North San Juan, California, in Northern Mines area of Sierra.

THE BOOTED BODIES OF BODIE

BAD MEN DIED EARLY IN BODIE
William Bodey

Rosa May would sell her charms to anyone but she favored only one lover, Ernest Marks. The pair now lie side by side in Bodie's famous Boot Hill. Not far away are the graves of Henry Chatterton, an alcoholic who lay on the street one cold night until he froze to death and James Madden who was fatally shot in the Palace Laurel Saloon; Felix DeGuire who murdered Patrick Coyle; opium den habitue David Mitchell.

These and dozens more lie in that spot outside the pale where "decent folks" were buried. The people of Bodie may have put up with prostitutes, opium addicts, horse thieves and murderers while they lived but once they had passed over, segregation was strictly enforced. Class distinction prevailed even with Indians and Chinese. The surviving countrymen of the latter periodically exhumed the bones, shipped them to China. In Boot Hill their souls would never attain a celestial heaven.

Occasional epidemics of pneumonia and diphtheria swelled the ranks of all classes on the hill with no discrimination. On this eastern fringe of the High Sierra winter temperatures often dipped to 40 below, blasting powder was used to open the frozen ground. The rattling of windows and shaking of the earth did little to aid recovery of those ill with the disease.

Bad men just naturally gravitated to Bodie, even undertakers and doctors. Shotgun Johnnie Heilshorn and Big Bill Monahan were partners in an undertaking concession for a time, the brick Heilshorn Morgue and County Hospital conveniently close to the cemetery. One night a hospital matron on late duty heard a strange noise in the graveyard and was able to make out the forms of two men carrying a casket away from the cemetery and into the morgue. She informed authorities who next day opened a freshly disturbed grave and found a body robbed of its wooden case. Although the greedy "ghouls" were brought to trial for appropriating and reselling caskets and corpse clothing, the articles could not be identified so Shotgun Johnnie and Big Bill went free. Retribution overtook both of them however, Johnnie being found dead in an opium parlor and Bill falling victim to a bullet fired by "an assailant unknown."

About the same time Bodie had two doctor partners. One of their patients, a prominent female member of Bodie society, died of some inexplicable cause. The doctors wished to perform a post mortem but the bereaved husband refused. Later a few of the family convinced him he should consent so the grave was opened and found—empty. The doctors were accused and there was strong talk of lynching but suddenly there was no one to lynch. The medicos had vamoosed.

French Joseph DeRoche was enamored of another man's wife, the beautiful Cornish lady, Mrs. Treloar. A long series of clandestine meetings between them was climaxed by their openly dancing together at a ball held in Miners' Union Hall. The affair was common knowledge and Treloar had frequently demanded the woman quit seeing the Frenchman.

Working on the late shift the night of the dance, he left the job and found his wife waltzing in DeRoche's arms. To avoid a scene Treloar took his wife by the arm, asking her to come home with him. DeRoche had been drinking and pulled the husband outdoors. In the snow he drew his gun and placed it against the head of the unarmed Treloar and pressed the trigger.

The Frenchman was placed in jail where he engaged the services of famous lawyer Pat Reddy, who attained fame later in other camps (e.g. Randsburg, Calif. See *Ghost Town Treasures*). But to make doubly sure of avoiding the noose he escaped to the French-owned goat ranch a few miles out of town. There a posse located him, returned him to jail under heavy guard.

That night a mob erected a wagon crane as a ready-made scaffold over the spot still red with Treloar's blood and DeRoche was dragged there from the jail. A rope was whipped around his neck, the other end passed over the pully and dragged away by some twenty men, the Frenchman dangling and twisting. Before being taken to Boot Hill the body was laid out with the rope artistically draped around the neck.

The event had no quieting effect on Bodie's rampant lawlessness for five days later David Banner was shot by H. Ryan, the affair described in the coroner's report as "A quarrel between sporting men." The two were added to those in the exposed yard below the properly fenced one on the hill.

On a sweltering day in July, 1859, William

VIEW LOOKS NORTHEAST from famed cemetery. Prominent in background is portion of Bodie Butte from which many millions in gold were taken. Slightly left of center is little Methodist church. At right of center, nearer foreground, is brick and board structure housing morgue, notorious during time of Shotgun Johnny Heilshorn and Bib Bill Monahan proprietors. Old cemetery was once filled with hundreds of wooden headboards, most long since rotted away, a few like one in right foreground still standing but without legible inscriptions after almost a hundred severe winters.

Bodey, a Dutchman from Poughkeepsie, N.Y., discovered gold where the mining camp of Bodie (spelling of name in this way not explained) was to be. The following winter, anticipating a snow storm, Bodey and his partner, Black Taylor, hurried down to Monoville for supplies. Overtaken by heavily falling snow on the return trip, the men became separated and Bodey was caught in drifts and died of exposure. His bones, gnawed bare by coyotes, were discovered by Taylor the next spring and he wrapped all he could find in a blanket, together with Bodey's belongings, and buried it in a shallow grave.

The town of Bodie grew rapidly to become a city of several thousand. In 1879, one of the biggest boom years, J. G. McClinton accidentally stumbled upon Bodey's grave, settling a much argued question as to its location. A wave of sentiment for the town's founder swept the place. The body would be exhumed and properly buried in an honored spot in the cemetery. A fine monument might even be carved and erected on the site.

A committee finished opening the grave, disclosing the skull, a few bones, gun, necktie, bowie knife, shoe button, part of a blanket and some cloth. On the following Sunday a funeral was held

in Masonic Hall, the remains placed on exhibition for all to see. At the graveside the Hon. R. D. Ferguson delivered an impressive eulogy, concluding: "Let a fitting monument be reared in his memory. Let it be wrought from the chiseled granite of these mountains. Let its shaft rise high with its sculptured urn o'ertopping, with the simple name of Bodey there to kiss the first golden rays of the coming sun, where his setting beams may linger in cloudless beauty and majesty, undisturbed forever."

In the latter part of the following year a sculptor was brought to Bodie to chisel just such a monument, right up to the urn on top. He was about to begin inscribing Bodey's name when the shocking news of the assassination of President Garfield was announced. The wave of sentiment over Bodey changed to one of confusion but the sculptor chiseled doggedly on, inscribing on the stone shaft the line that remains today — SACRED TO THE MEMORY OF JAMES A. GARFIELD.

BODIE JAIL possibly held more vicious characters than most mining camps, expression "Bad Man from Bodie" being widely used. Almost break-proof, only exit was to scaffold and Boothill. At least one man cheated gallows. Early in 1880 Bodie stage left for Carson City one morning with $30,000 in bullion. Two Mexican bandits held it up and removed gold. Next day sheriff and posse tracked them down, shooting and killing one who was buried on spot. Other man was locked in Bodie calaboose and was found dead in cell next morning, taking with him secret of bullion cache. Wells Fargo offered substantial reward to spur expert trackers McCullogh and Frank Holmes on two month search but they nor anyone else ever discovered treasure.

A TOWN THAT DIVIDED ITSELF

LONE PINE

MONUMENT PLACED OVER GRAVE of 16 out of 27 victims of earthquake in 1872 — located just north of Lone Pine, California, near turn off on U. S. 395. Lone Pine is base for mountain climbing and pack trips into High Sierra but has long history, first cabin being built there in winter of 1861-2. Town almost straddled earth fault running roughly north and south along eastern face of mountain range.

Sierra itself was formed in successions of alternately gradual and sudden uplifts along fault, western section rising in sheer escarpment, eastern settling to form low basin, now Owens Valley. Difference in altitude is about 9,000'. East facing side of Sierra is vertical in places where weathering has not been too pronounced, more gently sloping on west side. Mt. Langley, 14,402', in left background, shows both faces. Mt. Whitney, concealed here behind other peaks, is of similar contour.

PLAQUE ON MONUMENT over mass grave. Visible rift of much longer earthquake fault is about 12 miles long, parallels highway, "recent" fractures showing differences of 12' on sides.

DISASTER IN 1872

ON THE DATE OF MARCH 26, 1872, AN EARTHQUAKE OF MAJOR PROPORTIONS SHOOK OWENS VALLEY AND NEARLY DESTROYED THE TOWN OF LONE PINE. TWENTY SEVEN PERSONS WERE KILLED.

IN ADDITION TO SINGLE BURIALS, 16 OF THE VICTIMS WERE INTERRED IN A COMMON GRAVE ENCLOSED BY THIS FENCE.

EAST FACE OF MT. WHITNEY, highest mountain in conterminous states, 14,495', as seen in telephoto view from eminence in Alabama Hills, close to earthquake fault. White cross is unidentified, possibly remaining from shooting of movie or TV scene.

VIEW FROM SUMMIT OF MT. WHITNEY, looking north over top of Mt. Russell, 14,190'. Photo shows part of 3000' vertical face of earthquake escarpment, extreme right, wall dropping straight down to Owens Valley. Most Sierra peak photos show noon or afternoon lighting. This one was made in early morning, author and Dr. Mason having spent freezing night on summit.

TOWN OF HORNITOS is unchanged, lacking usual trappings to attract tourists. Exceptions are these "hornito" graves, "gussied up" with modern signs thought to add interest but desecrating scene in opinion of many.

"LITTLE BAKE OVENS" is English equivalent of Hornitos, Spanish name of Mother Lode mining town because above-ground graves had resemblance to Mexican outdoor ovens. Early native Mexicans laid body on surface or in slight depression on ground, walled it around with rocks, crude mortar, to reach average height of 30-36 inches, often with one end higher for placing of headstone. Grave in this photo is dated 1871.

Earliest graves here were marked merely by wooden board inserted in rock crevices and have long since rotted away, The "hornitos", in protecting confines of Catholic cemetery, have not been molested or vandalized in any way. Gently rolling hills of Sierra piedmont are idyllic in spring, as shown here. Little creek (left) once yielding gold nuggets in quantity, is clear and sparkling. Scattered oaks are barely leafing out, grass of slopes fresh and green.

SLANE FAMILY being Catholics, were buried in graveyard of St. Francis Xavier Church, first place of worship in Chinese Camp other than joss houses. Although this town in Mother Lode section of California's Sierra mines was settled mainly by Oriental workers, it was largely peopled by non-Asiatics and the Irish were heavily represented.

One wagon train coming to the area included members of Kerrick, Stubblefield, Keough and Alcorn families who left Kentucky in 1853. Along the way Oney Luticia Kerrick died in childbirth in camp on Platte River in Sioux Nation territory. Men of party hewed crude coffin from trunk of tree, buried dead mother on bank of stream, disguising site from Indians. Infant Oney Kerrick was carried on horseback remainder of journey, lived much of later life in Crimea (named after Crimean War 1853-56) and Chinese Camp. One descendant of party members, Alice Jones Kuch, still lives in Albany, Calif., not far from Chinese Camp.

"MOCCASIN" HILL

Disease was sweeping the tribe of Indians at the old Wascopam Mission near the site of what would later be the city of The Dalles — the time about 1844. An early victim of the malady was the young son of the chief whose constant companion and servant had been a slave boy captured from a neighboring tribe. Now the old chief said the slave must accompany his dead son to the spirit land.

The young man who would have been chief was stretched out on the ground and the slave-companion was forced down on the body so the two faced each other, ankles and wrists of living and dead bound tightly together. Then they were carried to a canoe which cut through the swift current to an island in the Columbia River.

The Indians readied a sarcophagus box by emptying it of fleshless bones which were cast into a repository pit. The live and dead boys were laid in the box and the mourners departed with the cries of the little slave boy in their ears.

When Mr. and Mrs. Perkins, in charge of the mission, heard of the incident, they went to the chief to plead for the release of the living boy. He refused the request and the Perkins approached the Indian custodian of the island and here found help. Before sunrise the next morning the rescuers paddled out to the island, cut the bonds and brought the boy to the mission where he was fed, the angry welts on his wrists and ankles treated.

The Perkins related later the wounds remained in evidence for months.

There are at least three small, rocky islands in the Columbia which were used by the Indians as burial grounds and were known as Memaloose or Place of the Dead. Upper Memaloose was used largely by Yakima tribes. The island is public domain, being withdrawn from entry and set aside as a burial ground for the Yakima Confederate Tribes by Public Law in an act of Congress approved June 24, 1926.

The island was surveyed as containing 4.70 acres of rocky land on which were erected three frame structures, the first containing 12 burial boxes with 17 bodies, the second 15 boxes with 30 bodies, the third 27 boxes and 45 bodies. There were also two common burial pits, one estimated to contain more than 500 bodies, the other at least 22 burial boxes with 26 bodies.

Due to the ancient use of the island, the Indian custom of placing more than a single body in a burial box, and the unnumbered bones and skeletal remains of older burials in the two common graves, it was impossible to determine the exact number of burials on the island. A concrete monument was erected there in 1935 to the memory of the Indians so buried. Included were three chiefs who joined in the signing of the Yakima Treaty of 1855.

Construction of The Dalles Dam by the Federal

UPPER MEMALOOSE ISLAND, now under waters backed up by The Dalles Dam. Shown is mass burial pit where bones were pushed as bodies decayed in burial boxes held temporarily in shelters. (Photo by courtesy of Oregon Historical Society.)

Government necessitated the removal of the remains to higher ground as the island would be inundated by backed up waters. A new cemetery was acquired by the government, located 1¼ miles north of the Wasco County Bridge in Klickitat County, Washington, known as Wish-ham Cemetery. The Yakima Tribal Council agreed to the transfer of bodies and relocation began in 1957.

All bodies were removed to the new location except those of one family, which upon request of a member of the family, were reburied in the existing Hartland Cemetery 10 miles northeast of Lyle, Washington.

A second Memaloose Island, called Grave to avoid confusion, was also inundated by waters impounded by The Dalles Dam. From this the bones of some 650 Indians had already been removed when the Portland OREGONIAN printed a news item concerning the operation January 6, 1957. They were to be reburied in a tomb at a lookout point above the dam on the Oregon shore. Grave Island had been used primarily by Warm Springs Indians of Oregon, who report there have been no burials there since the great flood of 1894, when raging waters washed away all burial structures, boxes and pit covers.

LOWER MEMALOOSE ISLAND—view made from U. S. Highway 30 with 180 mm telephoto lens, bringing island much closer but also making Washington shore appear closer than it is. Island lies about 12 miles downriver from city of The Dalles, some 15 miles below dam. Safe from those flooding waters, Lower Memaloose was nevertheless reduced to about ½ acre by fringes of pool formed by Bonneville Dam below. Shafted monument seen here toward lower end marks last resting place of Victor Trevitt, pioneer printer who moved to The Dalles in 1854. Member of first state legislature and state senator 1866 to 1874, he was buried in 1883 in accordance with his wishes in this old burial ground. "In the resurrection I'll take my chances with the Indians", he wrote. Highway builders have placed fine rest stop at this viewpoint, complete with picnic tables, etc.

LARGE SUBSTANTIAL HOUSES such as this were built by Indians in areas where cedar trees grew, particularly around Puget Sound. Down logs, even standing cedars were split to timber or plank width by bone wedges inserted along natural grain, each wedge tapped in turn until log split, then pieces sectioned to length by fire. Many Indian houses accommodated several families, each occupying cubicle like one shown at left and right. House required months, even years of labor, tribesmen invoking spirits before each task. Should death occur in such a house, curse was circumvented by removing body through space provided, by unfastening and taking out certain planks. If door was used "death devils" could be expected to bring misfortune to tribe. Photo Oregon Historical Society.

MOST TRIBES living close to water used canoes for temporary entombment. Canoe was simple or elaborate depending upon prominence or wealth of deceased. It was elevated on poles, holes made in bottom for drainage of rain water. Possessions of departed were placed in and around canoes — animal pets, horses, weapons, robes, etc. all "killed" by being broken or otherwise damaged. When body decomposed, bones were removed, buried in individual or communal pit, sometimes left exposed as on Memaloose Island in Columbia River. Famous, powerful Chief Concomly of Chinook tribe was first placed in canoe similar to this one. Photo Oregon Historical Society.

HISTORIC OLD PHOTO was made on Crow Indian reservation in Montana. Crows were great warrior tribe considered as subdivision of other tribes, mostly Sioux, part of family known familiarly as Dakotas. Crows followed several customs in disposal of dead, one being placement of body in wooden box, elevating it on poles to prevent molestation by coyotes, etc. When poles rotted and collapsed, bones were ready for normal burial if tribe had not departed for other locations. Photo Oregon Historical Society.

LOG TOMBS photographed at Ft. Wrangell, Alaska, in 1887. Most of these were too short for supine body so knees were drawn up to chin to fit. Short length was often occasioned by widespread custom of placing dead body in fetal position for burial. Carved wooden figures on top were similar to those on totem poles, usually denoted family connection of departed. Photo Oregon Historical Society.

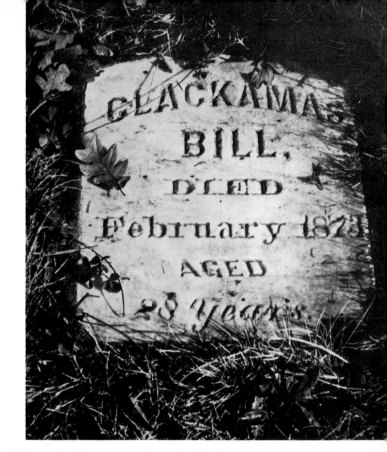

"MYSTERY" of Clackamas Bill remains unsolved while marble marker in Old Mountain View Cemetery at Oregon City, Oregon, has fallen to ground. Clackamas Bill was member of Clackamas tribe, subdivision of Chinooks living along Willamette River, but there is no record of why he merited tombstone.

UMATILLA INDIANS built simple teepees of mats woven of reeds from edges of rivers, marshes, lakes. If tribe members seemed near death in such a house he was moved outside to die, averting curse of death. Should it occur indoors, no recourse was left but to destroy shelter, usually by fire. Original caption on old photo read: "Sacajawea points out direction taken by Lewis and Clark" was scratched out. Photo Oregon Historical Society.

HOW GREEN WAS HER VALLEY?

AIR-DRIED BODY OF INDIAN GIRL, possibly about 18 years old. During process of excavation of Mesa Verde ruins many mummified bodies were discovered, most simply pushed into refuse heaps, or over cliffs with garbage. Some were found wrapped in turkey feather robes, others wore little or nothing, several in shrouds of reeds and surrounded by pottery. Mummies in good state of preservation were set aside for display in museum, identified by nicknames which have become more or less permanent. This young woman, known as "Esther", was found stuffed into crevice with 19 other mummified bodies. Large amount of cord made from human hair was found in cave with mummies, probably accounting for Esther's being shorter than usual.

MESA VERDE NATIONAL PARK contains 50,275 acres, set aside by Congress in 1906 to preserve the many prehistoric cliff dwellings, surface structures and Indian artifacts, including what are probably the best examples of genuine mummies in the U. S. First recorded observation of the area was made by Padre Escalante in 1776. Mesa Verde, meaning "Green Acres" in Spanish, is actually mound of earth and rock 15 x 8 miles, rising abruptly 2,000 feet above Montezuma Valley in southwestern Colorado.

First inhabitants of natural caves were likely mongoloid hunters using shelters after traversing Aleutian Islands from Asia. Later residents were "Basket Makers", roughly divided into two groups, the early from about 500 B. C., the later occupying dwellings up until drought period from 1276 to 1299. During last few hundred years Basket Makers were peacefully infiltrated by Pueblo Indians. Buildings were constructed of sandstone blocks, broken from rock sheets on mesa and lowered to site.

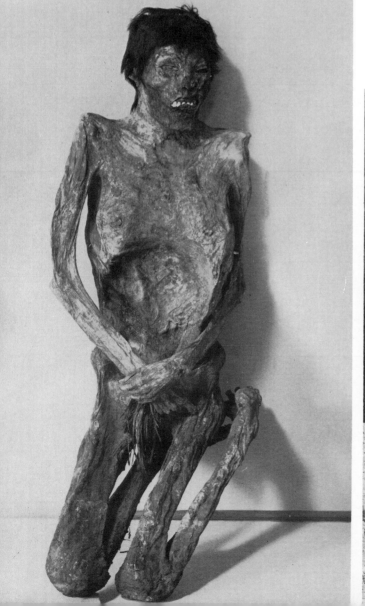

TO HEAVEN IN A HANDCART

THEY DIED FOR SILVER

Silver Reef's Boot Hills

The desert mining camp of Silver Reef in southern Utah had two special claims to fame. It was one of only two places in the world where silver was found in sandstone, and in a land where violent death was the rule, it notched a record number of violent fatalities per week. Had there been a special burying ground for the victims it would have been by far the largest known.

There were three cemeteries just below Silver Reef, one each for Catholics, Protestants and Chinese plus other "heathens." Sam Wing was the acknowledged custodian of the latter, conducting all funerals for the Celestials, seeing to the exhumation of their bones and shipping them home to China for permanent burial. Today it has virtually disappeared, sagebrush and cacti replacing whatever temporary markers there were.

The other burial grounds are easily identified by the comparative large number of marble and sandstone tombstones scattered over a large area, intervening spaces once filled by wooden headboards long since deteriorated. All traces of fencing have vanished, cattle and other stock roaming freely among the graves, nibbling at scanty forage. Large clumps of cacti, mostly of the Opuntia tribe display their satiny blooms.

Silver Reef had the usual quota of saloons, two of them with dance halls. One of the bordellos was the temporary stand of well-known "Soft Sophie", the toughest harlot in Utah. Sophie never worked anywhere very long, tolerating no suggestions from bosses, having her own ideas as to handling patrons. She displayed her charms on the little stage at the

Silver Lode for a week and the owner suggested she be more discreet in "rolling" her customers. Sophie's temper flared. She reached down into the recesses of her bodice, extracted her silver-plated derringer and used it with deadly effect. Then she packed her trunk and departed.

The incident would have caused no flurry in a town case-hardened to violence except for a long persisting rumor that the victim had stashed a large sum of money on the premises. A thorough search of the building failed to reveal any such treasure but after it deteriorated in a few years Peter Anderson bought it and started wrecking operations. Almost immediately a collapsing wall uncovered a stout leather bag stuffed with bills and gold coins. Being a thrifty farmer he did not gamble the money away but used it to improve and expand his ranch just north of the nearby town of Leeds, building it up into a showplace.

MICHAEL GARBIS was popular foreman of large mill at Silver Reef. Ordinarily getting along well with employes, he found intolerable the heavy drinking habits of a trouble-making laborer from Pioche, Nev. Reluctantly firing the man, he forgot the incident. A few weeks later, rounding the tailings dump, he came face-to-face with the discharged Nevadan who was evidently waiting for him with six-shooter ready, and Garbis was killed by several well-aimed bullets. Assailant was later captured, removed to St. George jail for safer keeping but mob of Garbis' friends removed him from cell and took him to famous hanging trees at edge of town. Beam was laid across limbs of huge cottonwoods and rope thrown over it, murderer jerked to death before sheriff could intervene.

Sacred to the memory of MICHAEL GARBIS departed this life October 3, 1880, AGED 48 Yrs. & 9 Mos. Native of Cornwall England. Dying is but going home.

Death thou art but another birth, freeing the spirit from the clogs of earth. Erected by his son MICHAEL.

LITTLE PARK MOREHOUSE occupies unique tomb in desert grave-yard. In early day mining camps doctors were scarce and infant mortality rates soared, but specific reason for Morehouse child's death is not known.

HENRY C. CLARK, born in New York State, March 13, 1853, met violent death beside spinning roulette wheel. Possessing fiery temper, Clark had been involved in several altercations, on one occasion shooting at a Navajo Indian for some fancied slight. The bullet missed its mark and Clark was prevented from firing again when bystanders tied him to wagon wheel.

Having a streak of luck one night in gambilng house, Clark being unable to pick wrong card or lose at craps, he was even more successful playing roulette, right up to the point of "breaking the wheel." With bank exhausted, proprietor attempted to eject Clark and the gambler's luck deserted him when he was beaten to the draw.

IN THE SHADOW OF ZION

Nancy Ferguson Ott

Pioneer Utah was a Mormon haven. The state's grandsires built their homes and towns solidly of mud, brick and logs, and because of a dry, preserving climate, there are now more evidences of early settlement there than in any other western state. On striking exception is the town of Duncan's Retreat.

Members of the Ott family have passed down a legend that Chapman Duncan, fugitive from a pursuing mob in Nevada fled to find refuge in a dense copse of willows on the banks of the Virgin River. In 1861, the "heat" fading, Duncan founded a settlement there, this was soon washed away by floods but resettled by other farmers a couple of years later.

In a sense "founded by a runagate", the Mormon settlement had for its heroine a woman outstanding among the original Mormons who pushed their hand carts from Nauvoo to Zion—Nancy Ferguson. She was born in Stokes County, North Carolina, August 27, 1822. With her family she joined the struggling and persecuted Mormon Church whose members, fleeing from place to place lost eighteen of their number in a massacre at Haun's Mill when intolerant mobs fell upon them. Young Nancy followed the Saints to what proved to be but temporary sanctuary at Nauvoo, Illinois. There she met and married Frederick Ott in 1841. Only five years later she found herself a widow with two children, Frederick and David.

In 1848 Nancy Ott followed her church members to "The Place", the broad valley at the foot of the Wasatch Mountains that would be Salt Lake City. On the trek Nancy suffered all the hardships of those pioneers, even losing one of her babies — Frederick — and the infant was laid in a tiny hollow in the earth, the grave unmarked.

In 1851 Nancy Ott joined another party of travelers, those designated by Brigham Young to settle the southern colony of Dixie, now centered by St. George, Utah. The group, including Mrs. Ott and son David, carved out homes on the banks of the Virgin River, the spot within sight of the outermost "Temples of Zion", Mount Kinesava.

Not long after the settling of Duncan's Retreat, a little Indian girl wandered into the Ott home and was adopted, Nancy giving her the name of Sarah, treating her as her natural child. With her home duties, Nancy served as nurse in the lonely outpost, even taking the place of doctor and midwife. Her brothers who had gone on to California, wrote that they had done very well financially and asked Nancy to join them so she would not have to work so hard and could live in comparative luxury. It was a strong temptation but Nancy could not bring herself to leave her church. Privation and work brought on her early death in 1863 and Nancy was buried in the small family plot at the upper edge of the cemetery.

Several years later heavy rains and suddenly melting snow on the heights of what is now Zion National Park swelled the Virgin River and all of Duncan's Retreat was washed away, most of the cemetery included. Only the grave of Mrs. Nancy Ferguson Ott, on slightly higher ground, was spared.

DAVID BENTON OTT, son of Nancy Ferguson Ott, migrated to Escalante area after destruction of Duncan's Retreat, and raised large family. In 1940, grandson James R. Ott, fascinated by story of heroic Nancy, determined to mark her grave in permanent way. He and other grandsons erected monument and placed plaque June 8, 1941, occasion marked by large family gathering at site. Lonely marker stands just north of road between Hurricane and Rockville on way to Zion National Park. Descendant Lily Ott Shakespeare researched story not included in annals of Utah.

RED LIGHT SIGNALS

HER BOOTS AND EVERY STITCH — WERE OFF

Julia Bulette

Julia Bulette, Queen of the Red Lights, did not die with her boots on. When her neighbor and friend, Gertrude Holmes, dropped over that Sunday morning to call Julia for breakfast, she found her dead and quite nude. Julia Bulette, respected in spite of her profession, well loved by the men of Virginia City, hated by most of the women, had obviously been brutally murdered. Was it by one of her patrons? The circumstances of the killing, apprehension of the suspected slayer, his trial and subsequent hanging as a public spectacle, had the famous silver camp of Virginia City, Nevada, on its ear for a year and three months.

The town owed its inception to a dramatic discovery of silver on Mount Davidson, east across the Sierra Nevada from where gold was discovered ten years earlier. The California gold rush had ground down to hard work and humdrum living for many, complete disappointment for most, and the argonauts who had flocked to the western foothills of the Sierra in 1849 now poured back over the mountains to the Washoe.

Previous finds of gold in subsidiary canyons of Mount Davidson resulted in the building of clusters of shacks, one of which bore the name of Gold Hill and another later one named Silver City for the newly discovered metal. But when silver was re-

puted to stick out of the ground in solid bars extending for miles in an area farther up the hill, a city sprang up never to be equalled by any other mining camp. It took such a promised land to lure a beautiful courtesan like Julia Bulette away from San Francisco.

Julia was born Jule of a miscegenation in London, England, in 1832. Her negro and white blood provided for a type of beauty unusual in England but commonplace in New Orleans where her family moved while she was still a child. Later, on her own, she went to Weaverville, California (see GHOST TOWN SHADOWS), and then to the brighter lights of San Francisco. When the newspapers of the Bay City ran glaring accounts of the new city on Mount Davidson, Julia took the stage to Virginia City.

A Rothschild representative who tried to interest his firm in financing early operations on the Comstock Lode, failed in his efforts, much to the company's chagrin when the lode began to pour out millions in silver. He did give his name to the mountain on which the city grew and it was the mountain that dictated the street plan and incidentally the location of the prostitutes' cribs.

The main business streets ran roughly north and south, angling slightly from northeast to southwest. The cross streets were so steep that wagon traffic had trouble on them so that most stores, hotels and other businesses faced the more level thoroughfares, named for the letters of the alphabet, at first exclusively on A Street, route of the original lode. As the silver deposit was found to extend downhill, so did the town, the main street becoming C.

This street also became the dividing line between the "upper class section" above and the riffraff below, lightly referred to as "four-bit and two-bit" sections, alluding to the price of drinks. Parades came down this street drawing large crowds in both sections, each on its own side of the street.

Naturally the "frail sisters", like the gambling and dance halls, were banished below C Street but the distance was only a short block, stretching along D Street for some distance at the height of Vir-

GRAVE ENCLOSURE OF JULIA BULETTE was almost intact when Dr. David Mason took this photo about 1950. Wooden headboard, apparently original, was inside at right, had been painted white with black initials "J B" faintly legible. This disproves stories giving headboard lettering as "Jule".

ginia's prosperity, shriveling to part of one block as times grew lean. Most of the houses were mere cubicles, with a bed, a chair or two, small table and space for a trunk which usually doubled as closet and bureau to hold its owner's temporary possessions.

The red light section was considered a necessity, a popular section of town. The men of Virginia City might well have thought they needed such comforts and pseudo touches of home. Their lot in the silver mines was a hard one, shafts extending so deep the heat was next to intolerable. Streams of cold water were played on the crews in some locations and actual working time limited to short periods with alternating spells at a "cooling station" where wet, cold cloths were swabbed over sweating bodies. Houses built for single miners usually afforded only rows of shelves for bunks, bedding being straw and a pair of blankets.

Julia Bulette occupied a crib at the corner of D and Union, her house one of the smaller ones, not equipped for cooking. Next door was the slightly larger cubicle of Julia's friend, Gertrude Holmes, having a small kitchen where Julia took her meals.

Julia's sparkling personality accented her mulatto beauty. She had a friendly greeting for every miner walking home from his shift. She could be depended upon for a sizable contribution to any charity seeking funds. During one of the several disastrous fires Julia took charge of an emergency hospital, nursing any and all casualties. Possibly it was this hospital work that started her popularity with the fire department, one that lasted until her death.

She was elected Queen of Engine 1, Virginia Fire Department, in her early days there and dressed in the regalia of a fire chief. In parades she rode in front of one of the engines and it was said

GRAVE ENCLOSURE re-photographed in 1965 shows few pickets remaining, effects of attrition by vandals, souvenir thieves. In background is famed old silver camp Virginia City. Most conspicuous landmark is St. Mary's In The Mountains, church built in 1877 after two previous structures were destroyed by town's frequent fires. Some of extensive tailing dumps are seen at right and in center are others, new and old, latter continually excavated by bottle collectors.

the silver trumpet she carried was filled with red roses but the source of them was not mentioned. Julia went to the fires too and at mop-up time she hurried coffee and sandwiches to the tired men.

Stories of Julia's love for display may be true — and maybe not. Did she "ride through the streets in a fancy carriage, doors emblazoned with four spread aces"? Zeke Daniels points out in his book on Julia Bulette the newspapers were sensitive to any such goings on and they mention no such performance. What about the truth of a magazine story that the courtesan maintained a large and fancy brothel termed "Julia's Palace"? If she did she must have had a "come-down" at the time of her murder.

Among her friends in the same business were Annie and Lucy Smith in Carson City at the foot of the mountain. On the crisp January 19, 1867, she visited them and upon leaving Annie gave her some jewelry for repair in Virginia, among other pieces a watch of unique design given her by a "boy friend", Henry Monk, a diamond pin and earrings. Julia placed the gems in her trunk with her own, the jewelry store being closed. She had dinner with Gertie, stayed to chat and went to her crib about eleven o'clock. This was Saturday night.

The next morning the man who delivered the

TERRITORIAL ENTERPRISE thought he heard a scream coming from Julia's house. Later in the morning the Chinese "house boy" employed by several of the girls entered the house, built a fire, brought in wood, swept and left, noticing nothing amiss. After that Gertie came to call her friend for breakfast, got no response, concluded Julia was sleeping in after a busy night. She came back later, this time suspicious, and pulled the covers down from the sleeper's face. What she saw made her scream and run for the police.

The body was lying on the left side, feet partially exposed. A pillow covered the face, apparently to silence any outcry. The neck bore marks of fingernails, bed clothes and head saturated with blood. A billet of wood lay near the pile showing particles of wool like the blanket material and on the bed were several splinters apparently from the stick. Conspicuously missing was Julia's small trunk.

Although doctors seemed uncertain as to the cause of death, whether by strangulation or blows on the head, the coroner's jury pronounced the verdict: "We find the deceased was named Jule Bulette, a native of England, aged about thirty-five years, and that she came to her death by strangulation on the 20th day of January, 1867, by the hands of some person or persons unknown to the jury."

Prepared for burial, the body was taken to the station of the Virginia Fire Department, Engine 1, on B Street and the funeral held from there the next day, Monday, at 3 P.M. The Rev. William H. Martin read the service, another departure from normal procedure at the death of a "fallen woman".

A long procession followed the hearse to Flower Hill Cemetery, a burial ground set aside for the regular members of the V.F.D., the line of mourners made up entirely of men led by 60 members of the band. As they passed the houses along the way many window shades were yanked down inside. Returning from the cemetery the band struck up the strains of "The Girl I Left Behind Me."

Although Police Chief W. E. Edwards put his entire force to work to find the murderer there were no developments for months, until one night another girl on the "row," Martha Camp, started

VIRGINIA CITY has been greatly commercialized but old camp still offers much of original to photographers. This view was made with 180mm telephoto lens over heads of thronging tourists.

screaming. She heard a noise in her little room and awoke to see a man with a large knife in his hand. Her lusty screams scared him away but she glimpsed his face and build and several days later saw the man on C Street, able now to give the police a better description. With this, Chief Edwards men brought him in — one Jean Marie Milleian — on charges of attempting to rob Martha Camp.

Now events happened thick and fast. The news of Milleian's arrest made Mrs. Cazentre do some thinking, then go to the police. She and her husband owned a restaurant in nearby Gold Hill and Milleian, who had done some odd jobs for her there, had approached her with some dress goods he wanted to sell. She refused his offer of $60 but bought it later at $40. The fabric was identified by the local dry goods store as an entire lot of a certain color and pattern sold to Julia Bulette.

Other articles belonging to her began to turn up, among them the diamond pin she brought from Annie Smith's to be repaired. It was found in the jewelry shop of Emanuel Nye who said Milleian sold it to him. The most important evidence seemed to be Julia's small trunk hidden in the attic of J. D. Ardaut, a friend of Milleian's who said the man brought it there.

Milleian's trial opened June 26. Henry Monk of Carson City identified the watch he had given to Annie, later found in a pawn shop, left there by the defendant. And Jean Marie Milleian was convicted of murder in the first degree, the man violently protesting he could not properly defend himself due to his lack of familiarity with the English language.

On April 27 of the following year Milleian was hanged in a level area just north of town, the hills supplying a natural amphitheater. The execution was set for noon but people began arriving early, some with lunches. The condemned man was accompanied by Father Patrick Manogue, priest of St. Mary's In The Mountains, two doctors and other personnel. Dropping of the trap was held up while the rope was adjusted, causing the crowd to grow restive, complaining they were hungry. If they brought sandwiches, they broke them out and opened the beer bottles as Milleian jerked convulsively at the end of his rope.

MANY OLD STONES raise more questions than can be answered, as this one. Baby Berry was born in Indiana when glamor of California gold was brightest. Sierra was pouring out golden flood, was generally regarded as El Dorado richer than any known. Could infant have been so named by romantic parents? If father had already departed for nugget-laden foothills in West, would he return with bags of gold dust or empty handed as so many did? And if he made a big strike would he ask: "What is that boy named Hubert for when a name like El Dorado is a better one for a kid worth his weight in gold dust?" Inscription "Gone But Not Forgotten", considered trite today, is actually rare on monuments, this being the only one ever observed by author.

WILLIAMS BOYS SPARK MASSACRE
Williams Station, Nev.

The earliest western-bound Argonauts were glad to see the placid, winding Carson River after the long dry stretch of desert, sighting it first about 30 miles east of where Carson City would later be. Samuel Sanford Buckland and his family were entranced with the stream with the adjacent fertile valley and when they failed to find El Dorado in California's Sierra, they returned to the Carson and settled there, in 1858. Buckland built a substantial ranch house beside the river and nearby a stage stop, hotel and trading post. Here for years crawling ox team caravans halted to partake of the Buckland hospitality.

With the Buckland station established, travel to the Comstock Lode at Virginia City increasing, three Williams brothers—David, James and Oscar— set up another trading post a few miles east of Buckland's and soon became equally successful.

The Paiutes were tolerant of this influx of whites, even friendly at first but friction soon developed. There were no white women about and the younger Williams brothers had eyes for the Indian girls who were always present at the post buying knick-knacks or acting coy. James Williams made the younger two keep their distance but when he was away on one business trip, Oscar and David abducted two Indian maidens and held them captive in their quarters. The girls were returned to the Paiute village and their enraged parents and brothers lost no time in attacking the post, killing the seven men present and leaving all buildings in ashes, some of the victims incinerated inside.

This was war and the whites in the territory sent out a call for volunteers to track down the murderers. 105 men answered the appeal and, gathered at Buckland's, they were separated into four companies, Major William Ormsby of Carson

PYRAMID LAKE, scene of disastrous engagement between Major Ormsby's detachment and Paiutes, is now about 30 miles long, only mere remnant of once huge Lahontan Lake. Water was then, as now, brackish, chemical elements combining with algae forms to make heavy deposits which build up to create tufa islands such as this "monument" standing on dry lake bed bordering present Pyramid Lake.

City placed in command of the "Carson" detachment. At nearby Pyramid Lake he brashly led his troops under the very noses of Indians encamped there and suffered almost total disaster, half the men being killed, Major Ormsby one of the first to fall.

In retaliation the U. S. Army sent a company of seasoned Indian fighters led by Col. Jack Hays, one time Texas Ranger, to the area. They made a concerted attack on the Paiutes at Pyramid Lake and completely routed them, sending them fleeing into the hills.

Soon after, Col. Hays recommended to the War Department that a substantial fort be built on the Carson River to protect this vital section of the immigrant trail. His suggestion was accepted and work began in 1860. Completed, it was named Fort Churchill and the adobe buildings could house 1,000 men, the average complement being around 500. Next year, 1861, Fort Churchill found itself in Nevada Territory, separated from Utah by signature of President Buchanan. That year saw the opening of the Civil War and a quarter of the space at the fort was utilized as recruiting headquarters and to hold Confederate sympathizers.

By 1869 fewer covered wagons were coming through, many travelers riding the newly laid iron rails. The Paiutes had long been made to bow their heads to the white man and Fort Churchill was no longer considered vital. It was abandoned on Sept. 29, 1869 and in 1871 was put on the auction block. Sam Buckland was high bidder, buying all remaining improvements for $750. He removed good roofing material, usable timbers and lumber. Exposed to the elements, the old fort began to melt away, falling into near complete ruin in a few years.

FORT CHURCHILL, established as quarters for soldiers protecting immigrant trail from attacks of Paiute Indians, was built largely of native materials. Adobe bricks were fabricated on spot, timbers for beams cut in nearby Sierra. In 1880 military authorities removed soldier dead from Fort Churchill's cemetery, some bodies reinterred in San Francisco, some at nearby Carson City. Only two were identifiable, one that of Major William Ormsby, slain by Paiutes near their village on Pyramid Lake, the other, Col. Charles McDermit, commanding officer at fort in 1865. He had kept friction with Indians at minimum, fed prisoners well, sent provisions to their families, was lenient in punishment, respected by most Paiutes. His death was ironic, meeting it in an Indian ambush.

Seen through arches formed by remains of officers' quarters are Pine Nut Mountains, higher summits Mineral Peak, Mt. Wilson, Como Peak. Fort, on Fernley-Yerington Highway, is now Nevada State Park. Grounds provide excellent camping sites and adjacent Carson River is full of placid swimming pools.

SAINTS AND SINNERS

"ALL YOU'LL EVER FIND IN THEM THERE
HILLS WILL BE YOUR TOMBSTONE"
Edward L. Schieffelin

Friends of Ed Schieffelin told him he was a fool
to go prospecting in the wild, Indian-infested country hemmed in by the Whetstone, Huachuca and
Dragoon Mountains. Muriel Sibel Wolle, in her
THE BONANZA TRAIL, feels that although Schieffelin did discover the enormously rich metal deposits responsible for the town of Tombstone, the
Apaches should have at least some of the credit.

Most of that part of Arizona was untenable in
1877 but Schieffelin was determined to prospect the
country and prudently made his headquarters at

Fort Huachuca. At first his forays into the hills
were under the protection of the soldiers stationed at
the fort, then when escort was not available and as
he gained knowledge of terrain, he cruised alone. It
was after he returned from one of these trips his
friends warned him: "All you'll ever find in them
there hills will be your tombstone". And when he
found a ledge of silver in August of 1877, he named
the first claim Tombstone and the second one
Graveyard.

Although both claims turned out to be shallow
pockets, two subsequent ones — Lucky Cuss and
Tough Nut — proved to be the foundation for the
most fabulous silver mining camp of all time, Tombstone, Arizona.

NATURAL GARDEN of desert
plants surrounds Schieffelin monument. Most conspicuous when in
bloom is **Yucca filamentosa,** blossoms of which are shown here.
Seldom seen at such close range,
flowers are placed on ten-foot
stems usually swaying in slightest
breeze. Thirty odd varieties of
yucca grow in U.S., half of these
in Southwest, species including un-
gainly Joshua Trees whose lily-
like blooms prove plant's mem-
bership in order of **Lilicacae.**
Yucca flowers require reciprocal
partnership with tiny moth, **Pro-
muba Yuccasella,** for successful
pollination, moth requiring blos-
som for survival of progeny. Tiny
insect emerges from pupa at
ground level when yucca flowers
are ready. Moth gathers ball of
pollen from several blossoms,
pushes it down against selected
bloom's ovary, unreachable for
fertilization by any other method.
At same time moth deposits egg
within ovary emerging grub later
consuming some of seeds resulting from pollenation, leaving
many for future germination. Full
grown larva drops to ground to
pupate, later emerging to repeat
natural cycle.

TRUNCATED CONE OF HUGE GRANITE BOULDERS stands among jumble of larger ones marking grave of famous prospector who found rich silver mines that gave rise to town of Tombstone. At base of unique monument is plaque reading: "Edward L. Schieffelin. Died May 12, 1897. Aged 49 years, 8 months. A dutiful son, a faithful husband, a kind brother, a true friend." Nearby is sign pleading respect for isolated and unprotected grave site.

THE SINNERS

JOHN HEATH and five others — Don Dowd, Red Sample, Tex Howard, Bill DeLaney, Dan Kelley — were accused of committing robbery and murder in Bisbee, all standing trial in Tombstone. Heath went up first and although acknowledged ringleader of gang, was convicted of second degree murder only. Next morning his body dangled from a telegraph pole a short distance from jail. Dan Dowd was tried that day, attorney for prosecution telling jury: "Consider carefully what happened last night before you render another such verdict." And the jury did consider, convicting Dowd and others of murder in first degree, all hanging together on one scaffold in courthouse yard.

MEMBERS OF "COWBOY FACTION" who were killed in famous fight at O. K. Corral. Surname of brothers Tom and Frank has been spelled as McLowery, here, McLowry as in newspapers of the day and McLaury as family is said to have used it. Originally three tall crosses stood on graves, poles once serving as uprights to support oil lamps on streets of Tombstone.

M. R. PEEL, mining engineer employed by Tombstone Mining and Milling Co., was sitting in his office at Millville when two masked men threw open door and fired two shots at him, one slug entering his body. Two suspects were located and city officer John Gillespie sent to arrest them, one suspect, Zwing Hunt, shooting him in the head. Retribution struck other suspect, William Grounds, when an officer blasted his face away. Wounded in same fracas, Hunt was taken to Tombstone jail, recovered and later escaped.

A STAIRWAY TO HELL—SPIRAL FIRE ESCAPE winds down Cochise County Courthouse wall into yard where many convicted men were hanged in turbulent years of Tombstone. Among victims of gallows were members of John Heath gang, leader having been lynched previously from telegraph pole. Courthouse was second in Tombstone, replacing older one in 1882, period of greatest number of killings.

TOMBSTONE'S CHINATOWN is represented in old Boot Hill cemetery by such names as Foo Kee, who owned a grocery and died of ptomaine poisoning; by Sung Wan and Quong Kee who ran a restaurant in the 1880s which thrived, then failed because generous proprietor could not turn down plea for free meal. Dying destitute Quong was buried in pauper's plot but those whom he had fed removed body to be near friends and countrymen. His grave is next to that of Mrs. Ah Lun, reputed to have had connections with powerful tong in China.

THE SAINTS

SCENE IN SANCTUARY of spectacular mission church, San Xavier del Bac near Tucson, Arizona. At upper left is figure representing the Christ wearing robe of rich red velvet. Below is replica of body of San Xavier, patron saint of Father Kino, who is buried in Golaghat, India.

At right is figure of St. Bonaventure. Plaster mouldings and paintings covering almost every square inch of walls and ceilings were conceived by Spanish artists in mode of period, largely executed by Indians. Figures have vividness and lack of subtlety characteristic of primitive workers. Construction of edifice, started in early 1700s, was not finished until 1797. Dedication was held in that year, many furnishings and ornaments being those brought by Father Kino.

OLD CEMETERY dating back to time church construction was begun in 1796, where missionaries buried many Christian Indians. Original burial records show some of these were slain by Apaches. All these graves were completely obliterated by milling cattle after church was abandoned and cemetery walls used as corral fence. Present mounds and crosses date from "modern" period between 1880 and 1905, one exception being grave of little Juanita Alegria who died at age of 9 months on Sept. 12, 1916. In 1939 baby girl's family built little monument shown here and each year on All Souls' Day Nov. 2, some member of family has placed flowers on grave. Cemetery walls bear at least two clusters of bullet holes, apparently made by .45 cal. gun, although holes have been enlarged by people digging out slugs. Tradition holds these were results of execution but no defiinte evidence supports this. Tree at left in exceptionally large mesquite.

CIRCULAR MORTUARY CHAPEL in rear of old Tumacacori Mission Church. It is believed structure served as place for bodies while religious ceremonies were consummated. Night long vigil usually preceded funeral next day. Chapel was never completed nor was main building. Apparently dome was planned for chapel but was not built, plastering not completed. Broken brick fragments were worked into walls possibly to provide bonding surface for plaster. Since much bare adobe surface was exposed and deteriorating, modern surfacing has been applied for protection. Top of main structure dome is shown in photo but not visible is line of built-in steps to permit access to lantern which was lighted at night.

TOTTERING WOODEN CROSSES seen in near-silhouette against sunset sky. Dos Cabezas has turbulent history as mining camp and stage stop. During negotiations ending in Gadsden Treaty and Purchase, Capt. Richard Stoddard Elwell and army unit camped at spring near this area in 1852 and "Elwell's Spring" became stopping place for first stage line. It was soon wiped out by Apaches, later reestablished only to suffer same fate again, setting pattern for early history of town.

ELABORATE CROSS may seem grotesque but does express certain medieval character which may have been designer's aim. Hand made of heavy zinc, cross was erected in 1901 according to almost obliterated marks at base, identity of person beneath lost in faded inscription. Old metal workers say zinc is "tricky to work with. If you get your soldering iron too hot it goes right through the metal". This particular art disappeared shortly after turn of century.

CEMETERY SYMMETRY
BEAUTIFULLY ORNATE example of wrought iron art is silhouetted against fading daylight in old cemetery in early Arizona town of Patagonia. All identifying marks are gone. Burial ground, neglected and filled with thorny brush and dead grass for many years has been improved in past year.

CRUDE BUT DISTINCTIVE GRAVE MARKER in Harshaw near from lead and silver ore are embedded in face of monument, Mexican border has several unique features. Pyrite crystals glittering in Arizona sunshine. Candelabra is placed inside, no doubt for use on night preceding All Saints' Day, Nov. 1, when many Catholics, especially those of Latin origin, place lighted candles on graves of relatives.

When Dr. Mason and this author walked across arroyo to little weedy cemetery at Harshaw they were accompanied by bright-eyed Mexican urchin and his three boisterous dogs. Imaginative boy reached hand up into miniature "belfry" and shook tiny, tinkling bell with this bi-lingual explanation: "The Father, he rings the bell every morning for Mass."

...FOR HIM THE BELL TINKLES

METAL MARKER, made of pipe and a steel plate, carries tantalizing, almost-readable inscription — the most nearly legible one in Ehrenberg's old Boot Hill cemetery. Historic town on Arizona side of Colorado River has almost vanished except for few pitiful remnants of adobe buildings. Faded and cacti-grown cemetery is most tangible remnant of once rip-roaring town.

Nell Murbarger, in her definitive book about Arizona's old mining camps, **Ghosts of the Adobe Walls,** says of this graveyard: "Saint and sinner, slayer and slain, most of those interred here died by violence. Here were bandits fallen before the guns of lawmen, peace officers slain by outlaws, desperados killed by their own confederates. Here were laid teamsters, stage drivers, ranchers and prospectors dry-gulched by hostile Indians, men trampled to death by wild mustangs, men drowned beneath the gray waters of the Colorado, men shot to death over card games and fickle dance hall girls. Ehrenberg, in the 1870s provided many avenues by which one might acquire six feet of space in Boot Hill."

OLD CEMETERY at edge of Dos Cabezas, Arizona, is crowded with victims of violent days when camp was subjected to Apache raids every few weeks, men killed in mines, young and old citizens succumbing to "plagues" often undiagnosed. Possibly this beautiful example of weathered wooden headboard marks grave of one of latter, a soon-to-disappear monument "IN MEMORY OF THE LITTLE GIRL", only 11 years old. Name of almost totally deserted mining camp —Dos Cabezas, meaning two heads — becomes significant to visitor when he notes mountains crowding close, nearest and most conspicuous crowned by pair of granite knobs.

Grave and board are beautified by exuberant growth of "Paradise Poinciana" or "Bird-of-Paradise", properly **Poinciana gillesii.** Shrub is straggling, unsymmetrical, but bears profusion of spectacular blossoms with yellow petals centered by cluster of brilliant red filament-like stamens. Related to more tree-like Royal Poinciana, this plant is adjusted to arid conditions in Southwest deserts.

WHEN "TAOS LIGHTNING" STRUCK

THE GOVERNOR WAS SCALPED

Gov. Charles Bent

He had just been appointed as the first governor of the new Territory of New Mexico in 1847 and hardly had time to take office when the fiery Mexican rebels broke into his home. Others of the family escaped but Gov. Bent fell victim to the mob. The insurrection foundered the next day and Taos was saved from chaos.

Taos, pronounced to rhyme with house, is actually a rather closely knit group of several communities stemming from a bloody past. There was the Spanish town—Don Fernando de Taos—and the Indian pueblo—San Geronimo de Taos—and the old Indian farming center—Ranchos de Taos. Postal clerks struggled doggedly to sort mail for this confusion of points until in 1884 a young official appealed to Washington to straighten things out.

This was partially accomplished by making the post office designation simply Taos, retaining Fernando Taos for legal purposes. By then the group of towns had existed in various forms for 344 years, Hernando de Alvarado having found a flourishing Indian village on the site in 1540. Near this pueblo other Spanish people settled in the 17th century.

The two villages, Indian and Spanish, might have grown together but too much togetherness between Spanish boys and Indian girls was causing trouble around 1610. A delegation of black-haired natives made a demand on the Alcalde of the Spanish section to make his people move a "league away," and they did put seven miles between town and pueblo.

Friar Pedro de Miranda built a little adobe church at the edge of the pueblo in 1617 but in disagreements between the two factions in 1631 the priest and two Spanish soldiers were killed, the first recorded deaths by violence in Taos. Ill feeling mounted. One Indian attempt to abolish the Spanish in 1650 failed but in 1680 the Indians led by Tewa Indian medicine man Pope successfully expelled all Spanish settlers, killing many and suffering some casualties themselves. In 1692 General De Vargas marched up the Rio Grande and re-established the settlement, again at the cost of blood on both sides.

Then came a succession of attacks from marauding Utes, Comanches, Apaches and Navajos, culminating in 1760 in a Comanche raid on Taos, killing men and carrying away 50 women and children. Soldiers overtook the Indians and slaughtered 400 of them to end the forays although other tribes continued sporadic attacks.

When Thomas Jefferson signed the Louisana Purchase bill, causing the center of the country to become part of the United States, American trappers and "mountain men" began coming through this part of the Southwest. One of these travelers, "just going through," was Ewing Young who was to settle later near Champoeg, acquire an estate and start meetings to establish law and order in Oregon. Ewing did not "go through" Taos until he met an attractive Indian woman and father a son named Joaquin. He left then to eventually aid in making the Oregon country a part of the United States.

During these years Padre Antonio Jose Martinez started a school for boys and girls, the first co-educational one in the Southwest. He also printed the first newspaper in New Mexico—El Crepusculo—on a press imported from Chihuahua, Mexico, the same one which figured in local politics in Cimarron, N. M. and came to a sad end in the Cimarron River.

In 1837 the Alcalde was arrested and imprisoned by the Mexican government at Santa Fe. Enraged, Taos Indians marched to the capitol, surprising authorities into promising to elect a Taos Indian as governor. Almost immediately a Santa Fe politician, Manuel Armijo, shot and killed the Taos official, claiming the governorship for himself.

In May of 1846, U. S. President Polk declared war against Mexico, announcing plans to invade New Mexico, Chihuahua and California. General Kearney, invading enemy territory through Raton Pass, took Las Vegas without resistance, then occupied Santa Fe. On Sept. 22 he organized New Mexico as an American territory and appointed Charles Bent as first governor. Bent had lived in New Mexico since 1826, was a partner in the largest fur trading company in the Southwest. He had always liked Taos and now established a home there, being in residence in January of 1847.

With Kearney moving toward California for further conquest, Mexicans in New Mexico set about to disrupt the hated American occupation. The revolutionary spirit flared out with a vengeance, homes of the American officials in Taos burned and most all killed. Gov. Bent was saved for special treatment. Guards were placed around his home to prevent escape while the Mexican attackers waited for reinforcements from the Indians of the pueblo. When they arrived they were given drinks of a fiery brand of locally made brandy aptly called Taos Lightning. At a signal Indians and Mexicans swarmed into Bent's home. During the seige the governor's family and servants were frantically digging into the soft adobe wall separating the house from its adjoining neighbor and at the last minute squeezed through a hole. Gov. Bent delayed too long and was seized by the drunken invaders. The mob leader whipped out a knife, carved a circle in his scalp, removed a piece with lock of hair attached and the howling marauders took turns plunging knives into his body.

When news of the massacre reached Santa Fe, authorities sent 350 soldiers to Taos. They surrounded the town, firing on Indians and Mexicans who had gathered in the church for sanctuary. On the next day the entire population surrendered. Taos would be peaceful at last.

INTERIOR OF CHURCH, photographed in available light, shows heavy hand-carved roof beams or vigas and simple altar also adorned by carvings. Tall painting of Jesus on Shores of Galilee at left is famous for luminosity when church is darkened. After eyes adjust to darkness painting shows background of garden in Gethsemane, Jesus appearing to bear heavy cross over right shoulder.

Phenomenon is unexplained although painting has been subjected to tests for common explanations such as accumulated luminescence, radium in paint, etc. Painted before turn of century by Henry Ault, study of Master was shown at St. Louis World's Fair in 1906 and Dore Galleries in London. Mrs. H. S. Griffin purchased it from U. S. art dealer and presented it to mission church.

OLD INDIAN MISSION of St. Francis de Assisi at Ranchos de Taos, N.M., started in 1772, is oldest unrestored structure of kind in state. Old adobe edifice is kept in repair by annual coat of clay mud. Indians make big fiesta of event, build scaffolds around walls — 10 feet thick at supporting corners — spread on gooey mixture, covering all small cracks before they can develop into larger, water-carrying ones.

Hard work is ended in evening by barbecue, fiesta, dancing. Church and grounds are scene of many other celebrations, especially in Christmas season, involving night processions by candle light, Indian dances around bonfire. Grounds within protecting adobe walls are solidly filled with graves of priests, Indians, some markers remaining but most wooden ones rotted away.

THE ROUGHER ELEMENT

JUVENILE DELINQUENT WITH A GUN
Billy the Kid

"He came directly towards me. Before he reached the bed I whispered: 'Who is it, Pete?' but received no reply for a moment. . . The intruder came close to me, leaned both hands on the bed, right hand almost touching my knee, and asked in a low tone: 'Who are they, Pete?' . . . at the same instant Maxwell whispered to me: 'That's him!' Simultaneously the Kid must have seen or felt the presence of a third person at the foot of the bed. He raised quickly a pistol, a self-cocker, within a foot of my breast. Retreating rapidly across the room he cried: 'Quien es? Quien es?' All this occurred in a moment. Quickly as possible I drew my revolver and fired, threw my body aside and fired again. The second shot was useless. The Kid fell dead. He never spoke. A struggle or two, a little strangling sound as he gasped for breath, and the Kid was with his many victims."

Well established seem to be the facts of Billy the Kid's death. The above account of it is chronicled in Pat Garrett's book—THE AUTHENTIC LIFE OF BILLY THE KID. Not so clear is the story of that life which has been subjected to many controversies. How many persons did he shoot? Where did he shoot them? And when? Even the account written by his slayer, Pat Garrett (or ghost writer Asa Upson) has been attacked for veracity. Even more questioned are events occurring after he was shot in Peter Maxwell's bedroom at Fort Sumner, N.M. Extensive research and much help from historians Ed Bartholomew of Toyahvale, Texas, and Phillip Cooke of Santa Fe, N.M. have exposed some fascinating details about the grave of the infamous Billy.

Garrett's "ball" struck him just above the heart and "must have cut through the ventricles", Garrett declared in print. On the following morning the alcalde (mayor judge) held an inquest on the body. The jury found a verdict that William H. Bonney had come to his death by gunshot wound from a weapon in the hands of Sheriff Pat Garrett, the homicide being justifiable. "The body was neatly and properly dressed," said Garrett, "and buried in the Military Cemetery at Fort Sumner, July 15, 1881. His exact age at death was 21 years, 7 months and 21 days."

Not mentioned by Garrett was the fact that while the demise of the bandit brought sighs of relief to lawmen, jailers and cattle owners throughout New Mexico and western Texas, the killing was not a popular one. The Kid had many admirers who felt he was unjustly persecuted, hunted down and killed. And they said so, even attempting to sue Garrett for outright murder. As Billy's body lay on a wooden bench in the Maxwell house overnight, all the women and most of the men employees of the establishment kept up a wailing demonstration, some of the women throwing themselves on the body.

In the next few years many reports circulated that this or the other grog shop or side show had

PALS
TOM. O'FOLLIARD DIED DEC. 1880
WILLIAM H. BONNEY ALIAS "BILLY THE KID" DIED JULY 1[...]
CHARLIE BOWDRE DIED DEC. 1880

MONUMENT popularly supposed to mark last resting place of three of New Mexico's "most wanted" bandits in center of old military cemetery of Fort Sumner. Fence protecting stone makes photography difficult. After wait of 2 hours for proper, glancing light, camera and tripod were leaned against fence, lens pushed through widest opening in mesh. Location of burial ground and entirely vanished Fort Sumner are several miles from town of same name. Many small coins lie scattered on ground and base of monument, tossed there by tourists.

on display the skull, fingers or other bones of the Kid. One claimed to be exhibiting the entire skeleton. Some even claimed that Garrett had prevented the actual burial and sold the remains to the highest bidder. Stung into action to disprove such accusations, Garrett opened the bandit's grave. "I wish to say," he wrote, "the body is there intact. Skull, fingers, toes, bones and every hair of his head that was buried with the body on that 15th day of July, doctors, newspapers and editors notwithstanding." He added that there could be many skeletons on display, all claiming to be that of Billy Bonney. "The banks of the Pecos from Fort Sumner to the Rio Grande are dotted with unmarked graves and skeletons of all sizes, ages and complexion. Any showman or ghastly curiosities can resurrect one or all of them and place them on exhibition as the remains of those of Billy the Kid. Again I say that the Kid's body lies undisturbed in the grave, and I speak of what I know."

About two years after the Kid's burial, January 16, 1882, the LAS VEGAS OPTIC carried this story. "The Bivouac of the Dead. A visit to an old burying ground at Fort Sumner. To the southwest of the abandoned and decaying Fort Sumner lies the grave yard surrounded by what was once an adobe wall, but from decay and neglect it is now only an outline around an acre of ground. We enter on the north, walking through the remains of a once handsome gate. To the left, in the northeast corner, are the graves of four rustlers, Grant, killed by Billy the Kid; Ferris, who was killed by Barney Mason at the instance of the Kid; O'Folliard and Bowdre, who were killed by Pat Garrett and posse. These graves are all unmarked and that of Bowdre shows the scratching of some hungry coyote who seems to have been scared away by something before he reached his prey.

"To the right of the entrance lies the grave of Billy the Kid marked by a plain board with the stenciled letters BILLY THE KID. It snowed last night, and the only marks on the grave were the

UNIQUE MONUMENT to fabulous pioneer, Lucien Bonaparte Maxwell and that of son Peter, about 25 feet apart, are likely in original situations, although author's surmise is that while Peter's stone is contemporary with time of his death, elder Maxwell's was placed much later.

PETER MAXWELL, born at Cimarron, original headquarters of Maxwell empire, disdained by father as "weak, profligate, unmanly", nevertheless inherited large estate including rambling adobe house father bought from army when Fort Sumner was abandoned. When notorious Kid was shot while visiting Maxwell in latter's bedroom, Maxwell fled outside trailing covers after him.

tracks of a skunk or rabbit. The southwest part of the cemetery is filled with the graves of soldiers who were killed in the fight with Indians near the Fort, as the few legible headboards all read July 7, 1866. Over in the southwest corner lies the grave of Lucien B. Maxwell, once so famous in New Mexico. . .”

Not long after, a drunken cowboy lassoed the headboard on the grave of Billy, dragging it away. Then the Pecos River, on one of its periodic rampaging floods carried away all wooden headboards (along with most of the adobe walls of the fort itself.). Another interval of a few years passed quietly over the ravaged cemetery. Then the U.S. Army moved in and made an effort to locate all the graves of soldiers buried there, finding many bones by a somewhat haphazard search because of complete absence of markers. They were reburied in an honored place in the National Cemetery at Santa Fe.

Many more years passed over the lonely cemetery. Automobiles began to chug their way along the highways and some of them stopped, tourists searching in vain for the headboard marking the grave of the famous Billy the Kid. They asked the owner of the adjoining property about it but he did not know where it was. More tourists came, asked him and finally in the early 1940s, tired of shaking his head, the property owner had a monument of black stone carved with the names of Billy, O'Folliard and Bowdre and placed in the center of the cemetery. Tourists came to stare, happily chipped away pieces of stone for souvenirs and went away with their hearts lifted—all but one who carried off the whole monument. It was then the present one was placed—a huge stone, much too heavy to remove but still subject to the picks and chisels of tourists. To thwart them the handsome stone was deromanced by enclosing it with heavy wire fence.

WHITE OAKS, N.M. (see **Ghost Town Album**) was favorite hang-out and rustling headquarters of Billy the Kid and gang. Street between adobe ruins and old bank building shown here often resounded to hoof beats of the Kid's horse.

IN THE BACKGROUND,
CHRISTIAN ENDEAVOR

MOST SPECTACULAR MINE in silver-rich Lake Valley was "room" lined with silver ore so rich rail spur line ran into it for direct loading. This one stope alone yielded $3 million. Accidents were frequent in shafts and tunnels, fatalities numbering several every month during period of greatest activity. Part of mine dump shows in left background of photo. Little false-front building visible in background just left of monument is one-time rooming house remodeled as non-denominational church by Christian Endeavor ladies (see story in **Ghost Town Album**).

Organization fenced cemetery, placed foot-thick slabs of concrete on some graves to foil digging coyotes. Buried here is George Lufkin, discoverer of silver deposits, his pauper's grave unmarked. Although Lufkin and partner sold original mine for $100,000, he died penniless, was buried by county. Only pretentious monument, with marble shaft surmounted by sculptured urn, center, marks plot of silver-wealthy Sherman family.

WOODEN CROSS surmounting this enclosure is well designed, glimpse between palings showing real masterpiece inside. Many graves in southwestern states were enclosed by fences as protection from digging animals, roaming livestock. Wrought iron fences as in Genoa, Nevada, seem non-existent here. Pine from nearby mountains is used for palings, split or sawed.

CARVED MARKER indicating beauty of conception and craftsmanship. Cross is nearest to "Formee" type, reminiscent of Maltese but with flattened ends and defies accurate classification.

SLAB OF ROCK, hacked out, faced and inscribed by hand. 36-year-old Fortunato Pezani of Italy lived in one of largest segregated sections of Dawson, N.M., an Italian colony hemmed in by nationalistic groups of Slavs, Greeks, Portuguese and other southern Europe types. Scandinavians and other workers of north Europe were less well represented.

Coal mines of New Mexico were particularly sensitive to catastrophe, Dawson possibly holding record. In one explosion 263 men were lost. Mine company had policy of paying $1500 compensation to each widow, adding $200 for each minor dependent. Also company provided uniform markers for graves of victims — white metal crosses (see **Ghost Town Treasures**). Families of some spurned uniformity, devised, manufactured, carved or wrought individual markers, some of much beauty, all distinctive.

GOLD! GOLD! THE CLARION CALL

LAST HOME IN A GOLD CAMP

Of 200 persons buried in this old graveyard in 1863, it is said only 28 died natural deaths. During this period Idaho City swarmed with thieves, highway men and murderers. Placer mining was at its height, Moore's and Grimes Creeks especially were yellow with gold nuggets. Some men panned the gravels, others got rich in easier ways by theft, force or gambling.

1863, it is said that only 28 died natural causes. During this period Idaho City swarmed with thieves, highway men and murderers. Placer mining was at its height, Moore's and Grimes Creeks especially were yellow with gold nuggets. Some men panned the gravels, others got rich in easier ways by theft, force or gambling.

On one occasion three road agents waylaid the daily stage as it swung around the bend near the confluence of Moore's and Grimes Creeks. In stunned surprise the messenger in charge of the strong box holding $90,000 in gold dust and nuggets handed it over without a murmur. Yet he had the last laugh — or did he?.

Aware of a short cut he turned the stage around and drove up a parallel and shorter canyon which intersected the robbers' route. When the three galloped into range of the messenger's waiting gun all were blasted from their horses. The gold? It was not found on their bodies and a diligent search of the short stretch of road taken by the bandits failed to reveal a trace of it.

GRAVE OF JOSEPH M. KELLEY. Born in 1827, Kelley was mucking gravel at 24 in the streams flowing seaward from the High Sierra, one of the Argonauts who left comfortable homes in the east for the California gold fields. When fortune eluded him here, itchy feet took him hither and yon to wherever he heard the clarion call of "Gold! Gold!" About 1860 he found better luck in the Boise Basin in Idaho but died before he could fully enjoy his gains and was buried in the Idaho City Cemetery in 1869. Since then this large Ponderosa pine has grown up inside enclosure completely wrecking marker. Stone monument has replaced original wooden headboard.

HEARSE HOUSE. Muriel Sybell Wolle reports in her book, **The Bonanza Trail:** "Across from the Joss House is Sampson's Livery Stable, a big red, barnlike structure, built in 1864. Silver had many livery barns in its busy days but in this one a hearse was kept 'ready for a fast run to the mines'. Many a time it returned with a mutilated body crushed in some stope or shaft.

SILVER CITY'S OLD CEMETERY was so close to center of town that white marble slabs and wooden headboards were clearly visible from all windows facing Slaughterhouse Gulch. People used to say first 20 men buried there were victims of gun play or other violence. Masons (Silver City had first Masonic Hall in Idaho) and Odd Fellows were buried in proper section at one side, non-affiliated next, then gamblers, saloon habitues and females termed "soiled doves" and in graves perched on very edge of gulch were numerous Chinese.

AND THEN THERE WERE NONE
Al Green, Jim Hayden, Don Coombs
and two others

Dan Coombs was one of a group of freighters captured by a band of roving Nez Perce Indians and held captive. Drunk from whiskey found in the wagons, the Indians were whooping it up, squaws jabbing the freighters with hot brands from the camp fire. Coombs took all of that he could and yelled: "The next squaw that pokes me is going to get this bull whip over her ears!" And when another burning stick was thrust in his face he brought the full weight of the loaded whip butt down on the woman's head. She dropped to the ground and the braves closed in on the almost defenseless white men.

It was the freighters' bad luck to be caught in the tribal hostilities of the Nez Perce War which exploded first in the White Bird area, then into more of Idaho. The Lemhi Range in the eastern part of the state runs in a northwest to southeast direction. Parallel to it runs the Beaverhead Range, forming the Continental Divide and boundary between Idaho and Montana. The long, narrow valley between the two ranges is split by a low, inconspicuous divide. The Lemhi River flows north from this division to join the Salmon at Salmon City, Birch Creek going south to sink into extensive lava beds along with Big Lost River. These streams supposedly proceed on southward under the tumbled lava to reappear at Thousand Springs near Hagerman. The valley of the Lemhi River and Birch Creek was the scene of some of the bitterest fighting of the Nez Perce War.

On an expedition to quell some of the uprisings here Gen. Howard and troops arrived at Bannack, Montana, on August 13, 1877. The main band of Nez Perce was 125 miles ahead on fresh horses, their destination uncertain. Howard recruited a company of scouts led by Alex Cruikshank to find

MONUMENT TO MASSACRED FREIGHTERS stands at west side of Highway 28 about 18 miles north of Terreton, Idaho, erected by Sheehan's Welding Co. of Idaho Falls and Du Bois Lions Club. There is a large turnoff at the spot, complete with litter barrels. Birch Creek runs alongside the shrubs in background and turnoff gives access to dozens of beautiful camping sites on stream. Area would be thronged with fishermen if less remote from centers of population. Mountain in background, part of Lemhi Range, received fresh sprinkling of snow overnight while photographer camped to get morning sunlight on it and monument.

out where the Indians were headed, whether the Salmon River, Medicine Lodge trail or Birch Creek trail, so Howard's men could head them off.

Cruikshank's men left Bannack on August 14, crossed the pass and headed down Agency Creek to the Lemhi River where they met Col. Shoup with 15 cavalry troopers. Five of the colonel's mule teams loaded with merchandise from Corinne, Utah Territory, were ahead making for Idaho Falls. When Shoup learned that a large party of Nez Perce might be in the Birch Creek valley, he was worried about his teams being ambushed.

The combined parties pushed on up the Lemhi and to the low pass near where Leadore is now. Not far from this point they learned from a band of 14 Bannocks that the Nez Perce had camped nearby and were aiming for Birch Creek. Now thoroughly alarmed for the safety of Col. Shoup's goods teams, Cruikshank reported: "Now we were sure the hostiles were headed for the Birch Creek crossing. We sent Dempsey, Turner and Sperry back to Bannack to inform Gen. Howard of what we had learned. We had proceeded only a short distance when we met two Chinamen, one a doctor, who could hardly speak coherently. However they made us understand the Nez Perce had attacked Col. Shoup's freight outfit the night before at Birch Creek. The two Chinese who were traveling with the freighters could hardly describe the massacre. We concluded that all had been killed except possibly one man, Al Lyons, who was

dressed in buckskin clothing like a wagon scout. They thought he had escaped."

Cruikshank's party pushed on somewhat ahead of Shoup's, which group had been reduced to Dave Woods and Billy Price, and arrived at the scene of the massacre first to find the wagons burned to ashes and nearby two of the freighters' bodies—Jim Hayden and Dan Coombs. The Indians had sorted through the merchandise, taken what they wanted and scattered the rest in every direction. When Shoup and his men came up with pack horses, supplies and shovels, the search produced the remains of Al Green in the creek where he had evidently been shot. Col. Shoup noticed a gathering of magpies farther up the creek and found there another freighter's body. Still another with $50 in the watch pocket was discovered some ten feet from where Green had fallen, his identity unknown. Al Lyons was missing and it was assumed he got away.

All the men died putting up a desperate fight. Hayden's gun was broken, hand still clutching the bent barrel. Dan Coombs still held his whip, the heavy loaded butt covered with blood and hair. One of the unidentified held a blood-covered axe. Cruikshank, Shoup and their men buried the bodies and returned to Salmon City.

When the two Chinese were calmed they were able to fill in some missing details of the tragedy. About 60 Nez Perce had surrounded the wagon train, holding the freighters in a knot while they searched for whiskey. They found a partially filled

BIRCH CREEK winds briskly along nearly level banks, is lined with poplars, willows, sagebrush. Banks are like lawns, grass closely cropped by range cattle. Area varies in elevation from 5000 to 6000 feet, temperatures cool, water of stream frigid. Freighter Al Lyons and two Chinamen had numbing experience in creek hiding from murdering Nez Perce.

keg and emptied it, putting the Chinese to work cooking food. Demanding more whiskey, the Indians grew rougher until Lyons, thinking they might drink themselves into a stupor, told them where they could find a full keg. But the more they drank the more vicious they became and one of the Chinamen was forced to his hands and knees and ridden by a brave who used the queue for reins. Then Coombs brained a squaw and all hell broke loose. Hayden fired once then used the gun as a club until he was beaten senseless. All the white men were finally killed except Lyons who submerged himself in the stream and lay unobserved. The Chinese also got in the water with only their noses above it. After they had burned the wagons the Indians plundered the merchandise and mutilated Hayden's body. When they rode off the Chinamen staggered in one direction, Lyons heading for Challis. His story of being without water for three days, no food for seven and of hiding in a cow's skeleton, was all but unbelievable to the people of Challis who considered him demented.

GRAVES OF REV. HENRY and wife, Eliza Spalding at historic Idaho site near Indian agency at Lapwai bearing their name. In 1836 the Spaldings made settlement here and exerted good influence on Nez Perce, establishing first school and church in Idaho, planting first seeds, building first grist mill and operating first printing press. Nearby is site of old Lapwai Mission, commemorated by 18-ton boulder and plaque at bridge over Clearwater River, same spot where Lewis and Clark pulled canoes up on bank to barter with Nez Perce.

FIRST ACTUAL BATTLE between military and Nez Perce in Idaho was brought on by Indian atrocities incited by encroachment of whites. On June 14, 1877 savages killed two settlers, carried off Mrs. John Manuel, killed John Chamberlain and raped his wife. They removed the tongue of the little Chamberlain girl and crushed her younger brother's skull — bloody deeds done without sanction of young Chief Joseph who was away taking care of his wife in childbirth.

Army detachment found guilty Nez Perce camped in White Bird Canyon, delayed on rim overnight and rode down into rolling valley next morning. Battle resulted in complete rout by Indians, soldiers chased back to canyon rim leaving 35 dead.

Years later when highway up tortuous hill was constructed, graders uncovered bones of one soldier and grave was made at edge of road just north of village of White Bird. From this point road winds steeply with many precarious sharp turns long considered one of most hazardous in state. Planned new one will ease grade, blunt turns.

JANE SILCOTT, buried under this elaborate tomb, on hill overlooking Clearwater River and Lewiston, Ida., was Nez Perce Indian girl of 16 who nursed wounded soldiers of Col. Steptoe's command when defeated by her father, Chief Timothy, and his braves. Later she guided goldseeking party of Capt. E. D. Pierce through Nez Perce lands when Chief Timothy refused, fearing uprisings and reprisals against his family. After death of her half-breed Nez Perce husband and her son, she married Virginian John Silcott who operated ferry across Clearwater at Ragtown, which became Lewiston. She clung to some Indian customs such as cooking over an open fire and burned to death, Silcott erecting handsome memorial. His own modest resting place is the little heap of stones alongside. (From Here Rolled the Covered Wagons: Albert and Jane Salisbury.)

BERNARD DE VOTO, native of Utah, transplanted to Cambridge, Mass. was outspoken, "terrible tempered" editor of **Harper's** for many years, Pulitzer Prize winner in historical writing in 1947. He was said to be at his best in this field, though being quoted as hating "detail and research of facts." De Voto admired such authors as Mark Twain about whom he was an authority and Stewart Holbrook whom he considered "mentor of western history." He often voiced loud criticism of communities for neglecting historical sites, in 1945 printing severe scolding of State of Washington for what he considered "unforgivable neglect" of site of Whitman mission and massacre—"an eyesore and disgrace". Oregon also felt lash for lack of care in preserving spots connected with over-winter camp of Lewis and Clark party. Student of that expedition, De Voto spent much time studying related manuscripts in peaceful surroundings of grove beside Lochsa River, actual site of portion of Lewis and Clark trail. Because of attachment to spot, De Voto expressed wish for cremation at death and that ashes be scattered among trees beside river. He collapsed at end of fiery broadcast for Columbia Broadcasting Co. in New York, Nov. 13, 1955, was pronounced dead at Presbyterian Hospital. Next year plans were pushed for establishing memorial beside Lochsa for De Voto, sponsored by the late senator from Oregon, Richard L. Neuberger. Records of rites, appearing in **Congressional Record,** included statement: "He understood fully how the West was being exploited and debauched."

AND THEY LEFT HIM TO THE SNOW
George Colgate

William Carlin was emphatic. He would never have hired Colgate had he known the man was subject to a chronic, recurring disease which caused his legs to swell and become unusable. And it was one of these attacks that brought about George Colgate's death in the mountains.

Young William Carlin had been planning a fall hunting trip for months in 1893. He selected Spokane, Washington, as a meeting place convenient for all men of the party which included his brother-in-law John Pierce and a friend L. A. Himmelwright who was coming from the east. Martin Spencer would serve as guide as he was familiar with the hunting grounds in the wild country of the upper Lochsa River at the summit of the Bitterroots in Idaho. Carlin interviewed several men who wanted to cook for the party and hired George Colgate, the

50-year-old father of seven children, well known as a mountain man, expert trapper and cook.

Horses, supplies, guns and equipment were shipped by train to the railroad terminus at Kendrick, then the climb to a camp close to the tumbling Lochsa and a hot meal prepared by George Colgate.

It was a hunter's paradise, the men bagging deer, elk and bear for a month. Then guide Martin Spencer, conscious of the late date, noted the sky and wind direction. "We've got to get out of here," he said. "Winter is about on us. It could snow any day now."

Carlin and the others told Spencer he was a killjoy. They were having such a wonderful time they would stay another week at least. After they did Carlin was willing to pull out. That night a howling wind came up and snow started falling. By morning it was a foot deep, pack and riding horses

GRAVE ON LOCHSA RIVER. After forced abandonment by rest of hunting party, George Colgate apparently struggled downstream for several miles. Grave marker was placed by U. S. Forest Service, location near modern, paved U. S. 12 close by turn-off and historical plaque. Route is often referred to as Lolo Pass, part of it followed by Lewis and Clark. Now paved over entire length, it offers beautiful way over mountains to Missoula, Montana.

had stampeded in the storm and their tracks were covered. And there was another snag — George Colgate's legs were so swollen he could hardly walk.

There seemed to be only one way out — locate the old Indian trail known as Lolo Pass which would be clearly marked and walk out. They dared not think about the distance which was 80 miles. Could they make it in the snow which was getting deeper every minute? Could they carry enough food to last them? The answers were unnecessary. The trail could not be located. It was hidden under the snow, so far unbroken by Indians.

Resourceful in their desperation, the men built two rafts, loading them with supplies and the now crippled cook, Colgate. On Oct. 5, with all on board, the rafts were let loose into the tearing current. Careening wildly, they swept the party down 30 miles, then broke up on rocks in impassable rapids. All made it safely to shore but most of the precious supplies were lost.

There was no way out of walking now. But what about George Colgate who had no use of his legs? It was a bitter decision but he was left. The others started down the canyon carrying what supplies they had salvaged, much of this jettisoned as the snow grew deeper and deeper, taking all the men's energies just to plow through the drifts. Days dragged by, food disappeared. All were now praying that friends at home would be alarmed and send out a search party.

They were and did. William's father, General Carlin, stationed at Vancouver, Washingon, organized a rescue party which set out from Lowell after the rail trip to Kendrick. It had great difficulty negotiating the snowdrifts but finally met with the younger Carlin and other men who were said to be "more dead than alive". Their clothing was almost torn off by brush, shoes nearly gone, food long before exhausted, the men almost as emaciated as skeletons. All agreed they could not possibly have survived another day.

After their return a hue and cry was raised by all newspapers in central Idaho and other cities. Headlines read: "The Carlin party was nothing but a bunch of murderers" . . . "Carlin accused of murder in abandoning Colgate to fate." There was talk of actually trying him for murder.

But such talk did not console Colgate's 18-year-old son. "I'm going into those mountains," he declared, "to find my father even if I leave my bones there." He recruited two others to go with him, one being a Billy Martin. They started Nov. 18 and when they came to the last cabin along the way the old miner who lived there told them:

FRINGE OF "DE VOTO GROVE" beside U.S. Highway 12, bordering Lochsa River, Idaho. Stately, renowned Western Red Cedar is victim of confusing technical nomenclature. Sometimes called Giant Arborvitae, it is properly listed as Thuja Plicata. Attaining height of at least 200 feet, with diameter of 15 at waist level and far more at widely flared base of trunk, characteristic forest tree of western slopes has unique features. Wood is enduring, resisting rot far beyond that of other coniferous trees. Remarkable splitting qualities enabled primitive Indian tribes to separate large slabs for building substantial dwellings especially around Puget Sound. Softness allowed them to fashion canoes from trunks, using bone and horn tools aided by fire.

"Boys — you're committing suicide. The snow 's more than seven feet deep now." But they went on and located the place, they thought, where the father had been abandoned. The boys tried hard to find the body, by now giving up all hope of finding the man alive. After digging in the snow for several days, they realized the search was useless and fought their way back to civilization with the last of their food.

As soon as the snow melted the next spring, a party was sent up the river to search for the body but to no avail as snow still covered the ground at higher elevations. But in early August two U.S. Army expeditions set out for the area, primarily to explore it, but with one eye out for the remains of George Colgate. One of the forays was led by Lt. Charles P. Elliott and he discovered the body beside the Lochsa, some eight miles below the point of abandonment. Elliott buried the body where it lay.

THE ORIGINAL MICKEY FINN AND HIS SLEEPING WAKE

THE CORPSE TURNED UP MISSING

Mickey Finn

The hell-raising in Beartown was the talk all over Montana, Missoula and Helena newspapers referring to its inhabitants as "Beartown Roughs." Notorious also was a special Beartown concoction reported as "having an unexpected effect upon a normally placid brain." While the ingredients were not noted on the bottle, reckless drinkers got a clue by its name—Benzine Botheration.

Driven up the wall by the fiery potion, one citizen broke windows in the red-light house down the street and poked a shotgun in, blasting shot over the heads of the terrified girls. He lived to sober up but one Finn did not.

Well liked by his fellow miners, Finn was familiarly called Mickey. He lived on his claim some distance down the gulch and the day he was missed it was assumed he was recuperating from a bout with a bottle of BB. When his friends went down to investigate they found him dead. Being a Catholic Mickey had often said he wanted to be buried in consecrated ground, so the boys decided to cart his body all the way to Deer Lodge, the nearest Catholic burying ground.

Early the following morning they wrapped Mickey in a blanket, tying it around his neck and feet and throwing it over an Arapahoe pack saddle cinched on a horse. The mourners got on their animals, led the horse hearse and the procession wound down the trail into the valley of Clark Fork. A man had set up a rip saw in the woods here and the escort got a few boards to make a crude coffin. A "democrat" wagon was borrowed as were two sets of harness made of shoddy Indian-made leather called shaganappy and the cortege set off again for Deer Lodge.

At the camp of Gold Creek the party turned south and eventually came to Pioneer where everybody made tracks for the Red Dog Saloon. It had been a hard day and one drink would hardly pick anybody up so they had several. Those led to several more and as the boys got emotional about their mission they said Mick was from the auld sod and

sure now, he would have to have a proper wake.

Two barrels were found out back and rolled to the middle of the dance floor, the coffin set on the ends of them. The lid was removed and lighted candles placed at each corner. This work was exhausting too and after drinks and more drinks somebody struck up a tune, the voices loud and raucous. Ribald stories went the rounds and the revelry lasted most of the night until a few mourners slumped out and bed rolls were spread on the floor around the coffin.

Daylight found the boys still dead to the world and the saloon keeper had to pour strong coffee down their raspy throats before he was able to get the rest of their bodies upright. The cortege moved on once more but by early afternoon inertia had set in and it bogged down. Two individuals were able to rouse themselves enough to go on to Deer Lodge and make arrangements for the funeral.

The pair found a priest and instructions as to where to dig the grave and when they had the hole deep enough the priest arrived in cassock and carrying a prayer book. It was almost dark when the coffin train showed up but everything seemed ready for the funeral, except—where was Mickey?

Faith and the lad was gone all right. The coffin had taken the devil's wings and flown away, sure as peat on the bog. Then somebody remembered, "We went down a sharp incline back there at the creek and the wagon bumped up against them skittish cayuses. It must have been when they jumped across the creek the coffin and poor Mickey slid out." By now it was black dark and the boys had that thirst trouble again. So to Pete Valton's Brewery they all trooped and made another night of it.

In the morning they took the wagon back to the stream and there, by the glory of the saints, was the coffin down in the water "with poor Mickey a-standin' on his head." The coffin and Mickey were dried off and once more the cortege moved toward the cemetery. Mickey Finn was shortly buried according to the book, his soul fluttering away to wherever the souls of Wild Irishmen go.

ALONG THIS WINDING "STREET" in old Pioneer, Montana, plodded Mickey Finn's funeral procession. At that time buildings lined both sides of the lane but later dredges pushed them to one side, burying all buildings in the way. Even those spared were badly treated by fire and ravages of time.

TOO ROUGH RIDE...

EVEN FOR A CORPSE

THEY PLAYED CATCH WITH HIS SKULL
Henry Plummer

Tu gras Hop Per digins
30 myle
Kepe the Trale next the bluffe

In 1862 men of every description were pouring into the new Montana location where a rich strike had been made on Grasshopper Creek, and it is said the above sign south of Dillon at the junction of Beaverhead River and Rattlesnake Creek was there to guide them. All the newcomers were expecting to find gold, either in the creek gravels or in the pockets of those who had already done the spade work. One of the latter breed was Henry Plummer.

Plummer may have been no worse than the rest of Bannack's unholy crowd but he came to be recognized as the natural leader because he had some formal education. Coming from a gently bred family in Connecticut he had the good manners necessary to carry on the double life he lived almost to the moment he faced the noose. He dressed in the finest buckskins and rode a beautiful horse. To further his reputation as a solid citizen he married Eliza Bryan, daughter of the most respected family in town. He was proud of his hands, his shapely fingers with nails well manicured, but they led to his ultimate undoing.

Somehow Plummer managed to get himself elected sheriff of Bannack and also, some say, of Virginia City, 90 miles away. He did not crave extra duties but liked to keep track of stage movements between the two towns. He also liked to know what was going on at higher levels of society and gave a dinner party to entertain the governor, as well as several vigilantes unaware of his undercover activities.

Plummer's gang included such smelly charac-

ters as horse thief George Shears, accomplished bandits Whiskey Bill and Mexican Frank and suspected cannibal Boone Helm. These and other members of the clique gathered periodically at several designated places such as Robbers' Roost near Sheridan, and even more boldly at Skinner's Saloon in the center of Bannack and almost across the street from the jail. Placed at strategic points along the stage road, the men could easily waylay and rob stages loaded with gold dust or bullion en route between Bannack and Virginia City. When passengers refused to give up their pokes they were shot on the spot. After more than a hundred men were so murdered, vigilantes of the two camps joined forces to exterminate the whole gang of road agents.

Plummer's role as first citizen began to be suspected when his absences seemed to occur when the hold-ups and murders did. Then it blew up in his face one day after Plummer and company successfully stopped a bullion-carrying stage. Incautiously he removed his gloves to open the strong box and one of the passengers, knowing Plummer in his other life, recognized the delicate hands.

Arrested in his home while washing those same tell-tale hands, Plummer asked for time to get his coat. The ruse did not work as he was unable to reach his gun. With little delay he was marched to a gallows erected behind Skinner's Saloon. Standing blindfolded before it the bandit-sheriff uttered an eloquent plea for clemency: "If you bring me my black horse, let me mount him and give me a few hours start, I'll give you your weight in gold. I want to live for my wife. I'm too wicked to die and should live to atone for all my misdeeds." Convinced of his certain doom, he made one more request: "As a last favor, gentlemen, let me beg that you will give me a good drop."

Bannack's carpenter French had been paid $43 to have a crude coffin ready and Plummer's strangled remains were placed in it to be lowered into a grave dug in the frozen ground.

But according to a story in the Hardin *Tribune*

BANNACK JAIL, constructed of logs with roof of brush plastered with dirt, grass taking root in rainy spring. Reportedly Sheriff Plummer built jail and owing to frailty of roof, had iron rings installed in floor. When he was apprehended, as bandit and sentenced to hang for numerous robberies and murders, he was incarcerated here and chained to his own rings.

Herald, Sept. 19, 1930, Plummer was to suffer more violence. Sometime before he had received a gunshot wound in the arm while carrying out a hold-up and forced a Bannack physician, Dr. John Glick, to treat the wound. Now, several weeks after Plummer's death, Dr. Glick decided to settle a doubt that bothered him—why had he not been able to find and remove the bullet from the wounded arm? Late at night he went to the grave, dug up Plummer's body, removed the arm for study, reinterring the bandit. On the way home he found a dance in progress at the town hall and hastily concealing the arm in a handy snowbank, he joined in the festivities.

Glick was just getting warmed up when a scream came from outside. The dancers crowded out and saw a hysterical young woman staring at a human arm her small dog laid at her feet. The doctor seems to have retrieved the grisly object and at home satisfied his curiosity that the bullet was there in the flesh.

The remainder of Henry Plummer rested in peace for a few months. The Dillon *Daily Tribune* on March 12, 1948 reprinted an old story to the effect that two of Bannack's citizens, full of grasshopper juice, dug into the grave and removed the head, now reduced to a mere skull. The two inebriates tossed it back and forth in a gruesome game of catch, then went into the Bank Exchange Saloon for another drink. Possibly the skull was tendered in payment, for it remained on display at the bar until the building burned some years later.

THE GRAVE BY THE GALLOWS contains the remains of Buck Stinson and Ned Ray. Hung the same night, just previous to Henry Plummer. Whether Plummer was buried with them is debated. Some say he was buried on the hill above.

OLD CEMETERY ON THE HILL where some say Plummer was reburied by the curious doctor. The five marble tombstones probably were freighted in by wagon freight from the east.

MONTANA-STYLE SALOON — Skinner's in Bannack, favorite rendezvous of notorious Henry Plummer and his bloody gang of desperados. As sheriff the dapper Plummer's obvious association with known criminals was questioned only privately, so great was public fear of bad men.

THOMAS MASSACRE is memorialized by this marker near Big Timber, Mont. In 1866, William Thomas and 8-year-old son, Charles, from Illinois, traveled west from Fort Laramie, Wyo., with another pioneer, Josenph Schultz of Ontario. Because of the intense hostility and fighting dexterity of the Blackfeet Indians, they were escorted by soldiers detailed to build Fort C. F. Smith on the Big Horn River. Becoming separated from the wagon train, Schultz, Thomas and the boy were slain by the Blackfeet. Another party found the bodies and buried them. (From Here Rolled the Covered Wagons: Albert and Jane Salisbury.)

TRAIL BLAZER BOZEMAN sought fortune and found death. Georgia-born John A. Bozeman prospected in Colorado in 1858, found the best diggings under claim and went on to Bannock, Mont., where the mining work was too rigorous. With John Jacobs he laid out a short route to the Montana gold fields, guided wagon trains and adventurers along it.

On April 17, 1867, with friend, Tom Cover, he started for Fort C. F. Smith and sighting Indians, waited for them to approach, thinking them Crows as they came with hands outstretched. Too late he saw they were Blackfeet. He was instantly killed, the wounded Cover escaping. (From Here Rolled the Covered Wagons: Albert and Jane Salisbury.)

THE LAST STAND GENERAL CUSTER

Their treaty with the whites violated by reckless miners in the Black Hills, the Sioux left their reservation and united their various bands as they moved into Montana. Ordered to intercept them, Generals Crook, Gibbon and Terry attempted a pincers movement, the strategy involving a meeting with General George A. Custer and the 7th Cavalry.

With no word from Crook at the Rosebud River, the forces of the other three generals were deployed to combine in an attack on the Indians at the Little Big Horn. Proceeding up the Rosebud, without knowledge of the Sioux being stirred to fighting pitch by medicine man Sitting Bull and defeating Crook's isolated army on June 17, Custer and men saw a large body of Indians ahead of them.

They then moved westward to the Little Big Horn and at dawn June 25, Custer saw a seemingly endless number of Sioux tents on the far shore of the river. He made his plan — Major Reno to attack the upper end of the encampment, Capt. MacDougal to follow with pack train and ammunition while Custer, with 231 men, struck the lower end.

Reno's command splashed across the river and advanced in columns of four, but when the Indians fired on them the horses stampeded. They were ordered to fight on foot and the Sioux swarmed over them, firing from under their horses' necks and dashing away. Men died, right and left. Now the major commanded the rest of his troops to mount but all discipline had vanished. In frantic haste the cavalrymen broke through the Indians,

THEIR SOULS go marching on . . . where the bodies of Custer and his men fell in the ever-tightening circle of Sioux and Cheyenne warriors.

jumped their horses into the river and fled up the eastern slope. They were rallied and dug in but the number of Sioux kept increasing and men were shot at long range as they lay in the rifle pits.

Meanwhile Custer sent an urgent message to Capt. Benteen and MacDougal' pack train to hurry extra ammunition. Benteen could hear the Reno battle and had his men charge the bluffs with drawn revolvers as they joined the entrenched men on the hilltop and fought with them for the rest of the day.

Moving rapidly down the east side of the Little Big Horn, Custer's troops saw the encampment from the top of the bluff and galloped eagerly down to battle. Histories and accounts of the events to follow vary but the stark results were complete annihilation of the brave but doomed men. The Sioux stampeded the horses, creating confusion and dust as they overran Calhoun's men. Many soldiers were killed at the bottom of the ravine just back of the ridge they had held, others as they rushed up the opposite slope. Custer and the remaining men made a last stand on the hilltop. The Indians rode in an ever-tightening circle and demolished them. (From *Here Rolled the Covered Wagons*: Albert and Jane Salisbury.)

MONUMENT TO MASSACRE. After the slaughter on the Little Big Horn, bodies of officers and men lay in grotesque shapes on the slopes of the grass-covered hills. Their first graves were merely trenches covered with dirt, marked with willow stakes on which cartridge shells containing soldiers' names were jammed, bodies easy prey to coyotes and weather. Months later graves were identified, bodies removed and placed in a common resting place, together with bones scattered over the hills and valleys, this large stone memorial erected over them.

SOLDIERS.
JAMES QUINN.   JNO. MILLER.
WM. REED.   PETER McCUE.
D. L. SYMMS.   W. B. ROGERS.
J. E. TROY.   CHAS. SCHMIDT.
W. B. WHALEY.   CHAS. SCOTT.
R. H. HUGHES.   AND. W. SNOW.
E. F. CLEAR.   E. O. TESSIER.
WM. CASHAN.   T. S. TWEED.
A. B. WARREN.   M. F. O'HARA.
JNO. SEILER.   H. M. SCOLLIN.
W. H. HEATH.   FRED'K STREING.
G. E. ADAMS.   HENRY GORDON.
JNO. BURKE.   GEO. LORENTZ.
WM. DYE.   W. D. MEYER.
JNO. DUGGAN.   G. E. SMITH.
J. J. CALVAN.   J. J. TAUNER.
LOUIS HAUGGI.   HENRY TURLEY.
F. F. HUGHES.   H. C. VOIGT.

ANTHONY ASSADILY.   T. E. MAXWELL.
WM. ANDREWS.   CHAS. McCARTHY.
ELMER BABCOCK.   D. J. O'CONNELL.
AMI CHEEVER.   CHRISTIAN REIBOLD.
W. B. CRISFIELD.   HENRY ROBERTS.
CHAS. GRAHAM.   BENT SIEMONSON.
WESTON HARRINGTON. BYRON TARBOX.
HENRY HAMILTON.   MICH'L VETTER.
T. G. KAVANAGH.   HENRY KLOTZBUCHER.
LOUIS LOBERING.   DAVID SUMMERS.
BARTHOLOMEW MAHONEY.

ARIKAREE INDIAN SCOUTS.
BLOODY KNIFE.   BOBTAILED BULL.
LITTLE SOLDIER.

CIVILIANS.
BOSTON CUSTER.   MARK KELLOGG.
ARTHUR REED.   CHAS. REYNOLDS.
MITCH BOYER.   F. G. MANN.   ISAIAH.

ON THE LONE PRAIR-E-E

OLD MEXICAN GROTTOS—Terlingua, Texas

The first whites discovering cinnabar on the north banks of the Rio Grande in the Big Bend country, found three Indian tribes camped in the area. All spoke different dialects which explained the name of the village—Terlingua or three languages. A variation of this tale gives the three languages as Spanish, Indian and English.

Cinnabar, from which mercury is refined, was discovered about 1890, the first mine put in operation in 1891 and named Chisos for the nearby mountains. In the following decades many more mines were opened and at the time of the town's largest expansion some 2,000 people, almost all Mexicans, lived and worked there. The premises now are pocked with at least 16 shafts, open and unguarded, and extremely dangerous. Shafts connect with 50 miles of tunnels extending under the whole town and even old cemetery at the foot of the hill.

Terlingua on the Rio Grande River, about a mile from the Mexican border, drew heavily on Spanish speaking laborers. The old cemetery is filled with Mexican-type graves, some for men killed almost directly below in tunnels of the quicksilver mines. Above ground vaults are still called "grottos" in south Texas, according to historian Ed Bartholomew of Toyahvale with word forms—grotto, grupta, crypta, krypte. The chamber was for displaying mementoes of departed and often contained artificial flowers, statuettes and even photographs. The opening was usually closed by glass in frame such as the one still sagging in front of the grotto at left serving as protection from weather and dust. Wire hoops hanging from crosses are remains of wreaths long since disintegrated.

EXTREME SOUTHERN BORDER OF TEXAS (and of United States) along Rio Grande presents varied terrain, vegetation. South of Shafter, ghost silver-mining camp, river once called Rio Bravo del Norte flows between moderately rocky banks of slight elevation. Near Terlingua Rio Grande enters spectacular canyon of Santa Elena, vertical walls of red rock hemming stream, preventing sun from reaching water most of the way. Above, roughly contoured plateau would seem too rocky, barren, to support plant growth. However, agaves, cacti, yuccas and other typical arid-land vegetation flourishes in such variety as to attract botanists and collectors from far places.

LARGE SECTION filled with burial places of Mexican laborers, once spending most waking hours in dark, rocky tunnels of extensive silver mines at Shafter. In background are foothills of Chinata Mountains, range topped by Chinata Peak, elevation about 7,750'. Summit of peak is said to display eerie ball of light at varying intervals. Observers describe light in various ways — as airplane beacon, auto headlight, beam from lighthouse. Some report bouncing, flashing effect, others steady glow. Such reports, dating from days of earliest explorations by white men to present time remain unaccounted for, legend explaining light as one from ghostly campfire of Indian chief driven to remote fastness by whites. L. Berger Copeman, writer for **The West** magazine, says phenomenon was observed by actor James Dean while making movie **Giant** in vicinity. He was fascinated, vowed to return later and organize expedition into rocky mountains to search for secret of illumination. Before this could be done Dean was killed in **auto wreck.**

ABOVE - GROUND CRYPTS called "grottos" are frequently seen in country along Texas-Mexico border. This one is outstanding because of exceptionally beautiful marker. Shafter, few miles north of Rio Grande, was silver mining camp, first mines being operated by partners John Spencer, silver discoverer, and capitalist Major Shafter about 1882. Previous to and even antedating establishment of Fort Davis, fifty miles distant, in 1854, Milton Faver established ranch-forts Cienega and Cibolo, not far from where Shafter would be. Many descendants of Faver are buried in this cemetery but his body lies on old Cibolo Ranch, now inaccessible.

THEY HAULED HIM UP THE HILL

BARKERVILLE, hub of gold rush to Williams Creek, British Columbia, starting in 1858, shared a cemetery with close neighbor, smaller and quicker fading Cameronton. Sign at entrance to burial ground on high bench overlooking camps, states history simply: "One of Cariboo Cameron's men died and they hauled him up the hill and buried him here.." While most of occupants died violently, many in mine accidents, passing of Griffith Lewis, whose headboard shows in photo, was attributed by **Cariboo Sentinel** to "inflammation of the bowels" which added that Griffith was "worth thousand dollars which he made in Cariboo."

At right is grave of Janet Allen, notorious but out-going saloon keeper. Almost illegible headboard is supported only by large spruce tree grown up inside elaborate paling, now falling apart. Janey spoke to everybody she saw, a fact which led to her undoing. Driving from Williams Creek to her emporium at Dunbar Flat on Lightning Creek, she became aware of a miner walking along behind buggy. Turning to speak to him she inadvertently pulled the rein on that side and her horse responded by turning off the road into thin air. Horse, buggy and garrulous Mrs. Allen all rolled off bank into creek far below.

Headboard is puzzler but seems to read: "Sacred to the memory of Janet White, wife of William White. Native of Fifeshire, Scotland, Who Departed this life Sept. 4th, 1870. Aged 42. **Sentinel** eulogized: "Mrs. Allen came to Cariboo in 1862 and acquired the respect of everyone by the numerous acts of kindness she performed in cases of sickness or distress. Whenever an accident occurred or any case of serious illness she volunteered her services to become the friend of the miner. She exhibited this humane disposition at a cost considerable to herself." At her death all flags in Barkerville were hung at halfmast..

JOSIAH CROSBY BEEDY is buried in tiny cemetery near Stanley, B.C. on road to Barkerville. He is best known for his ill-fated sponsorship of R. W. Thompson's Patent India Rubber Tire Road Steamers. Resembling steam rollers, cumbersome vehicles were hoped to be godsend to miners hauling supplies over rough country from Yale, head of navigation. Road steamers failed on first steep grade along Fraser River after panicking all pack animals encountered. For many years after fiasco, Beedy was partner in Beedy and Townsend Store in Lightning Creek, where gold-discovering Bill Cunningham exploded with favorite phrase— "Boys, this is lightning!"

"SAD" ART

GATES AJAR symbol is frequently seen on old gravestones but this one was cut deeply enough to survive weathering. Gates Ajar was once familiar funeral design in floral work, five-foot emblem required elaborate wire frame, many small flowers painstakingly wired. This author made several in latter period of their popularity.

CARVING on this stone in Mountain View Cemetery, Oregon City, Oregon is uniquely beautiful. If stone was placed in 1862 it is remarkably well preserved, marble being subject to early erosion, especially in wet climate of Willamette Valley.

DOVE OF PEACE is used with spray of stylized laurel leaves on stone marker for grave of young Ephraim Jamerson in Winona Cemetery, Tualatin, Oregon. When town received post office in 1869 its name and that of nearby river, meaning "sluggish", had been interpreted as Twality, Faladin, Twah-la-ti, Quality, Falatine, Nefalatine, Tuality.

MARKER FOR 10 YEAR OLD Jefferson Gilmour was re-erected in concrete base which obscured part of pathetic inscription. Erosive action of water on comparatively soft marble bottom of stone is clearly shown here. Frost hastens destruction, expanding drops of water in minute crevices, forcing off stone particles in same way mountains are eroded.

HEAVEN-POINTING FINGER AND CROWN, symbols usually seen separately, are used here in combination, on stone at Sand Ridge, Oregon. Old pioneer cemeteries contain many stones marking graves of the young, attesting to high death rate from tuberculosis.

LICHEN-ENCRUSTED MARBLE ANGEL stands on grave of little girl at St. Paul, Ore.

CONSOLING MESSAGES are often seen chiseled on marble tombstones dating back to turn of century. This one is at Sand Ridge, Oregon.

Mar. 30, 1870

Dear mother we miss th
But why should our tear
in sorrow flow when G
recalls his own and bid
them leave a world of w
for an immortal crown

SARAH E. COYL

FOR THE LAST LONG JOURNEY—HEARSE

The funeral hearse known to America bears little relation to the device of the same name used by early civilizations. In its Latin form the word hearse, derived from *hirpex* meaning a rake or harrow, was applied to a wooden frame placed in front of the bier. The arch-like frame was equipped with a row of upward projecting prongs to support candles burned during prayers. Handles were provided at either end so that later when the body was transported to the grave, the casket could be placed on the hirpex to carry it more easily. The Latin word passed through the French *herse* and English hearse which signified a conveyance with wheels.

The first wheeled hearses pulled by horses were built for the muddy, narrow roads of early towns and villages and were so short the casket extended over the axles, the driver sitting on the forward end. The hearse was gradually fashioned elaborately requiring the "careful combining of talents of other artisans, the blacksmith, the ornamental ironworker, the joiner or coachmaker, the carver, the upholsterer and the leather worker in building a vehicle upon which the painter, japanner and perhaps the heraldic device liner placed the finishing touches." In early America the more lavishly designed hearses were imported until about the middle of the 18th century.

TYPICAL HEARSE OF 19TH CENTURY stands in Rockerville, S.D. street. Earlier forms were often simple box wagons with beds open to sky, sometimes provided with dropping tail-gates. First enclosed hearses had panels of solid wood which later contained small, then larger glass windows. Some small hearses for transporting children's caskets were made almost entirely of glass, others often ornamented with huge shako-like plumes on corners. In early mining camps where services of undertaker were often unavailable, hearse could usually be rented to give show of opulence to funeral procession even though cemetery might be only few blocks away. In at least one instance, hearse was rented to Chinese who filled all space around casket with such delicacies as cooked pork and chickens. Although most food was consumed at graveside, some being placed on casket for use of departed, scraps and aroma remaining in hearse stopped this service to Orientals.